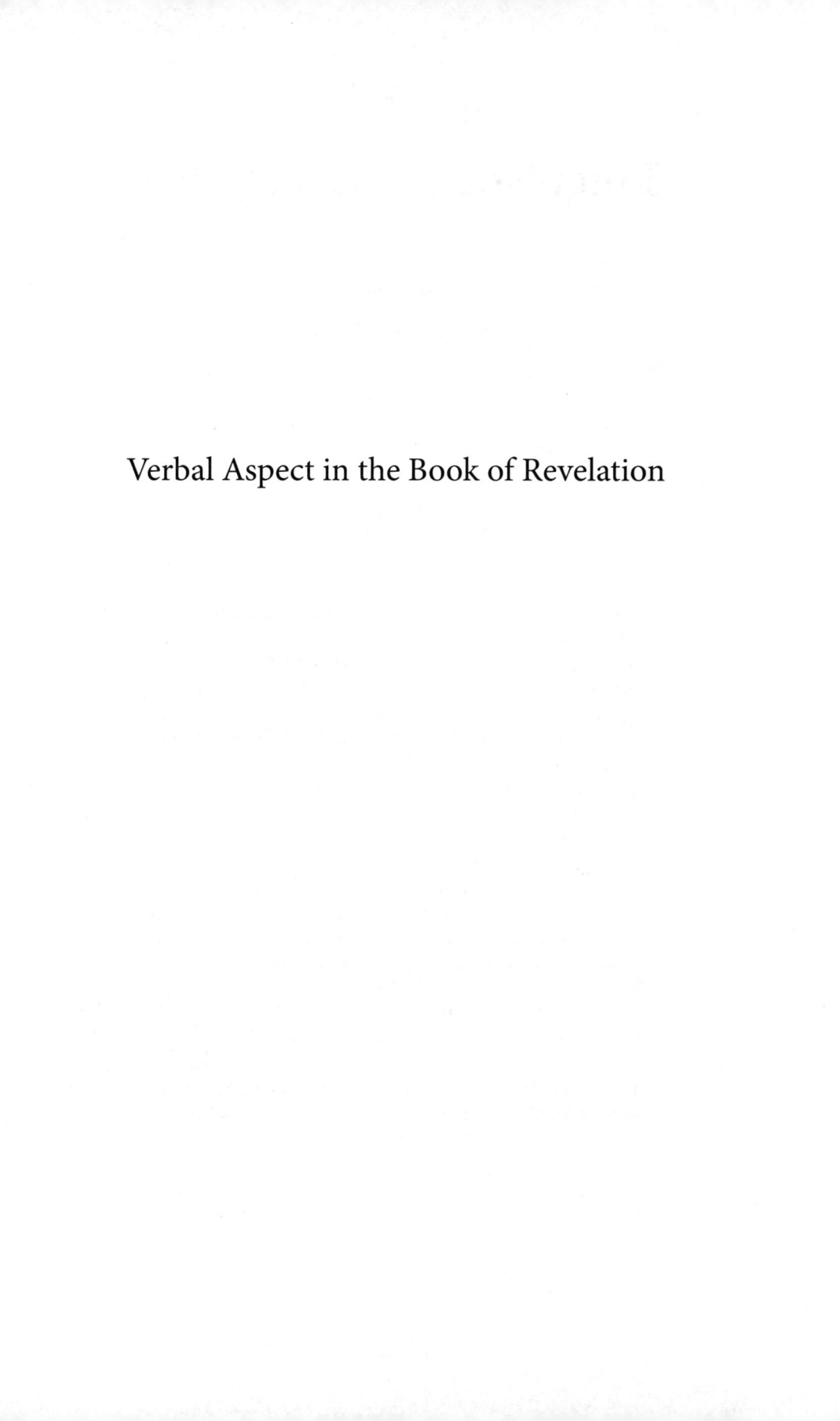

Verbal Aspect in the Book of Revelation

Linguistic Biblical Studies

Series Editor

Stanley E. Porter

Professor of New Testament at McMaster Divinity College
Hamilton, Ontario

VOLUME 4

This series, Linguistic Biblical Studies, is dedicated to the development and promotion of linguistically informed study of the Bible in its original languages. Biblical studies has greatly benefited from modern theoretical and applied linguistics, but stands poised to benefit from further integration of the two fields of study. Most linguistics has studied contemporary languages, and attempts to apply linguistic methods to study of ancient languages requires systematic re-assessment of their approaches. This series is designed to address such challenges, by providing a venue for linguistically based analysis of the languages of the Bible. As a result, monograph-length studies and collections of essays in the major areas of linguistics, such as syntax, semantics, pragmatics, discourse analysis and text linguistics, corpus linguistics, cognitive linguistics, comparative linguistics, and the like, will be encouraged, and any theoretical linguistic approach will be considered, both formal and functional. Primary consideration is given to the Greek of the New and Old Testaments and of other relevant ancient authors, but studies in Hebrew, Coptic, and other related languages will be entertained as appropriate.

Verbal Aspect
in the Book of Revelation

The Function of Greek Verb Tenses
in John's Apocalypse

By

David L. Mathewson

BRILL

LEIDEN • BOSTON
2010

This book is printed on acid-free paper.

Library of Congress Cataloging-in-Publication Data

Mathewson, David.
  Verbal aspect in the Book of Revelation : the function of Greek verb tenses in John's Apocalypse / by David L. Mathewson.
      p. cm. – (Linguistic Biblical studies, 1877-7554 ; v. 4)
  Includes bibliographical references and index.
  ISBN 978-90-04-18668-2 (hardback : alk. paper)
  1. Bible. N.T. Revelation–Language, style. 2. Greek language, Biblical–Aspect. 3. Greek language, Biblical–Tense. I. Title. II. Series.

  BS2825.6.L3M37 2010
  220.4'04–dc22

                                                                    2010020326

ISSN   1877-7554
ISBN   978 90 04 18668 2

Copyright 2010 by Koninklijke Brill NV, Leiden, The Netherlands.
Koninklijke Brill NV incorporates the imprints Brill, Hotei Publishing,
IDC Publishers, Martinus Nijhoff Publishers and VSP.

MIX
Papier van
verantwoorde herkomst
FSC
www.fsc.org   FSC® C004472

PRINTED BY DRUKKERIJ WILCO B.V. - AMERSFOORT, THE NETHERLANDS

CONTENTS

CHAPTER ONE

INTRODUCTION

The Challenge of Revelation's Language

Among the numerous interpretive challenges confronting students of the book of Revelation, the nature of the language of the Apocalypse continues to elicit considerable fascination and perplexity by both grammarians and commentators. The most disputed feature of John's[1] Greek is the apparent grammatical infelicities or solecisms, ostensible departures from "correct" Greek Grammar.[2] These apparent irregularities in the Greek of Revelation have led to judgments that its grammar is "*absolutely unique.*"[3] Consequently, much ink has been spilt in an attempt to explain this unique grammar of the Apocalypse. The presence of ostensible grammatical irregularities in the Apocalypse has engendered a variety of theories of explanation. Thus some see John's Greek as bad, sloppy, or careless (particularly when measured against Classical Greek standards), or perhaps the result of John's ecstatic visionary experience.[4] Some construe John's awkward or unusual grammar as a deliberate attempt to flaunt grammatical convention as a means of protest against the Greco-Roman empire.[5] Gregory K. Beale has recently argued that some of the grammatical solecisms are intentional authorial signals of Old Testament allusions, while Iwan M. Whitely thinks the solecisms are part of the hermeneutical strategy of the author.[6]

---

[1] I find it necessary to offer the same caveat that most everyone else does in discussing Revelation: by calling the author John I am not presupposing any particular view regarding the historical identity of the author. Rather, I simply refer to 'John' as the book's implied author.

[2] See the early comments of Dionysius of Alexandria cited by Eusebius, *Hist. Eccles.* 7.25.26–27.

[3] R.H. Charles, *Studies in the Apocalypse* (Edinburgh: T. & T. Clark, 1912) 81. Italics his.

[4] For this latter view see E.C. Selwyn, *The Christian Prophets and the Prophetic Apocalypse* (London: Macmillan, 1900) 258.

[5] A.D. Callahan, "The Language of the Apocalypse," *HTR* 88 (1995) 453–457.

[6] Gregory K. Beale, *John's Use of the Old Testament in Revelation* (JSNTSS 166;

Perhaps the most common assessment of the apparent grammatical incongruities in the Apocalypse is to posit some level of Semitic influence upon John's grammar. While speculations that Revelation is a translation from an original Hebrew or Aramaic source lack plausibility,[7] the grammatical solecisms in Revelation are frequently attributed to some degree of influence from the grammar of biblical Hebrew, perhaps deliberately to give it an Old Testament or prophetic flavor.[8] The well-known and oft-quoted dictum of R.H. Charles regarding Revelation is indicative of this approach: "while he writes in Greek, he thinks in Hebrew, and the thought has naturally affected the vehicle of expression."[9] Reflecting the perspective of Charles, Steven Thompson similarly writes that "at least in the Apc., the Greek language was little more than a membrane, stretched tightly over a Semitic framework, showing many essential contours beneath,"[10] or for a different metaphor, "Nowhere is the Greek 'ground cover' over Semitic 'subsoil' as thin as it is here."[11] More recently, David E. Aune has reiterated this persistent perspective: "The Greek of Revelation is the most peculiar Greek in the NT, in part because it exhibits interference from Semitic languages, perhaps both Hebrew and Aramaic."[12] Quite often this results in scholars postulating that the author of Revelation wrote in an extant hybrid Jewish Greek. "The Apc. can accurately be described ... and with no hesitancy be categorised as 'Jewish Greek', to the fullest extent of the term ...."[13] Additionally, conclusions to these various issues have sometimes been pressed into service to

---

Sheffield: Academic Press, 1998) 318–355; Iwan M. Whitely, "An Explanation for the Anacolutha in the Book of Revelation," *FN* 20 (2007) 33–50.

[7] See R.B.Y. Scott, *The Original Language of the Apocalypse* (Toronto: University of Toronto, 1928) and C.C. Torrey, *The Apocalypse of John* (New Haven: Yale University Press, 1958) respectively.

[8] For brief summaries cf. C.G. Ozanne, "The Language of the Apocalypse," *TynB* 16 (1965) 3–9; G. Mussies, "The Greek of the Book of Revelation," *L'Apocalypse johannique et l'Apocalyptique dans le Nouveau Testament* (ed, by J. Lambrecht; Leuven: Leuven University Press, 1980) 167–177; Nigel Turner, *A Grammar of New Testament Greek, Vol. IV, Style* (ed. by James H. Moulton; Edinburgh: T. & T. Clark) 145–158.

[9] Charles, *Studies*, 82.

[10] Steven Thompson, *The Apocalypse and Semitic Syntax* (SNTSMS 52; Cambridge: University Press, 1985) 108.

[11] Jürgen Roloff, *The Revelation of John: A Continental Commentary* (Transl. by John E. Alsop; Minneapolis: Fortress Press, 1993) 12.

[12] David E. Aune, *Revelation 1–5* (WBC 52a; Dallas: Word Books, 1997) clxii.

[13] Cf. Thompson, *Semitic Syntax*, 108. See also Nigel Turner, *A Grammar of New Testament Greek, Vol. III, Syntax* (ed. by James H. Moulton; Edinburgh: T. & T. Clark, 1963) 9. Cf. Brian K. Blount, *Revelation* (NTL; Louisville: Westminster John Knox, 2009) 8 ("he writes in a kind of Semitized Greek").

argue for a certain view of authorship, or to tease out underlying sources of the Apocalypse.[14] Furthermore, Daryl D. Schmidt has argued for the presence of numerous 'Septuagintalisms', rather than Semitisms, in the Apocalypse's grammar.[15]

The Problem of Verb Tenses

While much remains to be said concerning virtually all of these issues, the intention of this work is far less ambitious and will focus more narrowly on only one limited aspect of the issue of the Greek language of Revelation which seems to have attracted its share of the attention: the verb tenses in the Apocalypse. Mussies lamented that "the great shortcoming in the study of the morphology of the Apc. is the lack of a systematic description of the use of tense …."[16] One of the conspicuous features of John's use of Greek tenses is their appearance in contexts that seem to violate their assumed (temporal) values. Specifically, Revelation's visionary material commonly exemplifies a shifting between all the major Greek tenses (present, aorist, imperfect, future, perfect) while often apparently maintaining the same temporal sphere of reference (the narration of what John saw, εἶδον). Thus in recording his visions the author of the Apocalypse employs a full array of tense forms to depict the processes that make up his visionary narrative. Frequently, this use of tenses in Revelation is characterized as "irregular," "confused," or "inconsistent," due to the fact that John's use of tenses seems at odds with common conceptions of the values of Greek tenses (e.g. aorist = past and punctiliar; present = present time and linear; perfect = past action with present results). For example, in the throne vision of Ch. 5, the tenses of finite indicative verbs can be broken down according to the following number of occurrences:[17]

---

[14] Cf. R.H. Charles, *The Revelation of St. John* (2 vols.; ICC; New York: Charles Scribner's, 1920) I: cxvii–clix; Ozanne, "Language of the Apocalypse," 9.

[15] Daryl D. Schmidt, "Semitisms and Septuagintalisms in the Book of Revelation," *NTS* 37 (1991) 592–603. Schmidt defines Septuagintalisms as "syntactical peculiarities that are not typical of Semitic syntax, but are stylistic features characteristic of one of the varieties of translation Greek within the Septuagint" (596).

[16] G. Mussies, *The Morphology of Koine Greek as Used in the Apocalypse of John* (NovTSup 27; Leiden: Brill, 1971), 11.

[17] For reasons discussed below, I have only included the indicative forms of the verb. Furthermore, as will be explained below, I have not included forms of the verb εἰμί in my count.

Aorist: 16
Present: 3[18]
Imperfect: 3
Perfect: 1

This usage of various tense forms in identical temporal contexts has not escaped notice. Early on W. Bousset characterized this shift in tense forms as "das regellose Schwanken."[19] Thompson also observed the "sudden and seemingly inexplicable shifts among aorist/present/future tenses of verbs in connected narrative, without a corresponding shift in the time during which the action being described actually takes place."[20] Charles described the tense usage in 11.1–13 as temporally "confused,"[21] while E.C.A. Dougherty thought that the usage of tense forms in some visionary segments should be characterized as an "Inconsistency."[22]

How are we to account for the phenomenon of tense usage in the Apocalypse, a phenomenon which has often left not a few scholars with the impression that John's use of Greek verbal tenses is paradoxically un-Greek in character? Only a few commentaries have addressed the issue at any length, though several important book-length studies have appeared. Bousset, as already noted, highlighted "das regellose Schwanken" between the present and the future as characteristic of the author's visionary sections.[23] According to him, the use of the future tense in such cases is "ein Aus-der-Rolle-fallen."[24] In particular, Revelation 11 reflects an "irregular" change between present and future. Furthermore, the aorist and the perfect are frequently mixed (Vulgäre Vermischung) in the Apocalypse.[25] Bousset gives no clear rationale for the irregular uses that he notices, and says nothing in his introductory treatment of tenses regarding Semitic influence on Revelation's use of Greek tenses.

---

[18] The possible presence of a future tense form in this chapter depends on a delicate text-critical issue surrounding βασιλεύσουσιν/βασιλεύουσιν (present or future) in v. 10. If the verb in question is a future, this would reduce the number of presents to 2. See below.

[19] W. Bousset, Die Offenbarung Johannis (Göttingen: Vandenhoeck & Ruprecht, 1906) 168.

[20] Thompson, Semitic Syntax, 47. Thompson admits that such shifts are found elsewhere in the New Testament, but only to a limited degree, whereas these tense shifts are far more pronounced in the Apocalypse.

[21] Charles, Revelation, I, cxxiii n. 1.

[22] E.C.A. Dougherty, "The Syntax of the Apocalypse" (PhD Dissertation, Catholic University of America, Washington D.C., 1990) 428–447.

[23] Bousset, Offenbarung, 169.

[24] Bousset, Offenbarung, 169.

[25] Bousset, Offenbarung, 169.

Scholars have searched for an explanation for the ostensibly odd use of the tenses in Revelation. By far the most common approach, an approach used to explain the "odd" grammar throughout Revelation in general, is to posit some level of Semitic influence on the Greek tense system in Revelation. Charles noted the wavering between the present and future in Revelation, but concluded that it is not arbitrary.[26] The future is often correctly found in prophetic sections (7.16–17; 14.10; 17.14–15). In one instance, based on Hebrew idiom, it could be rendered by a past tense (4.9–10). In many cases the present tense in Revelation is used of future or past time. According to Charles this use of the present has been influenced by the Hebrew imperfect, which could refer to past, present, or future time (cf. 5.10; 9.8, 17–20; 13.11). At other times the present is used for past action "with a view to dramatic vividness."[27] The aorist tense in Revelation could 1) refer to pure past time; 2) be timeless; 3) refer to an event that has just happened.[28] And the perfect is sometimes used with the sense of an aorist (cf. 5.7; 7.14; 8.5; 19.3). In Ch. 11, however, the tenses are apparently confused, which Charles attributes to John's use of sources at this point.[29]

Hebrew influence on the Greek verbal system in Revelation was argued for at more length by A. Lancellotti, who suggested that the confusion in John's tense usage was due to underlying Semitic influence.[30] This confusion was the result of the author's native language being Hebrew. According to Lancellotti, though the aorist is often used with its normal (past) meaning in Revelation, at times the underlying Hebrew *qatal* has caused confusion in John's use of the aorist. Therefore, we find the aorist sometimes used of future time (the so-called proleptic usage or *perfectum confidentiae*). Cf. Rev 10.7.[31] The present tense in Revelation is

---

[26] Charles, *Revelation, I*, cxxiii.

[27] Charles, *Revelation, I*, cxxiii.

[28] Charles, *Revelation, I*, cxxiv–v.

[29] Charles, *Revelation, I*, cxxiii, n. 1.

[30] A. Lancellotti, *Sintassi ebraica nel Greco dell'Apocalisse, Vol. 1, Uso delle forme verbali* (Collectio Assisiensis I; Assisi: Studio Teologico, 1964). For summaries and brief evaluation of Lancellotti's work see Mussies, *Morphology*, 11, 335–336, 338–340; Thompson, *Semitic Syntax*, 5. Thompson criticizes Lancelloti's work for providing inadequate documentation and illustration from the LXX (5). Mussies criticizes Lancellotti for the following: "If the influence of Biblical Hebrew were so strong still that St. John could not clearly distinguish between present and future tenses it is difficult to understand why he did not avoid to use [sic] the Greek future at all. The present indicative could then be used either as a present, past or future tense and the aorist as a past tense" (*Morphology*, 335).

[31] Lancellotti, *Sintassi ebraica*, 56.

particularly abnormal. The timeless use of the present in the Apocalypse reflects the influence of the *yiqtol*, and even the perfect and future tense forms may reflect Hebrew influence.

Three significant and more recent studies on the Greek of Revelation by Mussies, Thompson, and Dougherty have appeared and have devoted sections of some length in their work to the issue of verb tenses. Though these studies treat the syntax of the Apocalypse more widely, they devote significant space to the verb tenses in Revelation. The works by Mussies and Thompson both discuss verb tenses within the broader linguistic context of Semitic influence, though they differ in the nature and level of Semitic influence they attribute to Revelation's tense usage. Within the context of his examination of the language and style of the Apocalypse, Mussies allots a lengthy section to verb tense usage in Revelation.[32] According to Mussies, the tense usage in the Apocalypse corresponds to the tense system of Mishnaic Hebrew and Aramaic. Thus he concludes that the Hebrew underlying Revelation's tenses "had developed to a great extent towards Mishnaic Hebrew or was perhaps already identical to it."[33] For indicative verb forms (the main concern of the present study) Mussies finds that the perfect (*qatal*) and imperfect (*yiqtol*) Semitic tense forms are reflected in Revelation in the 429 aorist indicatives and 118 future indicatives (according to his count) respectively.[34] Moreover, the Semitic "finite participle" is represented by the present indicative 238 times in Revelation. The imperfect tense "offers no special problem" in Revelation.[35]

Rev	*Mishnaic Hebrew*
Aorist	perfect
Present	participle
Future	imperfect
Perfect	—[36]

Yet Mussies finds nothing unusual about the use of the aorist tense in Revelation, concluding that it virtually always refers to past time (he only

---

[32] Mussies, *Morphology.*

[33] Mussies, *Morphology,* 336.

[34] Obviously, Mussies' verb count could be refined. Furthermore, according to Mussies the imperative and infinitive of non-durative verbs are reflected in the 59 aorist imperatives and 72 aorist infinitives in Revelation.

[35] Mussies, *Morphology,* 337.

[36] See Mussies' more extensive chart in *Morphology,* 349.

finds one or two clear examples of the proleptic use of the aorist).[37] The present is also used in a thoroughly Greek manner, referring to present time, but also as a "historical" and "futuristic" present.

In addressing the issue of the shifting tenses in John's visionary narrative, Mussies rejects the solution of Lancellotti that the tense shifts betray confusion on the part of the author and concludes that it is a reflection of the visionary experience of the author.[38] Mussies discerns a pattern where the author begins with aorist tenses which correspond to "the past time when the visions were actually seen," followed by present tenses to give a lively presentation of what is immediately before his eyes. The visions conclude with future tenses, which express "the prophetic character of the visions" (they depict future events).[39] Thus, according to Mussies, the tense shifts can be explained solely along temporal lines as a reflection of the apocalyptic genre.[40] As such, Mussies assumes as his starting point the temporal character of the Greek verbal system (aorist—past time; present—present time; future—future time), and concludes that while the tense usage in the Apocalypse conforms to the Semitic substrate (Mishnaic Hebrew and Aramaic), the tense forms are used in Revelation consistently with their Greek meanings. The influence, according to Mussies, is apparently not a matter of interference in the Greek tense system (so Lancellotti, Charles, Thompson below), but only a matter of style and enhancement. As Mussies summarizes,

> St. John betrays his Semitic vernacular therefore by the choice which he makes inadvertently of the Greek categories and not so much by striking Semitisms in the use of each category. The Greek verbs have their Greek values, but some of the aspects of their values occur more frequently due to the Semitic substrate .... The Semitic colour of the verb in the Apc. is therefore mainly a stylistic matter.[41]

In the most recent treatment of the syntax of the Apocalypse from a thoroughgoing perspective of Semitic influence, Thompson dedicates a lengthy section to the issue of verb tenses in the Apocalypse, noting also the problematic shifting of tenses within the visionary narrative.[42] In contrast to Mussies, Thompson sees the tense forms throughout

---

[37] See Mussies, *Morphology*, 338–340 for discussion of the examples.
[38] Mussies, *Morphology*, 330–349.
[39] Mussies, *Morphology*, 340.
[40] Mussies, *Morphology*, 349.
[41] Mussies, *Morphology*, 349.
[42] Thompson, *Semitic Syntax*, 29–53. For reviews of Thompson's monograph see Stanley E. Porter, "Review of S. Thompson, *The Apocalypse and Semitic Syntax*," *Journal for the*

the Apocalypse as *semantically* (not just stylistically) undergoing Semitic
interference. In his work he surveys individual tenses as well as the problem of shifting tenses in Revelation's visions. Thompson finds it strange
that present indicative verbs would be used in a future sense.[43] While
admitting that this phenomenon occurs in Classical and non-literary
Greek, Thompson, dissatisfied with Lancellotti's explanation of the future
use of the present due to the Hebrew perfect, attributes this use of the
present in the New Testament and the Apocalypse to the influence of
the Semitic participle.[44] Furthermore, the use of the present tense with
past meaning, the so-called "historical present" recognized by grammars,
is characteristically Greek with verbs of saying, but other verbs in the
present tense used of past time reflect the Semitic participle, which can
refer to past, present, or future action.[45]

Thompson is also further perplexed by examples of the aorist tense
that do not express "punctiliar past time."[46] He also finds aorist indicative verbs used with a present sense (1.2; 2.21, 24; 3.4, 8, 9 etc.), with
a future sense (10.7; 11.2; 11.10–13 etc.), and as timeless (5.9, 10; 14.4;
16.20 etc.). According to Thompson, this can only be accounted for by
the underlying Hebrew perfect, as is further demonstrated by the fact
that the LXX frequently uses the aorist tense to render the Hebrew perfect.[47] Thompson also notices that the perfect tense is used in Revelation
in conjunction with or in place of aorist tenses, where the meaning of the
perfect (understood as an anterior action with ongoing results) does not
seem to fit (e.g., 2.3; 5.7; 7.14; 8.5). While Mussies did not offer an underlying Hebrew construction for the Greek perfect tense, Thompson does
suggest one. According to Thompson, Revelation's use of the perfect can
be explained by Semitic influence of what he calls derived conjugations
(*niphal, piel, pual, hiphil*).

Study of the New Testament 29 (1987) 122–124; Barnabas Lindars, "Review of S. Thompson, *The Apocalypse and Semitic Syntax*," *JSS* 30 (1985) 289–291. Lindars is much more
sympathetic toward Thompson's conclusions.

[43] Thompson, *Semitic Syntax*, 29.

[44] Thompson, *Semitic Syntax*, 33.

[45] Thompson, *Semitic Syntax*, 35. He finds an example of this in the LXX Jud 14.4: ὅτι
ἐκδίκησιν αὐτὸς ζητεῖ ἐκ τῶν ἀλλοφύλων. Cf. Rev 9.9–11; 13.11–17 (36).

[46] Thompson, *Semitic Syntax*, 37–42.

[47] Thompson, *Semitic Syntax*, 37. See his chart on p. 37 which tabulates the various
Greek tenses used to express the Hebrew perfect from 95 occurrences of the Semitic
perfect that he checked. His comparison does show that at least for the 95 verbs the
majority are translated in the LXX with the aorist tense form, though other tense forms
are also well-represented.

Finally, Thompson notices examples of the future tense used apparently to refer to past time (4.9–10; 17.8), a phenomenon noted already by Charles. Thompson points to examples from the LXX where the future tense used of past action translates the Hebrew imperfect.[48] He concludes that this use of the future would be "intelligible primarily to readers familiar with Semitic languages. An ordinary non-Jew could hardly be expected to understand that the future tense contains a past reference ...."[49] Thus Thompson must assume that John and his readers shared knowledge of a hybrid Jewish-Greek, or else large numbers (if not all) of the Apocalypse's first readers would have found much of its language as confusing as modern-day scholars do! Presumably he would say something similar about the other tense forms in the Apocalypse. Generally, then, Thompson discovers the following correspondences between Revelation's use of Greek tenses and the assumed underlying Hebrew tense system:

Rev	Hebrew
Aorist	perfect
Present	participle
Future (past)	imperfect
Perfect	derived conjugations

The remainder of Thompson's discussion of Greek tenses in the Apocalypse is devoted to the "problem of shifting tenses," where he notes the "sudden and seemingly inexplicable shifts among aorist/present/future tense of verbs in connected narrative without a corresponding shift in the time during which the action being described actually takes place."[50] Thompson finds the conclusions of Charles, Lancellotti, and Mussies unsatisfying and suggests instead that the precedent for the phenomenon of shifting tenses be located in the underlying shifts in Semitic verb tenses. Thompson points to similar shifts in the Greek translation of a handful of Old Testament prophetic texts (Dan [Theod.] 4.31–32, 35, and LXX Hos 4.10; 9.3) and then deduces the following general pattern: aorist → Hebrew perfect; future → Hebrew imperfect; present → Hebrew participle. Thus, "One cannot escape the impression that the biblical Hebrew (and Aramaic) tense system, profoundly different from Greek, is to be

---

[48] Thompson, *Semitic Syntax*, 46. Cf. Ps. 103.6.
[49] Thompson, *Semitic Syntax*, 47.
[50] Thompson, *Semitic Syntax*, 47.

seen nearly everywhere in the language of the Apc.,"[51] Thompson's argument seems to be that Revelation's shifting verb tenses follows the parallel phenomena in the LXX and is due to a Semitic kind of Greek that both share.

The final major work, and the most extensive on this issue, was produced in 1990 by Dougherty. In his work, Dougherty begins by surveying the field of research on the grammar of Revelation, noting the propensity of scholars to have found a heavily semitized Greek.[52] His work is primarily a cataloging and classifying of the various grammatical constructions in Revelation illustrated with numerous examples. He also devotes a lengthy chapter to verb forms in Revelation, and discusses tense usage in some detail along with providing helpful statistics.[53] This following summary primarily focuses attention on his treatment of indicative verb forms in Revelation, with some brief comments on his treatment of non-indicative mood forms. Dougherty proceeds by categorizing the different tenses according to their various pragmatic functions throughout Revelation. Hence the present tense is discussed under the headings "Timeless," "Present Time in Contrast to Other Times," "Descriptive Present," "Historical Present,"[54] "Futuristic Present," "Present = Future," "Periphrastic Future," "Simple Present," "Perfect = Present."[55] The well-known "Historic Present" occurs only 16 times in Revelation according to Dougherty.[56] One could dispute some of these categories as valid (Present = Future; Perfect = Present) or necessary (Present Time in Contrast to Other Times; Periphrastic Future; Simple Present). However, Dougherty has at least demonstrated the variety of temporal and pragmatic contexts in which the present tense form occurs in Revelation.

Importantly, Dougherty begins his discussion by recognizing that the term "tense" is a misnomer, for the Greek tenses actually convey *aspect* (see below) rather than time. However, most of his explanations still

---

[51] Thompson, *Semitic Syntax*, 104. He goes on to state that "The conventional Greek time sense of past-present-future is equally foreign to verb tenses in the Apc. and in OT" (104).

[52] Dougherty, "Syntax," 1–33.

[53] Dougherty, "Syntax," 400–527. This section covers indicative as well as non-indicative mood verbal forms.

[54] Dougherty sees the "Historical Present" and the "Descriptive Present" as similar, perhaps the latter functioning as a subset of the former.

[55] For perfect = present Dougherty includes οἶδα and εἴρηκα as primary instances of this usage.

[56] By contrast Aune thinks that it occurs 43 times (*Revelation 1–5*, clxxxiv). Cf. Thompson, *Semitic Syntax*, 35–36.

assume temporal values as part of the meaning of the tense forms (present tense—present time; aorist, imperfect—past time; future—future time), so that he is ultimately unable to rid himself of time-based conceptions of the tense forms.[57]

The imperfect tense has one primary manifestation: it indicates a state or condition of the subject in the *past*; it is a true preterite. According to Dougherty, the future tense can be used in *future* or *timeless* contexts, and is found in a number of other syntactical environments (in conditional [εἰ] or purpose [ἵνα] clauses).[58]

For the aorist tense "aspect ... is primary, while any time involved is derivative and contextual."[59] Consequently, Dougherty sees the aorist occurring in three temporal contexts in Revelation: past in narration or in non-narrative sections, present, and future. He also sees the aorist used with perfective force 99 times, as an action in the past that is complete in the present.[60] Yet he still maintains a distinction between the two forms semantically, when he claims that while the aorist takes the place of a perfect "the perfect sense is not used."[61] Dougherty does not develop a semantically consistent meaning for the perfect tense form, but sees it used in the following ways: present sense (οἶδα and ἵστημι); past sense; perfective sense. The "past sense" of the perfect in Revelation occurs where the perfect "has a simple past sense typical of the aorist."[62]

The final section of Dougherty's treatment of tenses of the indicative mood in the Apocalypse is devoted to the issue of consistency in tense usage in larger segments of discourse. Dougherty finds the tenses used in John's visions in the following ways: consistency (e.g. 1.9–12); apparent inconsistency (e.g. 5.2–4);[63] inconsistency. For the latter category he lists 4.2–10; 5.8–9; 7.9–10, 14–17; 8.8–10; 9.1–6, 7–11, 17–19; 11.3–13; 12.1–6; 13.1–8, 11–17; 14.1–5; 15.2–3; 17.12–14; 18.4–20; 19.11–16;

---

[57] Dougherty appeals to the work of K.L. McKay ("On the Perfect and Other Aspects in New Testament Greek," *NovT* 23 [1981] 289–329) for the important insight that tenses do not communicate temporal information but aspect. See "Syntax," 401 n. 2.

[58] See Dougherty, "Syntax," 412–418. Dougherty sidesteps the question of whether the future is punctiliar or durative in meaning by showing (correctly in my opinion) that these features belong to the contexts in which the future form appears rather than to the meaning of the future tense form itself.

[59] Dougherty, "Syntax," 418.

[60] Dougherty, "Syntax," 420–422.

[61] Dougherty, "Syntax," 422.

[62] Dougherty, "Syntax," 425.

[63] As Dougherty describes, "Tenses are sometimes mixed for various reasons with no violation of consistency" ("Syntax," 427).

20.4–10; 21.15–16, 22–27; 22.1–5.[64] It appears that the criteria by which Dougherty thinks that these sections exhibit inconsistent tense usage consist of temporal understandings of the tenses: aorist and imperfect in past narration; present in present description; future in prediction, despite the fact that early on he claims that aspect rather than time is the essential feature of the tense forms.[65] Instances that fall outside of this temporal pattern or cannot be accordingly explained are "inconsistent." Throughout all of his discussion, he does not raise the question of ostensible Semitic influence. Overall, Dougherty has produced a detailed catalog of the various tense forms and their manifestations, temporal and otherwise, in Revelation, showing that the tense forms can be utilized in a variety of temporal contexts. Moreover, his work remains highly descriptive and classificatory, and he does not offer an interpretive framework or a consistent linguistic model for comprehending the Greek tense system in Revelation.

Most of the rest of his treatment of verb forms in Revelation, which is devoted to non-indicative verb forms, is basically a statistical analysis of the occurrence of various verbs in various tenses and moods. Though he does not develop a consistent explanatory model (again his work is descriptive and classificatory), he does at times draw conclusions regarding the semantics of the tense forms in various moods. However, he persists is seeing little meaningful distinction between the tense forms in various moods based on the fact that they occur in similar contexts. For example, with regard to subjunctive mood he notices "the occurrence of verbs in the present and aorist subjunctive in parallel constructions, in which there is little difference in meaning between the present and the aorist."[66] Similarly, for the imperative forms in Revelation, Dougherty hypothesizes that "there is on occasion a slight difference between the meanings of the present and of the aorist in the imperative mood,"[67]

---

[64] Dougherty, "Syntax," 428–447.

[65] Dougherty does think that some of these "inconsistencies" can be explained, whereas for other instances he concludes that there is no explanation ("Syntax," 428).

[66] Dougherty, "Syntax," 475. This problem will surface in several instances in the discussion of the tenses in Revelation below. There appears to be an overwhelming assumption that when different tense forms are used in identical contexts (e.g. temporal) this necessarily implies identical semantics. However, as will be shown below, it is just as likely that two different tense forms side-by-side in identical contexts implies a conscious semantic choice on the part of the author. In many instances in Revelation the same lexeme is used with different aspects.

[67] Dougherty, "Syntax," 477.

though he claims that ten times the aorist and present imperative are found in parallel with no difference in meaning.[68] As for the infinitive, like the subjunctive, Dougherty fails to see any appreciable difference between aorist and present tenses particularly when used in parallel fashion.[69] Apparently he operates with the assumption that lack of functional differentiation entails lack of semantic differentiation. With the participle in Revelation Dougherty does think that aspectual distinctions prevail, but his definitions of the "aspects" of the present, perfect, and aorist participles are the traditional temporal and *Aktionsart* ones.[70]

The most recent attempt at any length to analyze John's use of the tense forms is found in the more nuanced treatment in the introductory comments in the commentary by Aune.[71] He begins by recognizing that the verb tenses do not primarily indicate time, but, following recent study, they signal *aspect* which indicates the author's conception of the action (see below). Aune then surveys in summary fashion all the tense forms as they occur in Revelation, giving helpful statistics and summaries regarding their usage and function, referring to the works surveyed above as well as the most recent works on verbal aspect by Stanley E. Porter and Buist M. Fanning (see below). In regard to function Aune demonstrates that the verb tenses (aspect) in Revelation reveal a wide range of temporal implicatures. Thus the present tense is used both as a "historical" present (43×) as well as to refer to future time.[72] The aorist is the common narrative tense in Revelation, but is also used temporally to refer to the future (the so-called "proleptic" usage). Aune surveys several possible reasons for this, though he does not give his preferred explanation.[73]

There is apparently nothing unusual about the use of the future tense in Revelation, and the imperfect tense reflects its normal use in narrative. In one or two instances Aune's explanation is linguistically nuanced. For example, the imperfect is used to highlight or "foreground" action in opposition to the aorist, and the perfect in opposition to the aorist can be used to highlight or dramatize an action.[74] However, at other times

---

[68] He cites Rev 2.5; 3.2, 3, 19; 10.8; 11.1; 16.1; 19.10; 22.17.
[69] Dougherty, "Syntax," 489, 506.
[70] Dougherty, "Syntax," 517–527.
[71] Aune, *Revelation 1–5*, clxxxiv–clxxxviii.
[72] Aune, *Revelation 1–5*, clxxxiv–clxxxv.
[73] Aune, *Revelation 1–5*, clxxxvii.
[74] Aune, *Revelation 1–5*, clxxxvi, clxxxvii. Aune refers to the εἶχον in Rev 6.9 and εἴληφεν in 5.7. On the latter text see below.

his comments reflect more common, temporally oriented explanations. Thus the historical present can be used when the author assumes the role of an eyewitness (as if the author were present?). Or the aorist used of a future event may be explained by seeing the action as so certain that it is spoken of in a past tense.[75] Here Aune exchanges an aspectual explanation of the aorist for a temporal one. And Aune does not implement his perspective on verb tenses throughout his commentary, often opting for older, temporal explanations rather than the aspectual one that he seems to endorse in his introduction. For example, in 7.9–17 Aune describes the tense shift that take place in this segment in temporal language, where he sees irregularity in the shift from "a sequence of past tense verbs, then a sequence of present-tense verbs, followed by a sequence of future-tense verbs."[76]

Summary

Several concluding observations can be drawn concerning previous attention given to the issue of verb tenses in the Apocalypse. First, there is an overwhelming sense among interpreters that John's use of tenses is unique or odd or inconsistent and requires some sort of explanation. One of the most common theories for explaining Revelation's tense usage understands John's use of the Greek tenses in light of the Semitic tense system, though there are exceptions (Aune; Dougherty). Second, and most importantly, virtually all of the discussion related to the supposed confusion in tense usage in Revelation or supposed Semitic influence assumes that the Greek tense system should be understood according to a temporal model: aorist = past; present = present; perfect = past and present; future = future. Consequently, apparent deviations from this (temporal) "norm" in Revelation give rise to judgments regarding the aberrant Greek or the unique character of John's use of tenses. Thus according to Thompson the shift in tenses that takes place in Revelation is "inexplicable from a Greek viewpoint," by which he must mean a *temporal viewpoint*.[77] If Greek tenses grammaticalize absolute temporal

---

[75] Aune, *Revelation 1–5*, clxxxvii.
[76] David E. Aune, *Revelation 6–16* (WBC 52b; Nashville: Thomas Nelson, 1998) 438. Cf. also his comments on 11.1–13.
[77] Thompson, *Semitic Syntax*, 49.

relations, Revelation's use of tenses, especially where the author shifts tenses in his visionary material, understandably appears quite odd, aberrant, or inconsistent.[78] In one sense this state of affairs is not surprising since the grammars upon which these works rely perpetuate temporally-based descriptions of the tense system in Greek.

Third, when rendering judgments concerning Semitic influence on the tenses in Revelation, it is useful and necessary, following Porter, to distinguish between 1) *translations* of an underlying Semitic source; 2) *enhancement* of a rare though extant Greek grammatical construction through Semitic influence; 3) *intervention*, where a construction that is unparalleled in Greek can be attributed to direct Semitic influence.[79] Several of the above studies fail to observe these distinctions, often giving a false impression of the extent of Semitic influence; only the last example (intervention) can legitimately be labeled a true Semitism, according to Porter, since it represents an intrusion into the Greek verbal system. Revelation may contain examples of the first category (translation), since it alludes to or quotes from Old Testament texts at virtually every juncture, and even the second category. Fourth, there is inconsistency and a lack of a rigorous methodological approach which is linguistically grounded to the issue of verb tenses in this previous discussion. As seen below, our understanding of Greek grammar in general, and the Greek tense system in particular, has made significant strides in recent years, making it possible to readdress the issue with fresh questions. Virtually all of the attempts to account for the tenses usage in Revelation have proceeded from a temporal approach. Dougherty and Aune seem to be aware of the fact that the tense forms, even in the indicative, may not indicate temporal reference but aspect. Yet they fail to develop this important insight or implement these insights consistently throughout their work, usually opting for the time-based models that they initially question.

---

[78] It is not my intention to suggest that time-based conceptions of the Greek tense system cannot handle the tenses at all in Revelation or that it necessarily entails turning to Semitic influence for a solution. I am only suggesting that attempts to find Semitic influence stem largely from a temporal orientation to understanding the Greek tenses in Revelation. When these do not "fit," rather than looking at the Greek verbal edifice itself the Hebrew tense system is called upon to provide an explanation.

[79] Stanley E. Porter, "The Language of the Apocalypse in Recent Discussion," *NTS* 35 (1989) 587.

Method and Approach

Therefore, it is the intention of this work to revisit the issue of Greek tense usage in Revelation in light of recent linguistic advances in the field of Greek verb tenses. The suggested model for application is the theoretical, metalinguistic category of verbal aspect. Recent research into verbal aspect theory now requires that we rethink how we approach the tense system of New Testament Greek. With the production of two pioneering, significant efforts on the subject by Porter and Fanning, along with a significant cluster of subsequent works by K.L. McKay, Rodney J. Decker, M. Olsen, and Constantine R. Campbell,[80] it is becoming more common for grammarians of New Testament Greek to recognize aspect as a fundamental component of the tense system of Koine Greek.[81] According to verbal aspect theory, a concept explored more extensively in the following chapter, the verb tense endings indicate *the author's conception of a process* or *viewpoint on the action*. That is, aspect indicates how the author chooses to represent or portray the action, irrespective of *when* or *how* the action took place. Thus in contrast to older studies of Greek grammar, there is increasing recognition that Greek verbs grammaticalize aspect,

---

[80] Stanley E. Porter, *Verbal Aspect in the Greek of the New Testament, with Reference to Tense and Mood* (SBG 1; New York: Peter Lang, 1989); *Idioms of the Greek New Testament* (BLG 2; Sheffield: JSOT Press, 1992); Buist M. Fanning, *Verbal Aspect in New Testament Greek* (Oxford: Clarendon Press, 1990); K.L. McKay, *A New Syntax of the Verb in New Testament Greek: An Aspectual Approach* (SBG 5; New York: Peter Lang, 1994); Mari Olsen, *A Semantic and Pragmatic Model of Lexical and Grammatical Aspect* (Outstanding Dissertations in Linguistics; New York: Garland, 1997); Rodney J. Decker, *Temporal Deixis of the Greek Verb in the Gospel of Mark with Reference to Verbal Aspect* (SBG 10; New York: Peter Lang, 2001); Constantine R. Campbell, *Verbal Aspect, the Indicative Mood, and Narrative: Soundings in the Greek of the New Testament* (SBG 13; New York: Peter Lang, 2007); Constantine R. Campbell, *Verbal Aspect and Non-indicative Verbs: Further Soundings in the Greek of the New Testament* (SBG 15; New York: Peter Lang, 2008). The groundbreaking works of Porter and Fanning were very different, in that Porter's work is much more theoretically rigorous and linguistically grounded, whereas Fanning is more pragmatic in his approach to verbal aspect. The works of Porter and Fanning have also been followed by numerous article-length studies (see esp. *Filologia Neotestamentaria*) implementing and testing their approaches, especially Porter's.

[81] Moises Silva had the following praise for the works of Porter and Fanning: "It is only a mild exaggeration to say that, with the almost simultaneous publication of these volumes, our knowledge and understanding of the Greek verbal system has taken a quantum leap forward" ("Review of Buist M. Fanning, *Verbal Aspect in New Testament Greek*, and Stanley E. Porter, *Verbal Aspect in the Greek New Testament* (sic): *With Reference to Tense and Mood*," *WTJ* 54 [1992] 180). Without diminishing the significance of the ground-breaking works of McKay, would it be too much to conclude that Porter and Fanning are the "fathers of verbal aspect study in the New Testament?"

rather than time (past, present, future) or *Aktionsart* (kind of action, or how the action actually takes place, e.g. punctiliar, durative). Though this work on verbal aspect in the New Testament has been proceeding for two decades, to date there has been no comprehensive or systematic attempt to apply aspect theory to the Apocalypse, especially in light of the amount of attention that the tenses in Revelation have received and the varying accompanying judgments offered. Indeed, virtually all previous studies which addressed the issue of verb tenses in the Apocalypse surveyed above were produced well before the groundbreaking works of Porter and Fanning, having no recourse to the most important, recent work.[82] And since the works of Porter and Fanning have appeared aspect theory has had some time to undergo evaluation and development.

Aune, and to a limited extent Dougherty, stand alone in recognizing the potential value of insights from verbal aspect for understanding of the tense usage in the Apocalypse, though Dougherty did not have the benefit of the important works of Porter and Fanning. Furthermore, Aune's treatment is limited to a brief introduction, and as seen above he is inconsistent in his attempts to implement insights from verbal aspect into his treatment of various verb forms and into his exegesis throughout his commentary, often opting instead for an older, temporally-based model of explanation. And Dougherty, though aware of the work of McKay on aspect, does not develop a consistent aspectual approach to verb tenses in Revelation, also usually reverting to on an older, temporal- and *Aktionsart*-based model and categories for the tense forms, so that he is ultimately unable to shed time-based conceptions of the tenses. This inconsistency in which insights from aspect have been applied to Revelation suggests that the works on verbal aspect theory, especially Porter's, have not yet sufficiently been heard.

It appears, then, that the time is ripe, in view of the recent advances in aspect theory and its ongoing examination, testing, and development, and in light of the interest that John's use of verb tenses has garnered and the various theories which attempt to explain them, to revisit the topic of Greek tenses in Revelation. In the following chapter, therefore, it will be

---

[82] However, Thompson would have had access to the important nascent work on aspect by K.L. McKay produced in the early 1970's. See e.g. K.L. McKay, "Syntax in Exegesis," *TynB* 23 (1972) 39–57. As seen above, Dougherty relies on McKay's description of aspect, and in theory he seems to hold this view for verb tenses in Revelation. It is unclear, but doubtful, whether Dougherty was aware of the works of Porter or Fanning, since the publication date of these works are contemporaneous with Dougherty's. Most likely he did not have access to their works.

necessary to set out and summarize verbal aspect theory as advocated by Porter and others in more detail, in preparation for its application to the use of the tense system in the Apocalypse. In the remaining chapters I will examine and discuss the major tenses and their uses in the Apocalypse, as well as the issue of shifting tenses and possible patterns of usage in Revelation's visions in light of recent work done on aspect theory. It will become clear that I find Porter's approach to verbal aspect to offer a particularly compelling model with explanatory power to account for the verb tense usage in Revelation. While I will at times touch on non-indicative forms of the verbs, this study will focus primarily on indicative forms of the verbs since most of the debate lies with the usage of tense forms in the indicative mood, which are assumed to be temporal, in Revelation. A final chapter will briefly draw several conclusions regarding tense usage in Revelation and its relationship to the question of the nature of Revelation's Greek and ostensible Semitic influence.

CHAPTER TWO

VERBAL ASPECT THEORY

Verbal Aspect

The purpose of this chapter is not to provide a comprehensive account of verbal aspect and its development, nor to provide a detailed argument for its validity since these have already been done;[1] rather this section will summarize the salient features of the discussion surrounding verbal aspect theory and its significance for interpreting the New Testament in preparation for examining the function of verb tenses in the book of Revelation. The history and development of understanding of Greek verb tenses and the rise of verbal aspect has also adequately been documented elsewhere and will not be rehearsed here.[2] In the following discussion I will use the term "tense" or "tense form" to refer to the formal endings on verbs, without any necessary reference to actual tense (time). As will become clear, the primary semantic feature indicated by these tense forms is aspect, or how the author chooses to conceive of the action, rather than time or the procedural characteristics of the action (*Aktionsart*).

The study of the Greek tense system in the New Testament is undergoing somewhat of a revolution. As already noted, there is now increasing interest in verbal aspect as a metalinguistic semantic category with explanatory power to illuminate the verb tense system of New Testament Greek, a revolution sparked by the simultaneous appearance of the two major works by Porter and Fanning.[3] Since then, research contributing to our understanding of verbal aspect and its potential significance for exegesis has continued at a steady pace. The potential significance of aspect

---

[1] On the Greek of the New Testament see especially the works of Porter, Fanning, McKay, Olsen, Decker, Campbell.

[2] Cf. Porter, *Verbal Aspect*, chap. 1; Fanning, *Verbal Aspect*, chap. 1; Decker, *Temporal Deixis*, 5–26. Cf. Stanley E. Porter, "The Greek Language of the New Testament," in Stanley E. Porter (ed.), *Handbook to the Exegesis of the New Testament* (Leiden: Brill, 1997) 114–119 for a briefer, but helpful survey.

[3] Porter, *Verbal Aspect*; Fanning, *Verbal Aspect*.

as a viable category for perceiving the Greek tense system can best be seen
by contrasting it with more traditional approaches to Greek verbs. The
treatment of the Greek verb tense system in almost all Greek grammars
has tended to crystallize around two main concerns: time and *Aktionsart*
(kind of action). Though early on A.T. Robertson questioned the notion
that Greek verb tenses were primarily temporal in orientation, treatment
of Greek verb tenses largely proceeded from a temporal standpoint.[4] New
Testament Greek tense usage that apparently deviated from this temporal
model was deemed exceptional (the so-called "gnomic" aorist, or "historical" present), or could still be explained from the standpoint of the
assumed temporal value of the tense form (the "gnomic aorist" based
on a single, *past* occurrence; the "historic present" as if the reader were
present when the events took place in a temporal, rhetorical shift; the
"proleptic aorist" which views a future event as if it has already taken
place; etc.). Accordingly, in the indicative mood Greek verb tenses were
thought to communicate absolute temporal values, that is, time in relationship to the deictic center, usually the time of writing/speaking: past
(aorist, imperfect, pluperfect tense forms), present (present tense form),
combining past and present (perfect tense form), and future (future tense
form).[5] With little exception, this is the model that dominates most of
the discussion of the verb tense system in the treatments of tenses in the
Apocalypse surveyed in the previous chapter.

Moreover, alongside of temporal conceptions of Greek verbs, according to the category of *Aktionsart* Greek verb tenses were also regarded as
more or less indicating how the action objectively occurred.[6] As Porter
summarizes, under this approach "certain values are attached to the verb
tense-forms, such as punctiliar to the aorist, durative or linear to the
present."[7] Grammars have consequently developed a whole complex of
vocabulary to capture the various *Aktionsarten* supposedly communicated by verb tenses: durative, iterative, punctiliar, ingressive, culmina-

---

[4] A.T. Robertson, *A Grammar of the Greek New Testament in the Light of Historical Research* (Nashville: Broadman, 1934) 825: "Even in the indicative *the time element is subordinate* to the kind of action expressed." Italics mine. However, I would question Robertson's emphasis on kind of action. For a history of this (temporal) approach see Porter, *Verbal* Aspect, 22–26.

[5] On the deictic center see Olsen, *Semantic and Pragmatic Model*, 6.

[6] Cf. for example BDF § 318 and most other Greek grammars at beginning, interme-
diate and advanced levels. For a detailed discussion of this approach to Greek verb tenses, and some of the shortcomings of this method, see Porter, *Verbal Aspect*, 26–35.

[7] Porter, *Idioms*, 27.

tive, resultative, etc.[8] The following chart illustrates a standard approach to Greek verb tenses from the standpoint of time and *Aktionsart* reflected in a majority of Greek grammars.

Aorist	Punctiliar or undefined action in the past
Present	Continuous, durative action in the present
Imperfect	Continuous, durative action in the past
Perfect	Past action with present results
Pluperfect	Past action with past results
Future	Durative or punctiliar action in the future

The main difficulty with these models (time and *Aktionsart*) for understanding the Greek tense system is that numerous exceptions have to be accommodated. That is, identical tense forms are sometimes used in different temporal or situational contexts, or different tense forms are used in similar or identical contexts, a principle known as *contrastive substitution*.[9]

Present tense form used in different temporal contexts:[10]
Matt 8.25: κύριε ... ἀπολλύμεθα (present)
Mark 11.27: καὶ ἔρχονται πάλιν εἰς Ἰεροσόλυμα (past)
Matt 26.18: πρὸς σὲ ποιῶ τὸ πάσχα μετὰ τῶν μαθητῶν μου (future)
2 Cor 9.7: ἱλαρὸν γὰρ δότην ἀγαπᾷ ὁ θεός (temporally unrestricted)

Different tense forms used in similar (past time, speech) contexts:[11]
Luke 21.10: Τότε ἔλεγεν αὐτοῖς (imperfect)
Luke 20.41: εἶπεν ... πρὸς αὐτούς (aorist)
Acts 20.38: τῷ λόγῳ ᾧ εἰρήκει (perfect)
Mark 5.19: ἀλλὰ λέγει αὐτῷ (present)

---

[8] See Daniel B. Wallace, *Greek Grammar Beyond the Basics: An Exegetical Syntax of the New Testament* (Grand Rapids: Zondervan, 1996) 494–586. Fanning (*Verbal Aspect*) also follows this approach, though he attempts to ground it in a discussion and implementation of verbal aspect theory, raising the question of whether the more standard, older models can be integrated into the newer aspectual approach. For an example of the usage of these categories outside of biblical Greek see Herbert W. Smyth, *Greek Grammar* (Cambridge, MA: Harvard, 1956) 421–436.

[9] For discussion and examples see Porter, *Verbal Aspect*, 75–84; Decker, *Temporal Deixis*, 34, who is dependent on Porter at this point.

[10] The following examples are taken from Porter, *Verbal Aspect*, 75.

[11] See Porter, *Verbal Aspect*, 83 for these examples, to which I have added the Mark 5.19 reference with the present tense form of λέγει. The Mark 5.19 passage also presents a difficulty for notions that the present indicates "durative," "ongoing," or "continuous" action, since the speech that λέγει encompasses is of relatively short duration and does not continue for any appreciable length of time (he was not continually saying this).

It becomes clear that a strictly temporal approach or an approach from the standpoint of *Aktionsart* to Greek verb tenses is inadequate for accommodating the full range of tense usage in the New Testament. On the basis of the tendency of Greek not to waste multiple forms on the same function, one needs to explain why two or three tense forms are apparently used of similar *Aktionsarten* or temporal references.[12] According to Porter, the main proponent of aspect theory, a unified semantic theory is necessary to replace the prevailing model. The unifying semantic feature that is now being advocated is verbal aspect.

According to aspectual theory, verbal aspect refers to the way that the author chooses to represent, view, or conceive of the action indicated by the verb. The most linguistically rigorous and oft-quoted definition from its most ardent proponent is Porter's:

> Greek verbal aspect is a synthetic semantic category (realized in the forms of verbs) used of meaningful oppositions in a network of tense systems to grammaticalize the author's reasoned subjective choice of conception of a process.[13]

A somewhat more concise definition is presented by Fanning: aspect is "that category in grammar of the verb which reflects the focus or viewpoint of the speaker in regard to the action or condition which the verb describes."[14] Simplifying Porter's definition, "Aspect is the semantic category by which a speaker or writer grammaticalizes a view of the situation by the selection of a particular verb form in the verbal system."[15] Or according to K.L. McKay, aspect "is that category of the verb system by means of which an author (or speaker) shows how he views each event or activity ... in relation to its context."[16] What all these definitions possess in common is the express emphasis on the way the author chooses to portray or represent the action by his/her choice of a particular tense

---

[12] See Porter, *Verbal Aspect*, 83–84.

[13] Porter, *Verbal Aspect*, 88. Less technical is his definition in *Idioms*: "*verbal aspect is defined as a semantic (meaning) category by which a speaker or writer grammaticalizes (i.e. represents a meaning by choice of a word-form) a perspective on an action by the selection of a particular tense-form in the verbal system*" (20–21). Italics his.

[14] Fanning, *Verbal Aspect*, 84. Fanning argues that "viewpoint or perspective appears to be the residue of meaning left when the other features are stripped away or minimized by various means" (83).

[15] Decker, *Temporal Deixis*, 26.

[16] McKay, *New Syntax*, 27.

form.[17] The key feature of aspect is 'viewpoint', 'representation', or 'portrayal' of the action, as opposed to *when* (time) or *how* (*Aktionsart*) the action actually took place. Aspect is "perspectival."[18] Attached to each tense form (grammaticalization), then, is a particular way of portraying the action on the part of the author/speaker.

The potential significance of an aspectual approach can be seen by comparing the older and the more recent, aspectual approach to verb tenses in a text such as Rom 3.23. Paul states that πάντες γὰρ ἥμαρτον καὶ ὑστεροῦνται τῆς δόξης τοῦ θεοῦ ("all have sinned and fall short of the glory of God"). According to the older approach, the aorist ἥμαρτον would refer to past action that is punctiliar or undefined, while the present ὑστεροῦνται refers to ongoing present action. Under this view the two verbs together would in effect function like a perfect (traditionally conceived): a past, completed action, with ongoing results (all have sinned in the past, with the ongoing results of falling short continuing into the present). However, according to an aspectual approach, the difference has to do with the author's conception of the processes. The aorist ἥμαρτον summarizes the point argued in 1.18–3.19, that everyone has sinned, or it may simply state a timeless truth: all (πάντες) sin. The present tense ὑστεροῦνται, rather than referring to present ongoing action, further describes what sinning entails: it is falling short of God's glory. In this case the present tense form, rather than referring to a separate activity as a result of a past act, further defines and describes what sinning is.

Though there still remain areas of debate and disagreement in the way aspect theory is understood and applied, at least the following issues emerge as essential to aspect theory and represent areas of broad agreement among its proponents.[19] First of all, and perhaps most significantly, aspect takes precedence over time in the Greek verb tense system. According to Porter in particular (cf. Decker, Campbell), to some

---

[17] Cf. the helpful introduction in B. Comrie, *Aspect: An Introduction to the Study of Verbal Aspect and Related Problems* (Cambridge: University Press, 1976). Also, Maximilian Zerwick defines aspect as "the manner in which the action is regarded" (*Biblical Greek Illustrated by Examples* [Istituto Biblico: Roma, 2001] 77).

[18] J.W. Voelz, "Present and Aorist Verbal Aspect: A New Proposal," *Neot* 27 (1993) 157. See T.V. Evans, "Future Directions for Aspect Studies in Ancient Greek," in B.A. Taylor et al (eds.), *Biblical Greek Language and Lexicography: Essays in Honor of Frederick W. Danker* (Grand Rapids: Eerdmans, 2004) 201.

[19] For a survey of recent work and prospectus, see Robert E. Picirilli, "The Meaning of the Tenses in New Testament Greek: Where Are We?" *JETS* 48 (2005) 533–555.

extent to McKay, and less so to Fanning, the author's portrayal of the action (aspect) must clearly be distinguished from the absolute time at which the action takes place.[20] That is, the verb tense endings are not the conveyers of time; rather deixis and broader contextual and discourse features play this role.[21] In Porter's words, "when Greek speakers used a verb they had something other than temporal categories in mind with regard to what the verb form itself meant."[22] Though traditionally time was thought to be a major factor in at least the indicative mood, verbal aspect theory mitigates or even denies temporality even in the indicative mood. This is perhaps the most provocative claim of verbal aspect theory, especially as proposed by Porter, and one of the most potentially significant for our discussion, since as seen above most of the judgments regarding the tenses in the Apocalypse rely heavily on a temporal orientation toward Greek verb tenses. Deviations from their assumed temporal values must be explained. But as McKay adequately summarizes, "the tenses of ancient Greek do not signal time except by implication from their relationship to their context. Most of the tenses could be used with present, past or even future reference, depending on the time indicated mainly by other factors in the context."[23]

Thus, for example, in addition to the use of the present tense in present time contexts, most grammars make room for categories such as "historical present" and "futuristic present," or for the aorist, "gnomic aorist" or "futuristic (proleptic) aorist," though these are frequently regarded as exceptional uses, or as rhetorical applications of the common temporal value.[24] Yet according to verbal aspect theory, such usages are normal (rather than exceptional or odd) and can be explained from the standpoint that Greek verb tense forms only grammaticalize the author's

---

[20] Fanning initially claims that "aspect has nothing inherently to do with temporal sequence" (*Verbal Aspect*, 85), but he goes on to argue for "secondary" temporal nature of the aspect of verbs in the indicative mood (see 8–29). For further discussion of the relationship of aspect to time in Greek verbs see K.L. McKay, "Time and Aspect in New Testament Greek," *NovT* 34 (1992) 209–228. For a recent insistence on the temporal values of Greek verbs by a native speaker see Chrys C. Caragounis, *The Development of Greek in the New Testament* (Grand Rapids: Baker, 2006) 316–336. Cf. Moises Silva's response ("Biblical Greek and Modern Greek: A Review Article," *WTJ* 67 [2005] 391–404).

[21] For a concise treatment of temporal deixis cf. Decker, *Temporal Deixis*, 56–59.

[22] Stanley E. Porter, *Studies in the Greek of the New Testament: Theory and Practice* (SBG 6; New York: Peter Lang, 1996) 38. Cf. Porter, *Verbal Aspect*, 102–108.

[23] McKay, *New Syntax*, 39.

[24] See Wallace, *Greek Grammar*, 526–539; 562–565.

conception of a process and not temporal relations. Instead, temporal notions are resident in the broader context of the discourse.[25] This theory has been tested at a broader level over an extended discourse (Mark's Gospel) by Decker.[26]

Second, aspect is inextricably tied to the formal tense endings of Greek verbs. The synthetic aspects are grammaticalized morphologically in the tense endings (as opposed to time and *Aktionsarten* which are contextually determined), and are indicated by the author's selection of one of the tense forms from the verbal system (see below). Though Campbell sees this linkage between aspect and morphology as an assumption, he thinks that it is a reasonable one.[27] Thus by selecting the aorist tense form, for example, the author chooses to portray the action in a certain way irrespective of the time when the action occurred or the kind of action taking place. The selection of one tense form entails not selecting another, so that the selection of a given aspect, realized morphologically in the tense endings, entails a reasoned semantic choice. That the aspectual meanings are morphologically based appears to have garnered widespread acceptance among advocates of verbal aspect.

Third, the above definitions of aspect suggest a crucial distinction between aspect and *Aktionsart*.[28] This differentiation between aspect and *Aktionsart* now appears to have become commonplace in discussions of verbal aspect. As Evans notes, "A far greater precision has been achieved in defining the crucial category of aspect and in distinguishing it from closely interacting features."[29] Fanning refers to these features as *procedural characteristics*.[30] Though it is necessary to recognize that the distinction is somewhat overdrawn, the difference between *Aktionsart* and aspect is usually explained in terms of *objectivity* and *subjectivity*.[31] While

---

[25] For concise responses to a number of objections to the contention that Greek verbs grammaticalize aspect and not time see Decker, *Temporal Deixis*, 38–45.

[26] Decker, *Temporal Deixis*.

[27] Campbell, *Verbal Aspect*, 9.

[28] However, these two terms are still frequently confused in some grammatical discussion. For an example of this confusion see BDF §§ 166–167. BDF appears to distinguish the two when they suggest that Greek verbs indicated not time but "*Aktionsarten* (kinds of action) or aspects (points of view)" (166). However, in the rest of their treatment it is evident that they use the two terms interchangeably. Evans recognizes this distinction as one of the crucial gains of aspect studies ("Future Directions," 200–202).

[29] Evans, "Future Directions," 206. Cf. C. Bache, "Aspect and Aktionsart: Towards a Semantic Distinction," *Journal of Linguistics* 18 (1982) 57–72.

[30] Fanning, *Verbal Aspect*, ch. 3.

[31] Cf. Campbell, *Verbal Aspect*, 11: "The qualification that neither of these categories is *entirely* subjective or objective is simply a recognition that often aspect is determined by

Aktionsart has to do with the *objective* nature of the action itself (though *Aktionsart* is far from being completely objective)[32] as indicated by lexis and by broader contextual factors, aspect "depend[s] very largely on the *subjective* attitude of the speaker or writer"[33] as indicated by the choice of a given tense form. But as Porter himself points out, "patterns of usage, for example in various discourse types, mean that choice of verbal aspect is *not* random."[34] A view of Greek verbs from the standpoint of *Aktionsart* persists in standard characterizations of Greek verb tenses as punctiliar (aorist) or durative/continuous (present, imperfect) advocated in most grammars.[35] Yet such meanings are contextually and lexically determined, and attempt to describe how the action actually unfolds; cf. ingressive, instantaneous, repeated, culminative, etc. As Evans confidently predicts, "The days of explaining present and aorist forms in terms of durative and punctiliar aspect values are numbered."[36] In contrast to this approach, aspect refers to how the author chooses to represent the process being referred to irrespective of its procedural character. Hence it is illegitimate in exegesis to progress directly from the formal ending of the verb to the time or kind of action being described.[37]

Fourth, and related to the previous distinction, it is necessary in aspectual studies to draw a distinction between *semantics* and *pragmatics*.[38] The former refers to the invariable meaning of the tense endings, that is, aspect, which is *uncancellable*,[39] while the latter refers to the various con-

---

standardized usage and expression, or a lack of choice, and *Aktionsart* is still a matter of observation and interpretation." Cf. Buist M. Fanning, "Approaches to Verbal Aspect in New Testament Greek: Issues in Definition and Method," in *Biblical Greek Language and Linguistics: Open Questions in Current Research* (ed. Stanley E. Porter and D.A. Carson; JSNTSS 80; Sheffield: JSOT Press, 1993) 50–51; Richard A. Young, *Intermediate New Testament Greek* (Nashville: Broadman & Holman, 1994) 106.

[32] Cf. Porter, *Verbal Aspect*, 26–35.

[33] McKay, *New Syntax*, 27. Cf. Porter, *Verbal Aspect*, 86–88.

[34] Stanley E. Porter, "In Defence of Verbal Aspect," in *Biblical Greek Language and Linguistics: Open Questions in Current Research* (ed. Stanley E. Porter and D.A. Carson; JSNTSS 80; Sheffield: JSOT Press, 1993) 33.

[35] E.g. William D. Mounce, *Basics of Biblical Greek Grammar* (2nd edn; Grand Rapids: Zondervan, 2003).

[36] Evans, "Future Directions," 206.

[37] See Dave Mathewson, "Verbal Aspect in Imperatival Constructions in Pauline Ethical Injunctions," *FN* 9 (1996) 21.

[38] "Thus the failure to distinguish clearly between semantics and pragmatics appears to be a legitimate problem within traditional analysis" (Campbell, *Verbal Aspect*, 25). Cf. Olsen, *Semantic and Pragmatic Model*, 4.

[39] On uncancellability see Porter, *Verbal Aspect*, 114; Decker, *Temporal Deixis*, 45–48; Campbell, *Verbal Aspect*, 26–27; Olsen, *Semantic and Pragmatic Model*, 17.

textual realizations of the aspects. Much confusion results from a failure to distinguish these two features (defining a given tense based on a common pragmatic realization, e.g. present tense for present time). Porter also uses the term "implicature" to refer to that which can be inferred from the use of a certain aspect in a certain contextual environment (implication).[40] Consequently, the usage of a given tense in certain textual environments can implicate certain temporal meanings (e.g., aorist and imperfect in narrative).[41]

Fanning argues that aspect and the procedural character of verbs (*Aktionsart*) affect one another profoundly, so that aspect interacts with and is *shaped by* the context to produce various meanings.[42] Here Fanning is heavily dependent of the Vendler-Kenny taxonomy for classifying verbs.[43] Despite his insistence that the semantics of the tense forms and the pragmatics of the contexts in which they occur be kept separate, it is not clear that he consistently carries through with this. For Fanning talks in terms of other elements in the context having "an *important influence* on aspectual force," or that "Aspect *operates so closely* with such features [procedural characteristics] and is *so significantly affected* by them."[44] Fanning is apparently not just saying that these pragmatic meanings belong only to the context, but that the tense endings actually take these meanings "on board"[45] to create new meanings. But this is to confuse the

---

[40] Porter, *Verbal Aspect*, 103. Porter defines implicature as what can be inferred from a given grammatical construction, but which inference does not belong to the essential semantics of the construction. In the same way I will use the term implicature to refer to the implications that can be drawn from the use of an aspect in a given context.

[41] Porter, *Verbal Aspect*, 104–107.

[42] Fanning, *Verbal Aspect*, 50. Cf. Wallace, *Greek Grammar*, 500: "[T]enses combine with other linguistic features to form various fields of meaning."

[43] For a critique of the Vendler-Kenny classification, especially as it is applied to New Testament Greek verbs by Fanning, see Matthew D. Brook, "Authorial Choice and Verbal Aspect in the NT: An Investigation Using Corpus Linguistics to Identify Patterns of Aspectual Usage Linked with Lexis, Syntax and Context," (M.Div thesis, Gordon Conwell Theological Seminary, 1997) 58–63.

[44] Fanning, *Verbal Aspect*, 164, 50. Italics mine.

[45] D.A. Carson, "An Introduction to the Porter/Fanning Debate," 23. Fanning appears confusing or inconsistent at this point. For the distinction between aspect and "procedural characteristics" see *Verbal Aspect*, 49–50. "[A]spect is semantically distinct from these procedural characteristics: it is not to be equated with various characteristics of the *actual occurrence*" (49). For example, Fanning says of the aorist and its various usages: "the aorist itself does not bear these meanings" (*Verbal Aspect*, 97–98). Yet the overarching burden of Fanning's work is to demonstrate that the aspects are shaped and affected profoundly by the surrounding context. Statements that aspect interacts with and is profoundly affected by contextual features to produce new meanings are at odds with his

semantics of aspect with the pragmatics of the surrounding context, and "overloads" the meaning of the tense form with the totality of the information communicated by the broader context (an error we have learned to avoid at the lexical level). By contrast, Porter in more concerned with explicating the essential semantic feature of each aspect that finds realization in various contexts.[46] More balanced is Decker's view that "The web of semantic factors comprised by aspect, lexis, and *Aktionsart*, along with other grammatical and contextual factors (adjuncts, deixis, etc.) is referred to … as the verbal complex."[47] Therefore, aspect as grammaticalized in the tense endings only contributes the notion of the author's viewpoint or perspective to the verbal complex of ideas, but does not "pick up" the other features from the complex.[48] Thus aspect must be distinguished from this complex of ideas. Aspect communicates how the author chooses to view that action and must be distinguished from lexis, *Aktionsart*, and other contextual features. While aspect belongs to grammar, time and *Aktionsart* belong to pragmatics.

---

above statements. This can also be seen by the traditional labels that he uses to describe the various tense usages: progressive, iterative, customary, conative, ingressive, culminative, etc. It is not clear that Fanning has kept these two (semantics and pragmatics) sufficiently distinct.

[46] Porter, *Verbal Aspect*, 82: "I am primarily concerned with defining the essential semantic component(s) of tense usage in Greek, i.e. use of the tense forms at the level of code or network which allows various pragmatic manifestations at the level of text."

[47] Decker, *Temporal Deixis*, 27. Cf. also Brook, "Authorial Choice," 28, who sees the tense forms as not being shaped by the context, but as contributing to the composite of meaning made up of the individual parts.

[48] To confuse aspect and *Aktionsart* or other procedural characteristics, or semantics and pragmatics, is to commit at a grammatical level what James Barr has warned against at a lexical level, when he discouraged the confusion of word and concept endemic in much lexical work such as *TDNT*. Cf. James Barr, *The Semantics of Biblical Language* (Oxford: University Press, 1961). At a grammatical level this is reflected in the overloading of verbal aspect with meanings from the larger context (even the historical background of a document) to produce such labels as "durative present," "iterative present," "inceptive imperfect," "consummative aorist" and so on, as found in almost all grammars. As descriptive of the various tense forms, such labels are better abandoned as inappropriate and unnecessary, though this goes against a long tradition of grammatical discussion. Cf. Charles R. Smith, "Errant Aorist Interpreters," *GTJ* 2 (1981) 205–226 who also calls for the abandonment of such label for the aorist, though for different reasons. As Porter says, "a distinction between the meaning of an entire proposition in context and the individual semantic value of its component parts must be made. Because of confusion over the difference between a sentence with, for example, inceptive meaning and the meaning of the individual verb form, it may be better to abandon such descriptive labels" (*Verbal Aspect*, 184).

In summary, it is clear that the understanding of Greek verb tenses has undergone a significant reconceptualization. The linguistic notion of verbal aspect has risen to the forefront of discussion. According to aspect theory, as advocated by Porter, Fanning, McKay and others, Greek verb tense endings grammaticalize the author's viewpoint or portrayal of a process (aspect), irrespective of how the action took place (*Aktionsart*) or when the action took place (time) and must be clearly distinguished from these features. At the very least one must recognize that time is but a secondary feature in the Greek verb tense system (along with Robertson), and that the primary feature communicated by the tense endings is aspect.

Defining the Aspects

It was suggested above that verbal aspect is a semantic category grammaticalized in the Greek tense endings which indicates the author's perspective on a process. It remains to summarize the essential semantics of the aspects of Greek verb forms individually and in relation to each other. The starting point should be the two primary aspectual categories that are commonly agreed upon: perfective and imperfective aspect, or to draw on a metaphorical conception, external and internal viewpoints. According to Fanning, an action can be viewed from a vantage point outside of the action with a focus on the whole action and with no reference to its internal make-up (external viewpoint) or from a reference point within the action with a focus on the internal make-up of the action (internal viewpoint).[49] This is a useful way into the discussion of aspect. These two perspectives or aspects are grammaticalized by the aorist and the present/imperfect tense forms respectively. Thus according to the aorist aspect the action is presented "*in summary, viewed as a whole from the outside, without regard for the internal make-up of the occurrence.*"[50] By contrast, the present aspect "*focuses on its* [an action's] *development or progress* and sees the occurrence *in regard to its internal make-up, without*

---

[49] Fanning, *Verbal Aspect*, 85. In B. Comrie's words, "perfectivity indicates the view of a situation as a single whole, without distinction of the various separate phases that make up that situation; while the imperfective pays attention to the internal structure of the situation" (*Aspect*, 16). Cf. Campbell, *Verbal Aspect*, 8.

[50] Fanning, *Verbal Aspect*, 97. Italics his.

beginning or end in view."[51] Porter's understanding of the aorist and present/imperfect tenses is similar, though he substitutes the descriptive terminology "perfective" and "imperfective" respectively in order to avoid the confusing temporal implications of labels such as "present tense." The perfective aspect of the aorist portrays the action as a complete and undifferentiated whole, regardless of how or when the action actually takes place.[52] By contrast, the imperfective aspect grammaticalized in the present and imperfect tense forms conceives of the action as "*being in progress*. In other words, its internal structure is seen as unfolding."[53] In fact, Campbell concludes that the aspectual definitions of the present and aorist tense forms constitute one of the areas of aspect studies that is largely uncontested.[54] Thus in this area, aspect study is in general agreement that the aorist and present/imperfect tenses form the fundamental semantic opposition within the Greek tense system (the difference between the present and imperfect will be discussed below).

There is less agreement regarding a third potential aspect grammaticalized in the so-called perfect tense form. T.V. Evans identifies the perfect tense form as an area needing further attention.[55] Wallace proposed a fairly standard temporally oriented definition: the perfect "describes an event that, completed in the past ..., has results existing in the present time ...."[56] Fanning, however, regards it not as an additional aspect, but as a complex (too complex?) combination of three categories: *Aktionsart*

---

[51] Fanning, *Verbal Aspect*, 103. Italics his. See the similar distinction between perfective and imperfective aspect in Comrie, *Aspect*, 16–40.

[52] Porter, *Idioms*, 35. The use of the term "complete" to describe the aorist rather than "completed" is intentional. The latter designation suggests a temporal notion that is not the semantic property of the aorist tense form, though the aorist is well-suited for actions that are completed. It is also common to explain the aorist as "undefined" (from Greek ἀ–όριστος) Cf. Mounce, *Basics*, 126. While this label is innocuous in itself, the danger is that the interpreter might take this to mean that the aorist is void of semantic content. Thus Mounce (*Basics*, 126 n. 2) incorrectly understands the term this way when he concludes of the aorist: "The 'undefined aspect' is the absence of any specific aspect." Cf. Smith, "Errant Aorist Interpreters," who sees the aorist as an unmarked tense form in privative opposition to the other tenses. But the aorist is not void of meaning, but enters into meaningful opposition to the present and perfect. However, the term "undefined" may be unobjectionable if, in contrast to the present, it only means that the author does not describe the action's internal constituent makeup but only looks at the simple action, as a complete whole. In this way, the aorist tense form is still semantically weighted, though not in the same way as the present (or perfect).

[53] Porter, *Idioms*, 21. Italics his.

[54] Campbell, *Verbal Aspect*, 35, 103.

[55] Evans, "Further Directions," 205–206.

[56] Wallace, *Greek Grammar*, 573.

(stative action), tense (anterior action), and aspect (summary aspect). Evans sees the perfect as an imperfective (like the present) aspect expressing stative *Aktionsart*.[57] These definitions reflect studies that see the "stative" meaning as an *Aktionsart* rather than a third aspect.[58]

In distinction to Fanning, Porter, who follows McKay, has argued for a third distinct aspect: the stative aspect represented in the perfect and pluperfect tense forms, which regards the action as a given state of affairs.[59] Thus the perfect tense form conceives of the action as "the state or condition of the grammatical subject, as conceptualized by the speaker or writer."[60] In some transitive perfects the stative aspect also indicates the responsibility of the subject for the action that produced the state.[61] Aspectually, the perfect may or may not include a reference to an anterior action which produces the state: "Whether a previous event is alluded to or exists at all is a matter of lexis in context and not part of aspectual semantics."[62]

One of the most recent and significant challenges to this view of the perfect tense form has come from the recent work on verbal aspect by Campbell.[63] Campbell, a student of Evans, questions McKay's and Porter's analysis and instead sees the perfect tense form as grammaticalizing the aspectual feature of imperfectivity (like the present and imperfect tenses) along with the additional feature of "heightened proximity." Thus in addition to imperfective aspect, "the perfect semantically encodes a higher level of proximity."[64] It is sort of a "super present." Stativity, then, is an

---

[57] Fanning, *Verbal Aspect*, 119–120; Evans, "Further Directions," 206 and *Verbal Syntax in the Greek Pentateuch: Natural Greek Usage and Hebrew Interference* (New York: Oxford University Press, 2001) 30–32 (the latter work describes the perfect tense form as "a special type of imperfective, expressing stativity" [32]) respectively.

[58] Fanning, *Verbal Aspect*, 117.

[59] Porter, *Verbal Aspect*, chap. 5; *Idioms*, 21–22; McKay, *New Syntax*, 31–34. Cf. also K.L. McKay, "The Use of the Ancient Greek Perfect Down to the End of the Second Century," *Bulletin of the Institute of Classical Studies* 12 (1965) 1–21; McKay, "On the Perfect and Other Aspects."

[60] Porter, *Verbal Aspect*, 259. Or, as McKay says, "The perfect tense expresses the state or condition of the subject of the verb ..." (*New Syntax*, 49).

[61] McKay, *Syntax*, 32. Cf. his "On the Perfect and Other Aspects," 296–297.

[62] Porter, *Verbal* Aspect, 401. Cf. Porter, *Idioms*, 22. Thus this calls into question the traditional conception of the perfect as 'a past act with existing results', as sort of a combination between the aorist and present, temporally conceived. This view has wielded considerable but unnecessary influence on treatment of the perfect tense form in Revelation. See below.

[63] Campbell, *Verbal Aspect*, chap. 6.

[64] Campbell, *Verbal Aspect*, 197. Campbell's work is more of a treatment of levels of proximity than it is a treatment of the semantic category of verbal aspect. That is, levels

Aktionsart rather than an aspect, and is not part of the semantic property of the perfect form. Part of Campbell's argument depends on seeing the perfect tense form utilized in *similar contexts with the present* (imperfective) *tense form*, particularly within discourse (i.e. speech). Campbell concludes that at least in narrative "it is simply *very* rare to find a perfect outside discourse."[65] However, several criticisms can be leveled against Campbell's analysis of the perfect. First, Campbell places too much emphasis on his thesis regarding proximity.[66] His overall approach to the verb tense forms relies more on the spatial notion of proximity/remoteness rather than on aspect which plays a less significant role in his analysis. Second, in addition to the overemphasis on role that levels of proximity play in his construct, his conception of the perfect tense form experiences difficulties particularly in the non-indicative mood forms. In his second book on the topic, where he treats verbal aspect outside of the indicative mood form, Campbell admits that "remoteness" and "proximity" are no longer semantically encoded in non-indicative verbal forms.[67] However, this creates a problem for his approach with the perfect participle (and infinitive).[68] If the only semantic feature that dis-

---

of proximity end up playing a more important role and carry more interpretive weight in his scheme of treating verb tenses than the author's conception of a process.

[65] Campbell, *Verbal Aspect*, 187. Cf. also Evans, *Verbal Syntax*, ch. 6.

[66] For a similar criticism of Campbell's overdoing of the spatial notion see Buist M. Fanning, "Review of *Verbal Aspect, the Indicative Mood, and Narrative: Soundings in the Greek of the NT* by Constantine R. Campbell," *JETS* 51 / 2 (2008) 394–397. Campbell's view is somewhat lopsided in his treatment of the aspects, since there are four separate forms for the imperfective aspect (present, imperfect, perfect, pluperfect) distinguished by levels of remoteness/proximity, and only one form for the perfective aspect (aorist). Though Campbell does not explain this, perhaps it is because the aorist is the "external viewpoint" and only lends itself to remoteness. Campbell does see the future as also perfective (like the aorist), but it does not grammaticalize the semantic feature of remoteness. The following chart illustrates Campbell's scheme, and is adapted from his chart in *Verbal Aspect*, 243.

	Perfective	*Imperfective*
Heightened Proximity	–	Perfect
Proximity	–	Present
Remoteness	Aorist	Imperfect
Heightened Remoteness	–	Pluperfect

[67] This is much in the same way that more traditional grammarians conclude that *time* is no longer a feature outside of the indicative mood.

[68] Campbell does not discuss perfect infinitives, which are, however, comparatively rare. According to BibleWorks 7 it occurs 49 times in the New Testament (50 if one includes τεθῆναι from Rev 11.9).

tinguishes the present, imperfect, and perfect tense forms is the level of proximity, which is according to Campbell absent in the participle and other non-indicative tense-forms, then what distinguishes the perfect and present participle or infinitive? He must maintain the semantic feature of heightened proximity for these forms, otherwise the duplicate aspectual form would be unnecessary and would presumably drop out (e.g. there is no "imperfect" participle, since remoteness is not grammaticalized outside of the indicative mood). Campbell only asserts, but does not provide any compelling argumentation, that the notion of heightened proximity is still a semantic feature of the *non-indicative* perfect *participle* form.[69] But his inability to integrate his insights regarding levels of proximity into his discussion of non-indicative forms suggests that heightened proximity is not the semantic feature of the perfect tense in any of its forms.[70]

Third, Campbell's analysis is limited to narrative literature, and would need to demonstrate a distinction between the perfect and present tense-forms along the lines of proximity and heightened proximity rather than aspectuality in other literary types (e.g. epistolary). Fourth, though stativity may be an *Aktionsart* category, the perfect tense form may be an instance where aspect exhibits some overlap with a semantic (*Aktionsart*) category that is lexically and contextually determined. Fifth, in Revelation as well as elsewhere in the New Testament, the perfect tense form is found regularly along with the aorist rather than the present, which is problematic for Campbell's analysis.[71] In Revelation, Bousset noticed the mixing (*Vermischung*) of perfect and aorist tense-forms in Revelation (e.g. 5.7; 7.14; 8.5; 12.4; cf. 7.11 [pluperfect]).[72] And though Campbell may be generally correct that "it is simply very *rare* to find a perfect outside discourse,"[73] it does occur in narrative sections outside of the sections of discourse. But Campbell fails to note that the reason for this may

---

[69] Campbell, *Non-Indicative Verbs*, 28–29.

[70] Campbell's attempts to show the exegetical insights of this understanding of the perfect tense are unconvincing exegetically and are paradoxically dependent on an overly "temporal" (present time) translation. Hence he translates the perfects in 2 Tim 4.6–7 as "... the time of my departure **is coming** (ἐφέστηκεν), **I am fighting** (ἠγώνισμαι) the good fight, **I am finishing** (τετέλεκα) the race, **I am keeping** (τετήρηκα) the faith." See *Verbal Aspect*, 193–195. This is not an improvement over the more traditional ways of translating these texts.

[71] See the examples discussed in McKay, "On the Perfect and Other Aspects," 318–322.

[72] Bousset, *Offenbarung*, 169. For an example of a perfect (εἴληφας) in the midst of aorists (ἐβασίλευσας, ὠργίσθησαν, ἦλθεν) within discourse cf. 11.17–18.

[73] Campbell, *Verbal Aspect*, 187.

be the highly marked nature of the perfect tense form. Finally, much of
Campbell's analysis depends too much on translating the Greek perfect
in a certain way into English.

Given these shortcomings, this study will follow Porter and McKay
(see also Decker) and continue to view the perfect tense as a distinct
aspectual form which grammaticalizes the semantic feature of state of
affairs.[74] "The stative aspect distances itself from the process itself, referring to the state of the represented process."[75] This is the opposite of
Campbell's view that the perfect tense-form grammaticalizes "heightened proximity." Further, though Fanning and more traditional approaches add the feature of antecedent action to the perfect, as McKay
and Porter have argued the perfect tense as grammaticalizing a state of
affairs may or may not include an antecedent action of which it is a result
(cf. οἶδα, ἕστηκα).[76] The notion of prior action is lexically and contextually determined. Moreover, Porter and McKay's conception of the perfect
tense avoids the temporal dimensions of the more traditional approach
(a *past* action with *present* results) which run aground in numerous contexts. By understanding the perfect tense form as grammaticalizing a
state of affairs, it is possible to account for the variety of temporal contexts
in which it occurs.[77]

The three other tense forms require brief comment: imperfect, pluperfect, future. Aspectually, like the present the imperfect tense-form
grammaticalizes internal viewpoint, action seen as unfolding or developing.[78] Since both the present and imperfect tense forms grammaticalize
the identical semantic feature of internal viewpoint, this raises the question of what the distinction between the two forms might be. According
to Fanning's more temporal approach, the imperfect tense simply moves
the aspect of the present into past time.[79] However, though the imperfect

---

[74] Evans is close to this view, though he does not see "stativity" as an aspect. Nevertheless, he still apparently sees it as a semantic feature grammaticalized in the perfect tense
form (*Verbal Syntax*, 30–32).

[75] Porter, *Verbal Aspect*, 401.

[76] McKay, *New Syntax*, 31. Cf. also Evans, *Verbal Syntax*, 147.

[77] See examples and concise summary of the range of temporal reference in usage of
the perfect tense form in Porter, *Idioms*, 40–42.

[78] Cf. Porter, *Idioms*, 21.

[79] See Fanning, *Verbal Aspect*, 240. Cf. Wallace, *Greek Grammar*, 541, who also sees
it as imperfective in aspect, but with the added feature of past time, though Wallace
qualifies this by saying that when it comes to time, "the imperfect is almost always *past* ....
However, occasionally it portrays other than past time" (541). Cf. Young, *Intermediate*,
106.

tense is frequently attributed a preterite temporal quality, Porter, followed by Decker and Campbell, have argued that in addition to representing the aspectual value of action viewed internally as in progress, it also grammaticalizes the additional feature of "remoteness," which accounts also for the non-past contexts in which the imperfect can frequently be found.[80]

The imperfect "is used in contexts where the action is seen as more remote than the action described by the (non-remote) Present."[81] The notion of "remoteness" is a metaphorical application of a spatial notion suggesting distance, and like aspect concerns the viewpoint of the author.[82] This semantic feature of remoteness certainly includes remote (past) time as one of its pragmatic effects and would account for the numerous past-time contexts in which the imperfect tense occurs, but more broadly it includes action that is logically remote from the viewpoint of the speaker/writer.[83] It grammaticalizes "there" vs. "here." 'Then' vs. 'now' is a particular application of 'there' vs. 'here'. Therefore, "That past time predominates in the imperfect is not surprising given that this would be the most common type of remoteness in narrative literature."[84] The imperfect frequently stands alongside of the aorist in narrative contexts to fill in descriptive details.[85] That is, the "imperfect, semantically more heavily marked than the aorist" often occurs "in past contexts as the foreground narrative tense."[86] In addition, Decker suggests that the imperfect is also used "to record events simultaneous with other events (that may be either aorist or present)."[87] In contrast to the present, the imperfect is used when the author's perspective on the action is felt to be more remote. A final aspectual form, the pluperfect tense, stands in

---

[80] Cf. Porter, *Verbal Aspect*, 207; Decker, *Temporal Deixis*, 104–107; Campbell, *Verbal Aspect*, 84–85; Roy R. Millhouse, "The Use of the Imperfect Verb Form in the New Testament: An Investigation into Aspectual and Tense Relationships in Hellenistic Greek" (M.A. Thesis, Trinity Evangelical Divinity School, 1999) 57–80.

[81] Porter, *Verbal Aspect*, 207.

[82] Decker, *Temporal Deixis*, 106–107; Porter, *Verbal Aspect*, 207.

[83] Porter says that the imperfect tense form "is the closest that the Greek language comes to a form actually related to time" (*Idioms*, 33–34). Something similar could be said about the pluperfect tense form, which also grammaticalizes the constituent semantic feature of 'remoteness'. Porter concludes that the pluperfect tense "is not past-bound but appears predominantly in contexts with this implicature" (*Verbal Aspect*, 289).

[84] Decker, *Temporal Deixis*, 107. See also Porter, *Idioms*, 33–34.

[85] Decker, *Temporal Deixis*, 107: "Narrative writers normally employ the imperfective aspect for descriptive purposes."

[86] Porter, *Verbal Aspect*, 199. For Revelation see Aune, *Revelation 1–5*, clxxxvi.

[87] Decker, *Temporal Deixis*, 107.

relationship to the perfect as the imperfect does to the present. Like the imperfect, the pluperfect tense, in addition to the aspectual feature of action viewed as a state of affairs (stative), grammaticalizes the semantic feature of remoteness. Since the pluperfect occurs only one time in Revelation (7.11, εἱστήκεισαν) it will not be discussed here at any more length (see below on 7.9–17).[88]

The future tense presents a particular challenge for the grammarian, and there is much disagreement as to its precise nature, though there seems to be agreement that it is somewhat of a distinct form from the other aspects. McKay thinks that the future is a fourth aspect, grammaticalizing the semantic feature of *intention*, though virtually no one has followed him.[89] At the same time, McKay recognizes that the future is an anomaly in the Greek verb system.[90] Wallace regards the future as communicating aoristic, external aspect along with future time, while also recognizing that it is an enigma in the tense system.[91] Campbell treats the future as possessing both time (future) and aspect, regarding it as aspectually perfective.[92] His conclusion depends on seeing the future used with similar (ingressive) *Aktionsart* as the aorist. But many of his examples are not necessarily ingressive, and ultimately fail to prove his theory. It is more common to treat the future tense form as non-aspectual. Therefore, others treat it as primarily a modal form, being formally related to the subjunctive.[93]

Given this diversity of opinion, Porter argues that it has a unique place in the Greek verb system because of its odd formal paradigm (it consists of a single form with no choice in the other moods) and is therefore aspectually undetermined.[94] According to Porter, the future tense form should not be conceived of temporally (future time); rather "*the future*

---

[88]　See Aune, *Revelation 1–5*, clxxxvii–vii.

[89]　McKay, *New Syntax*, 34.

[90]　McKay, *New Syntax*, 34.

[91]　Wallace, *Greek Grammar*, 566. Wallace observes that "This tense is still something of an enigma, rendering any statements less than iron-clad" (566 n. 1). This is a significant admission from a temporally oriented approach.

[92]　Campbell, *Verbal Aspect*, 140–149.

[93]　Cf. C.F.D. Moule, *An Idiom Book of New Testament Greek* (2nd edn; Cambridge: Cambridge University Press, 1959) 21–23. For problems with taking the future as a modal form see Porter, *Verbal Aspect*, 406–407.

[94]　"Since the Future comprises a single paradigmatic edifice, and is morphologically undifferentiated (though it may have done this at one time with duplicate forms, and allows for an objective interpretation of an individual act [*Aktionsart*]), the Future offers no clear aspectual choice in establishing an author's conception of the constituency of a process" (*Verbal Aspect*, 410).

form grammaticalizes the semantic (meaning) feature of expectation."[95]
Due to the fact that the future appears to be mixed in the action it refers
to, Fanning argues that the future is non-aspectual, and refers instead to
action that is *subsequent* to some reference point.[96] Given the variety of
discussion, in this work the future tense will not be treated as an aspect in
relationship to the aorist, present/imperfect, and perfect/pluperfect, but
will be regarded as either a tense or a non-aspectual form semantically
indicating action that can be expected to take place. The primary realization of the future tense form is future referring action (prospective or
predictive). In Porter's words,

> The future is thus a unique form in Greek, similar both to the aspects and
> to the attitudes, but fully neither, and realizing not a temporal conception
> but a marked and emphatic expectation toward a process.[97]

On the basis of the preceding discussion, the following tense forms and
their aspectual values can be compared and summarized:

Aorist	External viewpoint, action portrayed in its entirety
Present	Internal viewpoint, action portrayed as in progress, developing
Imperfect	Internal viewpoint, action portrayed as in progress, developing, [+remoteness]
Perfect	Action portrayed as a state of affairs
Pluperfect	Action portrayed as a state of affairs, [+remoteness]
Future[98]	Action that can be expected to take place, often future

The shortcoming of much grammatical discussion regarding Greek
tenses is the propensity to treat the various tenses individually and in
isolation from one another.[99] Rather that treating the various aspects
in isolation, as most traditional grammars are prone to do, they should
be seen as "meaningful oppositions in a network of tense systems."[100]
Here Porter exploits the concept of systemic linguistics, that is, language consists of a system of meaningful choices arranged within a

---

[95] Porter, *Idioms*, 44. Cf. at more length Porter, *Verbal Aspect*, ch. 9.

[96] Fanning, *Verbal Aspect*, 122–123.

[97] Porter, *Verbal Aspect*, 414. Cf. his *Idioms*, 43–44.

[98] The separation of the future from the other tense forms reflects the unique role this
form plays in the Greek tense system.

[99] See e.g. Wallace, *Greek Grammar*, 513–586.

[100] Porter, *Verbal Aspect*, 88. Cf. G.P.V. du Plooy, "Aspect and Biblical Exegesis," *Neot* 25
(1991) 165: "Methodologically the old approach to grammar was an explanation of items
in isolation. Discourse analysis exchanges items for function."

network.[101] "The Greek language is not to be considered a series of discreet, disjoint forms but is to be viewed as a coordinated network of verbal semantic choices arranged in coherent systems."[102] Hence an author chooses a tense form from within the system, a system consisting of marked pairs in opposition. The following display is adapted from Porter.[103]

$$
\textit{Verbal Aspect} \rightarrow
\begin{cases}
+ \text{ perfective (aorist)} \\
- \text{ perfective} \rightarrow
\begin{cases}
+ \text{ imperfective (present, imperfect)} \\
+ \text{ stative (perfect, pluperfect)}
\end{cases}
\end{cases}
$$

According to this display, the fundamental opposition is between the perfective (aorist) aspect and the imperfective (present, imperfect) aspect. The perfective aspect is the less marked (default), and the imperfective the more marked form of the opposition.[104] The present is even more marked than the imperfect (+ remoteness), being used frequently as the so-called "historical present" in narrative.[105] Furthermore, the stative (perfect, pluperfect) aspect is more well-defined and the most heavily marked member of the opposition (semantically and distributionally) and provides the most specific semantic choice on the part of the author. This framework highlights the fact that the aspects derive meaning in relationship to one another within a system, and the author's choice of a tense form usually entails a meaningful semantic choice of a particular way of viewing the action. Following Porter, McKay and Campbell, the contrast between the verb forms should be understood as an *equipollent* one, rather than as strict binary opposites (*privative*). Thus, all the forms are marked for meaning, though not identically weighted.[106]

---

[101] Porter, *Verbal Aspect*, 1–16. Cf. M.A.K. Halliday, *An Introduction to Functional Grammar* (3rd edn; rev. by Christian M.I.M. Matthiessen; London: Arnold, 2004).

[102] Porter, *Verbal Aspect*, 97. However, Porter also suggests that this is "not meant to imply that the choice by a language user was always (or ever!) conscious, but that the 'choice' was presented or required by the structure of the verbal system of the language" ("In Defence," 32). That is, since the aspects exist in systemic relationship, the use of an aspect inevitably implies a choice, which also implies not choosing the other aspects.

[103] Porter, *Verbal Aspect*, 90.

[104] As Comrie observes, when there is an opposition between two or more members (perfective vs. imperfective), "it is often the case that one member of the opposition is felt to be more usual, more normal, less specific than the other" (*Aspect*, 111).

[105] Porter, *Verbal Aspect*, 199.

[106] See Porter, *Verbal Aspect*, 89–90; Fanning, *Verbal Aspect*, 65–72; Campbell, *Verbal Aspect*, 19–21.

Important for discussion is also the fact that some verbs are what Porter labels "aspectually vague."[107] According to Porter, "there is a handful of verbs in the Greek language that appear quite clearly not to realize paradigmatic opposition in their tense forms."[108] That is, they do not offer a full paradigm of formal choice, especially between aorist and present tense forms. The most significant example is the ubiquitous verb εἰμί, which does not offer a formal choice in the aorist aspect. Therefore, no particular significance should be attached aspectually to its occurrence in the imperfective forms, since the author's choice is formally restricted.[109] However, though such verbs may not offer a semantic choice at the more important level of aspect, they may still offer a semantic choice at the level of +/- remoteness or even mood (e.g. indicative vs. subjunctive).

Summary

In conclusion, it has been suggested that, based on recent research into the Greek verbal system, Greek verbs do not indicate when an action occurs (time) or how it occurs (*Aktionsart*). Rather, the tense forms grammaticalize verbal aspect, that is, how the author chooses to view or represent a process. Based on this understanding the various aspects can occur in a variety of temporal and situational contexts, and a given process can be portrayed by more than one aspect. Furthermore, the various aspects exist within a coordinated system of opposing choices, so that in choosing a given tense form a speaker/writer makes a meaningful semantic choice of a particular way of conceiving of the action: perfectively (aorist), imperfectively (present, imperfect), or statively (perfect, pluperfect). An additional form, the future, can be used when the author wants to emphasize that an action can be expected to take place (e.g. future).

---

[107] For discussion of aspectually vague verbs see Porter, *Verbal Aspect*, 94, 441–447.

[108] Porter, *Verbal Aspect*, 441. *Contra* Campbell, *Verbal Aspect*, 27–28, who sees, for example, the aorist of γίνομαι (ἐγενόμην) forming a suppletive tense form for εἰμί.

[109] In addition to εἰμί, Porter lists also as aspectually vague in the New Testament κεῖμαι, φημί, ἧμαι (*Verbal Aspect*, 443). In a later list Porter also includes κάθημαι as an aspectually vague verb ("Aspect Theory and Lexicography," in Bernard A. Taylor et al. [eds.], *Biblical Greek Language and Lexicography: Essays in Honor of Frederick W. Danker* [Grand Rapids: Eerdmans, 2004] 212).

Aspect and Discourse Analysis

If Greek verb tenses do not signal time but aspect, why would an author utilize the various aspects? There has been much discussion regarding the possible discourse function of verbal aspect. There is general agreement that verbal aspect, rather than being used to communicate temporal information, plays a role in structuring discourse and indicating discourse prominence. "Often further analysis of what are held to be arbitrary choices yields appreciation for development of the argument."[110] However, there is disagreement as to the precise role that verbal aspect plays. Within the discipline of discourse analysis there has been much discussion regarding the concept of prominence in discourse (salience, foregrounding, emphasis), a concept related to information flow, or the change in the status of information within discourse.[111] "The very idea of discourse as a structured entity demands that some parts of discourse be more prominent than others."[112] In light of this, prominence can usefully be defined as the *"semantic and grammatical elements of discourse that serve to set aside certain subjects, ideas or motifs of the author as more or less semantically or pragmatically significant than others."*[113]

---

[110] Porter, *Verbal Aspect*, 197.

[111] For important studies on prominence see H.A. Dry, "Foregrounding: An Assessment," in S.J.J. Hwang and W.R. Merrifield (eds.), *Language in Context: Essays for Robert E. Longacre* (Dallas: Summer Institute of Linguistics, 1992) 435–450; P.J. Hopper, "Aspect and Foregrounding in Discourse," in T. Givón (ed.), *Discourse and Syntax* (New York: Academic, 1979) 213–241; P.J. Hopper, "Aspect Between Discourse and Grammar: An Introductory Essay for this Volume," in P.J. Hopper (ed.), *Tense-Aspect: Between Semantics and Pragmatics* (Amsterdam: Benjamins, 1982) 1–18; R.E. Longacre, "Discourse Peak as a Zone of Turbulence," in J.R. Worth (ed.), *Beyond the Sentence: Discourse and Sentential Form* (Ann Arbor: Karoma, 1985) 81–98; S. Wallace, "Figure and Ground: The Interrelationship of Linguistic Categories," in Hopper (ed.), *Tense-Aspect*, 201–223. For NT studies in particular see Kathleen Callow, *Discourse Considerations in Translating the Word of God* (Grand Rapids: Zondervan, 1974); David A. Black, Katharine Barnwell, and Stephen H. Levinsohn, *Linguistics and New Testament Interpretation: Essays in Discourse Analysis* (Nashville: Broadman, 1992); Steven H. Levinsohn, *Discourse Features of New Testament Greek: A Coursebook* (2nd edn; Dallas: Summer Institute of Linguistics, 2000) 169–213; Porter, *Verbal Aspect*, 92–93; Jeffry T. Reed, *Discourse Analysis of Philippians: Method and Rhetoric in the Debate over Literary Integrity* (JSNTSS 136; Sheffield: Academic Press, 1997) 16–22; Cynthia Long Westfall, *A Discourse Analysis of the Letter to the Hebrews: The Relationship Between Form and Meaning* (Library of New Testament Studies 297; London: T. & T. Clark, 2005) 55–75; Stanley E. Porter and Matthew B. O'Donnell (eds.), *The Linguist as Pedagogue: Trends in the Teaching and Linguistic Analysis of the Greek New Testament* (NTM 11; Sheffield: Sheffield Phoenix Press, 2009).

[112] Longacre, "Discourse Peak," 83.

[113] Reed, *Philippians*, 106. Italics his. See Gustavo Martín-Asensio, *Transitivity-Based*

Discourse analysts have postulated two or more levels of prominence in discourse, especially narrative. Drawing ultimately upon the language of perceptual psychology, linguists make a distinction between what could be labeled *background* (ground) and *foreground* (figure) information. By definition the foreground material stands out distinctively against the background information. The background information in a discourse includes subsidiary characters or events that are of lesser importance which support by way of comment, elaboration, or summary.[114] This does not mean that background material is of no importance, but that it plays a supporting or secondary role in the discourse. By contrast, foreground material refers to those characters or events that are of major importance and stand out against the background material. Often it signifies "information central to the author's message."[115] In addition, a third category, *frontground*, has also been suggested as a referring to those elements within a discourse that stand out unexpectedly and which are the particular focus of the author.[116] This would be equivalent to all spotlights aimed at a particular character center-stage during a play.

There has been some discussion on what grammatical devices an author might employ to signal various levels of prominence in a discourse (background, foreground, frontground). It is not the purpose of this chapter to give a comprehensive account of various markers of discourse prominence.[117] However, there is general agreement among linguists that verbal aspect can have as one of its pragmatic functions (though not the only one) the signaling of levels of discourse prominence.[118] Therefore, the various aspects "have as at least one of their functions the sorting of information conveyed by linguistic means into greater

---

Foregrounding in the Acts of the Apostles: A Functional-Grammatical Approach to the Lukan Perspective (JSNTSS 202; Sheffield: Academic Press, 2000) 43: "The need of writers to mark varying degrees of saliency in narrative seems to be a universal one. By investing the text with diverse viewpoints on the action, and highlighting key elements or episodes through lexico-grammatical means, the skilled narrator is able to impose an 'evaluating superstructure' upon the text, aimed at effecting the desired response(s) in the reader."

[114] See Wallace, "Figure and Ground," 208.

[115] Reed, *Philippians*, 107.

[116] Porter, *Verbal Aspect*, 92–93. Reed labels this level "focus" or "focal prominence" (*Philippians*, 108). While Porter uses the terminology "background," "foreground," and "frontground," Reed refers to the same three levels with "background," "theme," and "focus." Due to the uniformity of the visual language I will stick with "background," "foreground," and "frontground" to refer to the three levels of discourse prominence.

[117] For brief but helpful discussion of how grammatical systems can create prominence see Westfall, *Hebrews*, 56–76.

[118] Hopper, "Aspect and Foregrounding"; Porter, *Verbal Aspect*, 92–93.

and lesser degrees of salience."[119] The reason for this is that like prominence, aspect is concerned with the author's perspective on happenings
within the discourse, thus lending itself to indicating levels of prominence.[120]

In narrative, for example, the aorist and imperfective aspects, as seen
above, provide the principle opposition and are the primary means of
structuring the discourse.[121] "When a Greek speaker narrated events,
the Aorist, used alongside the Imperfect, formed the basis for carrying
the narrative ...."[122] There is a sense among grammarians that the aorist
tense, often felt to be the "default tense," is the more usual tense in discourse and functions to summarize a sequence of events and propel the
narrative forward. In narrative texts, it is the tense form which provides
the basic "backbone" of the narrative. As McKay says, the aorist "is virtually a residue aspect, used when the speaker or writer had no special
reason to use any other."[123] According to Decker, the aorist is "the prin-
cipal means of structuring the narrative and sketching the background
events that carry the storyline."[124]

The imperfect tense is used, then, against the backdrop of the aorist, as
the foreground tense.[125] It selects certain actions in the narrative to dwell
on in more detail. Together the aorist and imperfect implicate past-time
narrative. Campbell thinks that the aorist is more the foreground tense in
narrative, while the remote imperfect form is offline, and indicates supporting information.[126] However, given that both the aorist and imper-

---

[119] Wallace, "Figure and Ground," 216.

[120] See Martín-Asensio, *Transitivity-Based Foregrounding*, 47.

[121] Porter, *Verbal Aspect*, 198; Robertson, *Grammar*, 883 ("The aorist tells the simple
story. The imperfect draws the picture"); Evans, *Verbal Syntax*, 208; Albert Rijksbaron,
The Syntax and Semantics of the Verb in Classical Greek: An Introduction (3rd edn; Chicago
and London: University of Chicago Press, 2002) 11.

[122] Porter, *Verbal Aspect*, 198.

[123] McKay, "Syntax," 46. Or in the oft-quoted words of Robertson, "the aorist is the
tense used as a matter of course, unless there was special reason for using some other
tense" (*Grammar*, 831). Cf. Comrie, *Aspect*, 111–114.

[124] Decker, *Temporal Deixis*, 98–99.

[125] Porter, *Verbal Aspect*, 199: "The Aorist as semantically the least heavily marked
verb is aspectually perfective, frequently occurring in past contexts as the background
narrative tense. The Imperfect, semantically more heavily marked than the Aorist, is
aspectually imperfective ..., also often occurring in past contexts as the foreground
narrative tense."

[126] Campbell, *Verbal Aspect*, 95. Campbell describes the imperfect as indicating "offline" material. He suggests that the "offline usage of the imperfect tense form is a pragmatic outworking of its semantic value" (*Verbal Aspect*, 96). Cf. also Decker, *Temporal
Deixis*, 107. Campbell's use of terminology at this point is somewhat confusing. Campbell

fect grammaticalize remoteness in Campbell's scheme, and given that verbal aspect is what distinguishes the two forms (perfective vs. imperfective), the aspectual value of imperfective aspect suggests that it stands in opposition to the default aorist as a foreground tense form.[127] Furthermore, the present tense also enters into narrative contexts (the so-called "historical present") for action that is even more marked, or vivid, and "is used in those places where the author feels that he wishes to draw attention to an event or series of events."[128] According to Porter, the present can be used in two ways: 1) at the beginning of a discourse unit to highlight the transition to the new unit; 2) within discourse units for events selected for special significance (such as a climactic turning point), to introduce important dialogue, and to describe final closing events in a discourse.[129] As such, the present selects events to describe in more detail. Descriptions of the present in past time contexts as "vivid" are valid, as long as vividness is not tied to a rhetorical temporal transfer (as if the reader is present), but to aspect and the speaker/writer's desire to attach

---

does not apparently see background as = level of prominence ("it is important to remember that the term *background* with the position off the mainline, rather than prominence" [p. 14]). But this is to confuse the function of this label as it is used by discourse analysts.

[127] Porter, *Verbal Aspect*, 199. On Revelation see Aune, *Revelation 1–5*, clxxxvi: "The imperfect is sometimes used in a narrative context dominated by aorists to highlight or emphasize a particular action."

[128] Porter, *Verbal Aspect*, 196. Its pragmatic effect is "*drawing attention to crucial events* or *highlighting new scenes or actors* in the narrative" (Fanning, *Verbal Aspect*, 231). Italics his. However, Fanning, like Wallace (*Greek Grammar*, 527), ultimately opts for a temporal conception of the use of the present in past-time contexts: "It is a presentation of a clearly past occurrence as though it were simultaneous with the writer/reader which produces the vivid or immediate effect" (*Verbal Aspect*, 228). Wallace argues that the so-called "historical present" has "suppressed its aspect, but not its time. But the time element is rhetorical rather than real" (*Greek Grammar*, 527). However, this is unnecessarily dependent on a temporal understanding of the present tense form, and given the uncancellability of aspect, Wallace's explanation is unsatisfactory. For the historical present in narrative in classical Greek see Rijksbaron, *Syntax and Semantics*, 22–25. I prefer the term "narrative present" over "historical present," as the former is more of a functional and pragmatic label, while the latter, though more common, is more of a temporal label.

[129] Porter, *Verbal Aspect*, 196. See also Fanning, *Verbal Aspect*, 231–232. Fanning sees the present used to begin a paragraph, to introduce new participants into the story, to show participants moving to a new location, to begin a specific unit. See also Stephen H. Levinsohn, "Preliminary Observations on the Use of the Historical Present in Mark," *Notes on Translation* 65 (1977) 13–28, who sees it used with verbs of speaking to give new direction to a discussion. With other verbs it gives prominence or with verbs of 'arrival' a participant is brought to a place of significant interaction. Furthermore, an "inciting" event for further development is indicated by the present.

greater significance to the process.[130] To see the effect of the present tense as a temporal transfer simply for the sake of vividness or for lively narration, however, does not explain why some verbs are selected for this feature and not others. The imperfect and present tense forms stand in opposition to the aorist in narrative as the tense forms which provide descriptive detail and foreground information, though the imperfect (+remoteness) is not as heavily weighted as the present.[131]

The perfect tense form, as the most heavily weighted aspect, functions to focus on elements within the discourse that stand out in an unexpected way; it is the *frontground* tense form.[132] Since it seldom enters into narrative contexts, it has a marked and special effect in narrative. In McKay's words, "In narrative accounts of past events it is clear that the aorist and imperfect are the dominant tenses, with the pluperfect occasionally used parallel to the imperfect, while the present and perfect are only used for special effect."[133] Hence, the perfect tense seems to signal a change created in the status of the discourse through utilizing a more marked aspectual form. Thus due to its semantic weight, one of the pragmatic functions of the perfect tense form is to view the action as highly prominent. Generally, then, the following scheme based on the discourse function of tense forms in their contexts presents itself:[134]

---

[130] McKay combines both of these: this use of the present is "a stylistic variant used by some writers to *enliven* the more *significant* parts of their narrative" (*New Syntax*, 42). Italics mine. Fanning (*Verbal Aspect*, 228) and Wallace (*Greek Grammar*, 527) tie their understanding of "vividness" too closely to a supposed temporal rhetorical transfer. But if this is the case, the question still remains: why are some verbs vivid in narrative and others are not? I would suggest that it is due to verbal aspect and the author's desire to establish prominence. In this light it is not necessary to reject "vividness" as an explanation for the use of the narrative present, *contra* Decker, *Temporal Deixis*, 104.

[131] See Porter, *Verbal Aspect*, 199; Decker, *Temporal Deixis*, 107. *Contra* Campbell, *Verbal Aspect*, 95.

[132] Porter, *Idioms*, 23. McKay, "On the Perfect and Other Aspects," 318–322, sees the perfect in opposition to the aorist as more vivid and as drawing more attention to the action.

[133] McKay, "Time and Aspect," 226. Campbell distinguishes between two functions of the perfect tense form: *intensification* and *prominence*. Yet since his description of both is so similar, it is difficult to meaningfully distinguish these two functions. Campbell variously describes the pragmatic effect of the perfect as intensifying in terms of "heightening the significance," "regarded as highly significant," "dramatic," having "special urgency" (*Verbal Aspect*, 205). But it is virtually impossible to distinguish this from his descriptions of the perfect's prominent implicature as indicating "significance" or highlighting (207).

[134] See also Porter, *Idioms*, 23.

Aorist	Background, backbone of narrative
Present (Imperfect)	Foreground
Perfect	Frontground

In addition, the future form, though not indicating aspect, may also denote action that is foregrounded in that it portrays actions with a strong expectation of taking place.[135]

It must be emphasized that it would be illegitimate to conclude that the aspects always function to indicate levels of discourse prominence. Discourse prominence is not part of the semantic value of verbal aspect grammaticalized within the verb tense endings, but is a pragmatic function of the aspects within discourse. The invariant feature of Greek verbs is always verbal aspect, and often an aspect was chosen simply because it expressed the nuance which the author wanted to communicate. As Jeffrey T. Reed correctly observes, "the use of verbal aspect ... to indicate prominence is a secondary role—a pragmatic function of grammar—and, thus, a *discourse function*, not a morphological function of Greek grammar."[136] Thus while such a scheme as suggested above cannot be simply assumed to be present, whether the tense forms indicate levels of prominence (background, foreground, frontground) is certainly worth exploring when considering the author's aspectual choice within discourse. It will be tested on the use of verbal aspect in Revelation later in this work to determine its usefulness in explaining the presence and function of the various tense forms.

Aspect and the Genre of Revelation

Before considering the issue of verbal aspect as surveyed above in Revelation, it is necessary to discuss briefly the genre of Revelation. Much work has been done on the genre of Revelation, usually placing it within the matrix of Jewish apocalyptic.[137] Though Revelation is also framed by an

---

[135] See Reed, *Philippians*, 113–114. This is at least consistent with Porter's explanation of the future form as "realizing ... a *marked* and *emphatic* expectation toward a process" (*Verbal Aspect*, 414). Italics mine.

[136] Reed, *Philippians*, 114. Italics his.

[137] See Brook R.W. Pearson and Stanley E. Porter, "The Genres of the New Testament," in Stanley E. Porter (ed.), *A Handbook to the Exegesis of the New Testament* (Leiden: Brill, 1997) 155–161, though they correctly note the many differences between Revelation and

epistolary prescript and postscript (1.4, 5; 22.21), the rest of Revelation presents an episodic autobiographical narrative of the author's revelatory experience. The "narrative framework" of Revelation and apocalyptic literature is the most agreed upon and verifiable formal feature of the book.[138] As Aune explains, formally, Revelation is "an apocalypse in prose narrative, in autobiographical form, of revelatory visions experienced by the author."[139] The visionary segments are frequently prefaced by καὶ εἶδον, and at times the author is a participant in his own vision reflected in the use of the first person (cf. Rev 5.4, ἔκλαιον). Within the autobiographical framework, the visions are generally cast as 3rd person depictions of what the author saw. For purposes of analyzing verbal aspect in the Apocalypse, Revelation will be treated as an autobiographical narrative of a visionary experience. Hence, the above observations on verbal aspect within narrative discourse will be applied to Revelation. Though the relationship of the visions to temporal concerns is an extremely difficult one, the narrative framework of Revelation suggests that as a narrative, the main temporal frame is past-time; temporally the Apocalypse records the "past" visionary experience of the author, although referentially the visions of Revelation are often timeless or future.

Conclusion

There is increasing recognition that the tense forms in the Greek of the New Testament indicate verbal aspect. The most rigorous and linguistically informed articulation of this view of the Greek verb tense system is that of Porter.[140] Though there are still issues to be resolved with regard to aspect, the remainder of this work will attempt to apply insights from verbal aspect to Revelation. Verbal aspect is a semantic category which grammaticalizes the author's perspective on a process. Aspect is indicated by the author's choice of a particular tense-form from within a

---

Jewish apocalyptic works. Cf. J.J. Collins, *The Apocalyptic Imagination: An Introduction to the Jewish Matrix of Christianity* (2nd edn; Grand Rapids: Eerdmans, 1998). This is obviously not the place to discuss the relationship between apocalyptic and prophecy.

[138] See the definition of Collins, *Apocalyptic Imagination*, 5; David E. Aune, "The Apocalypse of John and the Problem of Genre," *Sem* 36 (1986) 86 ("prose narrative"); W.S. Vorster, "'Genre' and the Revelation of John: A Study in Text, Context, and Intertext," *Neot* 22 (1988) 114–116.

[139] Aune, "Problem of Genre," 86. Cf. Vorster, "'Genre' and the Revelation of John," 114.

[140] See Porter, *Verbal Aspect*, 88, followed by Decker, Campbell; cf. Fanning.

verbal network of New Testament Greek. As such it is to be clearly distinguished from time and *Aktionsart* which are semantic features resident in the wider context of the discourse through lexis and deictic indicators. Furthermore, the aspectual system of the Greek New Testament implies choice; that is, by the selection of a particular tense ending, which grammaticalizes aspect, within the verbal system the author semantically communicates a perspective on the action (perfective, imperfective, stative). Furthermore, verbal aspect, by indicating the author's particular perspective on a process, can at times also function pragmatically in narrative to structure the discourse and indicate levels of prominence (background, foreground, frontground).

Based on the recent discussion surrounding verbal aspect, the rest of this study will apply these insights from aspect to the vexing question of tense usage in the Apocalypse. The ensuing treatment will be divided into two main sections: first, the treatment of the major verb tense forms in Revelation in the indicative mood individually; second, the question of shifting tense forms in sections of Revelation's visions. Though it is possible that Revelation is doing something very different from the rest of the New Testament in regard to its use of tense forms, this study will apply verbal aspect as a working hypothesis to the question of tense usage in Revelation. In the following chapters verbal aspect will be seen to provide a compelling model with explanatory power to account for the tense usage in Revelation.

CHAPTER THREE

VERBAL ASPECT IN REVELATION

Introduction

Though there has been some significant research done on verb tenses in Revelation on the one hand, and much recent important work done on verbal aspect theory on the other, there is no comprehensive study that applies verbal aspect theory to the question of verb tenses in Revelation. As already suggested, virtually all of the previous study addressing the topic of verb tenses in Revelation was produced prior to the most significant research on verbal aspect. Though Aune in his commentary is aware of the works of Porter and Fanning on aspect, he fails to develop a consistent aspectual approach throughout his work, opting instead for older more temporally-based explanations of the tense forms.[1] The rest of this study will apply the insights from verbal aspect theory discussed in the previous chapter, especially as developed by Porter, to the vexed question of verb tenses in Revelation.

The following two chapters will examine in turn the major tense forms in Revelation: aorist, present, imperfect, perfect, and future. In addition it will also consider the issue of shifting tenses in the visionary sections.[2] In both of these sections I will argue that verbal aspect has the explanatory power to account for verb tense usage, and that there is no need to conclude that Revelation's use of tenses is irregular or inconsistent, nor is there a need to appeal to Semitic influence, as is frequently done, to explain the author's use of tenses. In the following sections I will pay particular attention to indicative mood verbs, since most of the judgments regarding the use of verb tenses in Revelation center around indicative mood forms, which are thought to carry temporal significance. I will in

---

[1] Aune, *Revelation 1–5*, clxxxiv–viii. As seen in the previous chapters, the major works on verb tenses in Revelation were produced prior to the most significant work on verbal aspect theory.

[2] The major works on the syntax of Revelation by Mussies, Thompson, and Dougherty address both of these issues separately as well.

places briefly include consideration of the aspect of non-indicative verbs as well when they seem to be significant. Since εἰμί is "aspectually vague" (following Porter, see above) discussion of it will not be included in the following treatment of tense forms.

Before examining the tense forms in detail, the following chart itemizes the number of occurrences of the tense forms in the indicative mood as distributed in Revelation. I have included for comparison non-indicative forms as well.[3]

	Aor	Pres	Fut	Impf	Perf	Pluperf	Totals
Indicative	451	175	106	23	34	1	790
Subjunctive	69	17	–	–	–	–	86
Imperative	61	27	–	–	–	–	88
Participle	12	295	–	–	83	–	390
Infinitive	84	17	–	–	1[4]	–	102
Total	677	531	106	23	118	1	1456
	45.8 %	36.5 %	7.3 %	1.6 %	8.1 %	.1 %	

Overall, the distribution of the aorist and present tense forms in the indicative mood is generally what one would expect to find in narrative, with the aorist, as the standard narrative tense form, enjoying a distributional advantage over the present, even more so when one realizes that present participles comprise well over half of the present tense forms. The more heavily marked perfect, then, occurs much less frequently, which is consistent with the insight that as the most heavily marked form it enters into narrative infrequently. Perhaps the most conspicuous feature revealed from this comparison is the high number of future tense forms, as well as the high number of present and perfect participle forms. Though the focus of this study is primarily on the aspect of

---

[3] All tense-form statistics in this study are based on searches done with BibleWorks 7. The following verb counts exclude forms of εἰμί (there are 110 occurrences of εἰμί in Revelation in the present indicative, present participle, imperfect, future, and present infinitive forms), since it is considered aspectually vague as it does not offer a semantic choice at the level of aspect in its formal paradigm. Included in the above count is one usage of the aspectually vague κεῖμαι (21.16) in the present tense and one in the imperfect (ἔκειτο) in 4.2, that could have been excluded. Cf. also κάθημαι (Porter, "Aspect Theory and Lexicography," 212). κάθημαι occurs 3 time as a present indicative verb (17.9, 15; 18.7). It occurs an additional 30 times as a present participle.

[4] This deviates from Bible Works 7 which parses the infinitive τεθῆναι in Rev 11.9 as an aorist. However, it should be seen as a perfect (stative) and the total for aorist infinitives has been adjusted accordingly.

indicative verbs, the following discussion will briefly attempt to address some of these issues. The following discussion does not attempt to analyze and classify every tense form in Revelation, but considers a sufficiently large representative sampling to demonstrate the distribution of aspectual forms and their pragmatic functions.

The Major Greek Tenses in Revelation

The Aorist Tense

There are 451 instances of the aorist indicative in Revelation. As discussed in the previous chapter, the aorist grammaticalizes the author's conception of a process as perfective. That is, the action is viewed in its entirety from a perspective external to the action. Moreover, in narration it is the common narrative tense, functioning to lay down the basic structure of the narrative and propel the story line forward. However, the treatment of the aorist tense in Revelation, as is often the case elsewhere in the New Testament, has been influenced primarily by temporal and *Aktionsart* models. In looking to the LXX to illustrate John's use of the aorist, Thompson seems surprised to find "in the LXX a number of aorist verbs which cannot be made to bear the Greek punctiliar sense."[5] Therefore he postulates Semitic influence by means of the Hebrew *qatal* stem. However, Thompson reflects the tendency of (mis)construing the aorist tense form from the standpoint of *Aktionsart*.[6]

Noteworthy of attempts to evaluate the aorist tense in terms of *Aktionsart* is L. Morris' commentary on Revelation.[7] Commenting on the aorist tense form in "*has triumphed*" (his translation) in 5.5 with reference to the Lamb, Morris concludes that "the aorist tense may well indicate a victory once and for all."[8] Or in 12.11 where the saints "*overcame*" him (the accuser), the aorist tense indicates "the completeness of the victory."[9] Morris' commentary casts up a number of examples of such outmoded

---

[5] Thompson, *Semitic Syntax*, 37.

[6] Cf. also Turner, *Syntax*, 71; BDF § 318. Yet the work of Frank Stagg, which has now become somewhat of a classic ("The Abused Aorist," *JBL* 91 [1972] 222–231) and was available to Thompson, should have been sufficient to dispel him of this notion of the aorist.

[7] Leon Morris, *Revelation* (rev. edn; TNTC; Grand Rapids: Eerdmans, 1987).

[8] Morris, *Revelation*, 94.

[9] Morris, *Revelation*, 157.

construals of the aorist.[10] Though common in several treatments of the
aorist tense, such an understanding confuses aspect and *Aktionsart*, or
semantics and pragmatics.[11] When examined in light of its pragmatic
function in Revelation, the aorist can also be used of action that is varied
in character. Compare the following texts:

> Rev 5.8: καὶ ὅτε **ἔλαβεν** τὸ βιβλίον, τὰ τέσσαρα ζῷα καὶ οἱ εἴκοσι
> τέσσαρες πρεσβύτεροι **ἔπεσαν** ἐνώπιον τοῦ ἀρνίου
> Rev 13.5: καὶ **ἐδόθη** αὐτῷ ἐξουσία **ποιῆσαι** μῆνας τεσσεράκοντα δύο
> Rev 20.4: καὶ **ἐβασίλευσαν** μετὰ τοῦ Χριστοῦ χίλια ἔτη
> Rev 19.6: ὅτι **ἐβασίλευσεν** κύριος

In the above examples only the first reference can be construed in any
sense as referring to punctiliar-type action, since the context and lexical character of the verbs seem to suggest that the two activities (ἔλαβεν, ἔπεσαν) procedurally and contextually are of short duration. The
next two examples, however, envelop periods, at least at the visionary
level, of much longer duration, indicated by the deictic temporal indicators μῆνας τεσσεράκοντα δύο (42 months) and χίλια ἔτη (1000 years)
respectively.[12] The final example from 19.6 appears to be a timeless statement ("the Lord reigns") rather than a reference to any specific event
or events at all. In all four cases, though the nature of the action differs, the author chooses the aorist tense form in order to grammaticalize
the conception of the action as a complete and undifferentiated whole.
Thus all four of the above examples are comprehensible in light of verbal
aspect.

Lancellotti thought that the timeless Hebrew *qatal* was the source of
confusion in the author of Revelation's use of the aorist, resulting in the
aorist tense form being used in non-past time (future) contexts (proleptically).[13] However, Mussies, while admitting only limited future usage
of the aorist, and while seeing the aorist corresponding to the Mishnaic Hebrew *qatal*, disputes the examples adduced by Lancellotti, and

---

[10] See also Morris, *Revelation*, 60–61 (on 2.5), 75 (on 3.3), 97 (on 5.9–10), 115 (7.13–
14). The classic refutation of such erroneous readings based on the aorist is Stagg, "Abused
Aorist."

[11] Porter, *Verbal Aspect*, 91; *Idioms*, 35; Fanning, *Verbal Aspect*, 255; McKay, *New
Syntax*, 30; Campbell, *Verbal Aspect*, 103–104.

[12] On Rev 20.4 see Robertson, *Grammar*, 833, though his description of the aorist here
as a point could be improved upon. To what extent the 1000 year period corresponds to
an actual time period embroils the interpreter in issues related to millennial views: pre-,
post-, and a-millennialism.

[13] Cf. Lancellotti, *Sintassi ebraica*, 42, 56.

maintains that most of these examples could be understood as past in time. According to Mussies, the aorists reflect the actual time of the vision: the author is recording what for him is past.[14] Therefore, beginning with a temporal conception of the aorist (past time) he concludes that with the use of the aorist there is "nothing peculiar in the Apocalypse."[15] Out of 95 occurrences of the Hebrew perfect that he selected (he does not tell us from which texts they are selected or his criteria for selection), Thompson found that 45 (47%) were translated by an aorist tense in the LXX. Similarly, a number of instances of the aorist in Revelation "must be rendered with the sense of the Semitic perfect."[16] Thus Thompson finds the aorist tense used in three temporal contexts which reflect three temporal spheres of usage of the Hebrew perfect:

> Present aorist for stative perfect: 1.2; 2.21, 24; 3.4, 8, 9, 10; 11.17; 13.14; 14.4–5; 22.16
> Future aorist for prophetic perfect: 10.7; 11.2; 11.10–13[17]
> Timeless aorist for timeless perfect: 5.9, 10; 14.4; 16.20; 17.17; 19.2, 6; 20.11, 12

Likewise, Dougherty offers the following classifications for the use of the aorist tense in Revelation, though he does not posit Semitic influence:

> Past (narration and non-narration): e.g. 1.9; 2.8; 5.8, 11; 11.1, 11; 12.16; 16.17; 17.7[18]
> Perfective usage: e.g. 1.2; 2.2, 3; 3.3; 7.13; 11.17; 18.3[19]
> Present sense: 1.19, 20; 2.24; 17.8, 12, 15, 16, 18
> Futuristic usage: 10.7; 15.1

The purpose of this treatment is not to dispute these examples or to examine them all in detail, though some of them are patient of a different analysis; it appears that Thompson and Dougherty have effectively demonstrated the range of pragmatic and temporal functions for the aorist in Revelation. However, based on the assumption that the aorist

---

[14] Fanning seems to subscribe to Mussies' view of the aorist as reflecting the time of the vision: past (*Verbal Aspect*, 274 n. 163). He repeats the contention of Mussies that the aorist often occurs in groups, indicating a shift in perspective.

[15] Mussies, *Morphology*, 337.

[16] Thompson, *Semitic Syntax*, 40.

[17] Thompson also lists 12.8; 14.8; 18.17–19; 21.23, but thinks that these might better fit a timeless use of the aorist (*Semitic Syntax*, 41).

[18] For a more comprehensive listing see Dougherty, "Syntax," 419–420.

[19] For a more comprehensive listing see Dougherty, "Syntax," 421–422. However, Dougherty recognizes that the emphasis is on the action of the verb rather than the resultant state of the subject, hence the aorist tense.

grammaticalizes past time action, Thompson in particular attributes this varied temporal usage to Semitic influence. Nevertheless, if as argued above the aorist tense grammaticalizes the author's conception of the process irrespective of temporal relations, then these instances do not need to be explained in light of supposed Hebrew influence. Rather, temporal relations are determined by the broader context and deictic indicators of time. As Thompson himself recognizes, "In determining the date or time of the aorist verbs ..., one must always rely upon the context of the passage in question."[20] This is true based not upon an underlying Hebrew perfect, but upon the semantics of the aorist tense itself as grammaticalizing verbal aspect.

Past Time

There should be no difficulty in seeing the aorist used with past-time reference in Revelation, which is one of the aorist tense's principle pragmatic manifestations in narrative: John is narrating what he saw. This function of the aorist is not disputed. The aorist "is the primary tense used in the narration of past events, and this is the way in which it is primarily used in Revelation."[21] A clear example of this which functions to introduce the visionary segments is the ubiquitous καὶ εἶδον which punctuates the visionary narrative at numerous points (cf. ἤκουσα which often introduces audition within the narration).[22] According to Aune καὶ εἶδον functions in three ways throughout Revelation: 1) as an introduction to a new vision narrative; 2) as an introduction to a major scene within a continuing visionary narrative; 3) to focus on a new or important figure or activity within the vision.[23] There is no need to provide or discuss an extended list of specific examples here to justify the past-referring usage of the aorist in Revelation.[24] One short example will suffice.

---

[20] Thompson, *Semitic Syntax*, 42.

[21] Aune, *Revelation 1–5*, clxxxvii. Cf. Robertson, *Grammar*, 835–836: the aorist "is the tense in which a verb in ordinary narrative is put unless there is reason for using some other tense."

[22] On the discourse significance of this construction see Stephen Pattemore, *Souls under the Altar: Relevance Theory and the Discourse Structure of Revelation* (UBS Monograph Series 9; New York: UBS, 2003) 115–117.

[23] Aune, *Revelation 1–5*, 338. Cf. also Blount, *Revelation*, 99. On these two terms in Revelation more generally see David Hill, *New Testament Prophecy* (Atlanta: John Knox Press, 1979) 76–77.

[24] See the list of potential examples in Dougherty, "Syntax," 419–420.

καὶ ὁ τρίτος ἄγγελος **ἐσάλπισεν**· καὶ **ἔπεσεν** ἐκ τοῦ οὐρανοῦ ἀστὴρ μέγας καιόμενος ὡς λαμπὰς καὶ **ἔπεσεν** ἐπὶ τὸ τρίτον τῶν ποταμῶν καὶ τὰς πηγὰς τῶν ὑδάτων, καὶ τὸ ὄνομα τοῦ ἀστέρος λέγεται ὁ Ἄψινθος, καὶ **ἐγένετο** τὸ τρίτον τῶν ὑδάτων εἰς ἄψινθον καὶ πολλοὶ τῶν ἀνθρώπων **ἀπέθανον** ἐκ τῶν ὑδάτων ὅτι **ἐπικράνθησαν**   (Revelation 8.10–11)

Examples of this function of the aorist in Revelation could be multiplied. Yet as Thompson and others have demonstrated the aorist is found in other temporal contexts in the Apocalypse.

Present Time

In several instances in Revelation, the aorist refers to present time from the standpoint of the speaker.[25] Most of the examples of this use of the aorist occur outside of the narrative proper in the speeches scattered throughout Revelation, or in the prophetic messages to the churches in Chs. 2–3. The following examples appear to establish this usage. One group of texts refers to an action that has just taken place, but whose effects are present. As part of the speech of a heavenly voice, in Rev 12.10 (ἄρτι **ἐγένετο** ἡ σωτηρία καὶ ἡ δύναμις) the temporal deictic indicator ἄρτι suggests that the aorist ἐγένετο refers at least in part to the present time. McKay points to the use of the aorist for events that have just taken place—their arrival is complete.[26] However, it is often difficult to distinguish an event that has taken place in the immediate past from the present; rather such actions tend to encompass a broader period of time including the present moment.[27] The aorist can be used where there is

---

[25] Cf. Thompson, *Semitic Syntax*, 40. Grammarians often label this the "Dramatic" use of the aorist. Cf. Robertson, *Grammar*, 841–843; Wallace, *Greek Grammar*, 564–565.

[26] McKay, "Time," 219. Charles, *Revelation, I*, cxxv. Charles refers to *"events that have just happened."* He lists 1.19; 2.21; 11.2, 15, 17; 12.12; 14.15, 18; 16.5; 18.16, 19, 20; 19.2, 7, 8; 22.16 as having this same force. This use is sometimes referred to in grammars as the "Dramatic Aorist" (though often temporally conceived). Cf. Fanning, *Verbal Aspect*, 275–281; Wallace, *Greek Grammar*, 564–565.

[27] Porter, *Verbal Aspect*, 77, 226; Porter gives a number of possible examples of this use of the aorist. Cf. Decker, *Temporal Deixis*, 96. Thus in recording many present moments the action would be past by the time it is recorded. Even many usages of the present tense would not refer exclusively to present action, since as Comrie realizes, "a ... characteristic use of the present tense is in referring to situations which occupy a much larger period of time than the present moment" (*Aspect*, 37). Both Fanning (*Verbal Aspect*, 275) and Wallace (*Greek Grammar*, 565) admit that it is often difficult to distinguish a recent past event from the immediate present.

no interval between the event and time of speaking.[28] In this case, the presence of ἄρτι in 12.10 suggests that ἐγένετο at least overlaps with the present time and does not merely refer to past time, however recent. Something similar could be said about 19.7. With reference to the marriage supper of the Lamb and his followers, a voice proclaims ὅτι **ἦλθεν** ὁ γάμος τοῦ ἀρνίου καὶ ἡ γυνὴ αὐτοῦ **ἡτοίμασεν** ἑαυτήν. The sense of ἦλθεν and ἡτοίμασεν seems to be that the marriage of the Lamb has finally arrived and is present and the bride is prepared. While the arrival and preparation have just happened, they overlap with present time, the aorist covering the entire process. In 14.7 the hour of God's judgment is now upon (or has just arrived upon) humanity (ἦλθεν), providing the reason for the angel's call for repentance, like 12.10 and 19.7, referring to a process that encompasses both past and present temporal sphere. For other possible examples see 6.17 (ἦλθεν); 11.15 (ἐγένετο). Alternatively, however, it is possible that all of these examples do reflect past time value, action that has just taken place in the immediate past.[29]

More convincing is 11.17 where the 24 elders proclaim that εἴληφας τὴν δύναμέν σου τὴν μεγάλην καὶ **ἐβασίλευσας**. The aorist ἐβασίλευσας is not a reference to a past act of reigning, but to the present reign of God based on his possession of great power. Aune thinks that the aorist here is ingressive, and translates it "you have begun to reign."[30] Verbs that indicate states can often implicate an ingressive notion when used with the aorist tense.[31] However, the aorist can also simply refer to the entire state rather than the entrance into that state.[32] While βασιλεύω suggests a state of reigning, apart from contextual indicators that the entrance into that state of reigning is being signified, the aorist ἐβασίλευσας refers to the simple act of reigning.

Even more clearly, in 2.24 the description of the Thyatirans as those who do not know (ἔγνωσαν) the deep things of Satan is not a reference to some past act of knowing, but to a present lack of knowledge. Osborne's

---

[28] For this explanation see E.D.W. Burton, *Syntax of the Moods and Tenses in New Testament Greek* (3rd edn; Edinburgh: T. & T. Clark, 1898) 26–27.

[29] BDAG classifies Rev 12.10 under the category of "**ref. to the immediate past**, *just (now)*" (136).

[30] Aune, *Revelation 6–16*, 642–643.

[31] Cf. Wallace, *Greek Grammar*, 558.

[32] In his discussion of ingressive aorists (aorists used with verbs indicating a state) Fanning admits that the aorist may be used with stative type verbs to "take a summary view of the entire situation" (*Verbal Aspect*, 262). Rijksbaron concludes that the aorist with verbs of states can indicate ingressive meaning, but concludes that this ultimately depends on the context (*Syntax and Semantics*, 20–21).

translation "they have never known" is unnecessarily motivated by temporal concerns.[33] Included in this category could also be 3.9 where the reference to God loving (ἠγάπησα) refers to, or at least includes, God's present love (not just past) for his people ("I have loved" or "I love"). Some grammarians attribute the aorists for present time to the direct influence of the Hebrew stative perfect, since they have already determined that past time reference belongs to the semantics of the aorist tense form; therefore they must look elsewhere for this function.[34] If the aorist tense, however, does not grammaticalize absolute temporal reference, but verbal aspect, then there is no need to resort to direct Semitic influence to account for usage of the aorist in present time contexts. There should be no difficultly in taking most of these usages as temporally present referring to some degree and as a valid use of the aorist aspect.

Timeless

More difficult to assess are possible examples of the aorist which are temporally unrestricted (the so-called "gnomic aorist;" see Porter's categories "omnitemporal" and "timeless").[35] Some of Thompson's examples of this usage may more naturally refer to specific activities which are past from a visionary standpoint, or future, rather than timeless aorists (cf. 16.20; 17.17; 19.2; 20.11; 21.12).[36] Yet other examples seem to have timeless or omnitemporal implications. Thompson cites 5.9 as an example: καὶ **ἠγόρασας** τῷ θεῷ ἐν τῷ αἵματί σου, which he translates "and *are ransoming* men for God by your blood." While the reference to "his blood" may suggest a past act (temporal deictic indicator), the crucifixion of Christ, since the rest of Revelation unfolds God's plan for redeeming humanity, it is possible that this should be construed as a timeless statement.[37] Especially pertinent is the universal reference ἐκ πάσης φυλῆς καὶ γλώσσης καὶ λαοῦ καὶ ἔθνους in 5.9d. Likewise, the **ἐποίησας** in

---

[33] Grant R. Osborne, *Revelation* (BECNT; Grand Rapids: Baker, 2002) 162. The classic example of a present referring use of the aorist is Luke 16.4 (ἔγνων). Cf. McKay, "Time," 219 n. 28.

[34] Fanning, *Verbal* Aspect, 275; Wallace, *Greek Grammar*, 565; Thompson, *Semitic Syntax*, 37–38, 40.

[35] I will not debate the value or validity of Porter's distinction between "omnitemporal" and "timeless" reference. For a helpful explanation and defense see Porter, *Idioms*, 29, 32–33. Cf. Moulton, *Prolegomena*, 134–135 who discusses the timeless use of the aorist.

[36] Thompson, *Semitic Syntax*, 41.

[37] That Christ's death on the cross secured our redemption in the past is a theological argument and does not depend on a specific grammatical construction.

5.10 describes what God does, not just what he has done in the past, since this is what God accomplishes throughout the rest of the book. A somewhat clearer example can be found in 19.6, where a loud voice proclaims Ἀλληλουιά followed by the reason: ὅτι ἐβασίλευσεν κύριος. The aorist ἐβασίλευσεν depicts a timeless truth ("the Lord reigns" or "is king") as a result of the overthrow of the harlot in Chs. 17–18; this is clearly not a reference to a past act of reigning (or even entrance into that reign) but a timeless statement (cf. ἐβασίλευσας in 11.17, either timeless or present).[38] It is also possible that a text like 3.9 (ἠγάπησα) belongs here: "I love." Once again, unless one insists on attaching past time semantics to the aorist tense form, there should be no difficulty in seeing the aorist in some instances used in timeless or temporally unrestricted contexts.

Future Time

Though rare in occurrence, the future use of the aorist (proleptic or futuristic aorist) in Revelation has not gone unnoticed by scholars and grammarians.[39] This is understood, for example by Lancellotti and Thompson, as reflecting the well-known Hebrew "prophetic perfect," usually consisting of a rhetorical temporal transfer for the sake of certainty or vividness (a future action is seen as if it has already occurred) predicated upon the past time of the aorist.[40] But as Fanning recognizes, the future referring aorist "is not a non-Greek idiom."[41] Therefore "[i]n some instances the speaker seems to conceive of a future process as complete and he used the Aorist for this conception."[42] According to Decker, the significance of this use of the aorist is that the future tense form is aspectually vague, and so the use of the aorist for temporally future processes allows the

---

[38] On the timeless use of the aorist in the New Testament see Porter, *Verbal Aspect*, 217–225, 233–237. While this could also be taken as another example of an ingressive use of the aorist (entrance into the action), apart from other contextual indicators it probably refers to the entire act of reigning.

[39] Cf. Wallace, *Greek Grammar*, 563; McKay, *Syntax*, 48; Porter, *Idioms*, 37–38.

[40] Lancellott, *Sintassi ebraica*, 42, 56; Thompson, *Semitic Syntax*, 40. For a lengthy discussion of the proleptic or futuristic aorist from this perspective see Fanning, *Verbal Aspect*, 269–274. For this standard description outside of biblical Greek, cf. Smyth, *Grammar*, 432.

[41] Fanning, *Verbal Aspect*, 273. For discussion of the futuristic use of the aorist in the New Testament see Porter, *Verbal Aspect*, 232–233.

[42] Porter, *Verbal Aspect*, 232.

author to grammaticalize verbal aspect.[43] As a starting point, Fanning lists four texts in Revelation which have future time reference: 10.7; 11.2; 14.8; 15.1.[44] Each of these will be examined for possible future time implicature.

Rev 10.7: ἐτελέσθη τὸ μυστήριον τοῦ θεοῦ

The aorist ἐτελέσθη here is frequently understood as indicating future time reference.[45] While Thompson posits that it reflects Semitic influence from the Hebrew perfect, alternatively Bousset suggested that it "ist einfacher Hebraismus und entspricht dem ו consecutivum mit dem Perf."[46] Though Fanning admits that it is not un-Greek, he still thinks that its occurrence has been *enhanced* by Semitic influence.[47] In this case, the action is seen as if it has already taken place, a common way to conceive of the futuristic use of the aorist.[48] Lupieri describes it with the confusing conflation of temporal language, "past in the future."[49] Yet such conceptions of the future referring aorist stem from the controlling assumption that the aorist tense must grammaticalize past time reference. Verbal aspect can explain its usage here.

The deictic indicator ἐν ταῖς ἡμέραις, along with the temporal clause ὅταν μέλλῃ σαλπίζειν, serve to establish the temporal frame of reference of v. 7. Both point to the seventh trumpet which has not yet been blown, but is delayed until 11.15–19. Furthermore, the construction μέλλω +

---

[43] Decker, *Temporal Deixis*, 97: "It may be that the speaker uses the aorist form for future time, at least in part, to express aspect. Since the future form is aspectually vague, there is no explicit way to convey a view of the action as a complete event using the future form."

[44] Fanning, *Verbal Aspect*, 274. Dougherty only lists two: 10.7; 15.1 ("Syntax," 423). In addition to the texts adduced by Fanning, Thompson adds 11.10–13; 12.8; 18.17–19; 21.23 (*Semitic Syntax*, 41).

[45] Thompson, *Semitic Syntax*, 40; Mussies, *Morphology*, 337; Robertson, *Grammar*, 847; Wallace, *Greek Grammar*, 564; Fanning, *Verbal Aspect*, 274; Dougherty, "Syntax," 423; Gregory K. Beale, *The Book of Revelation* (NIGTC; Grand Rapids: Eerdmans, 1999) 539; Heinz Giesen, *Die Offenbarung des Johannes* (RNT; Regensburg: Pustet, 1997) 235–236; Stephen S. Smalley, *The Revelation to John* (Downers Grove: Inter Varsity Press, 2005) 265.

[46] Bousset, *Offenbarung*, 310.

[47] Fanning, *Verbal Aspect*, 274. Charles labels it a Hebraism (*Revelation, I*, 265). Though he clearly seems to suggest that 10.7 reflects the prophetic perfect, Giesen says this is not an example of a futuristic sense due to the Semitic perfect, but is to be understood in the sense of a prophetic perfect which gives the vision's fulfillment certainty (*Offenbarung*, 235–236).

[48] Cf. Fanning, *Verbal Aspect*, 274; Wallace, *Greek Grammar*, 564; Edmondo F. Lupieri, *A Commentary on the Apocalypse of John* (Grand Rapids: Eerdmans, 2006) 170.

[49] Lupieri, *Apocalypse*, 170.

infinitive often functions like a future tense form to indicate future time.[50] This suggests that ἐτελέσθη is future in its temporal sphere of reference (Dan 12.7 upon which Rev 10.7 is based has the future passive form συντελεσθήσεται in the LXX).[51] Interestingly, as an allusion to Dan 12.7 John's ἐτελέσθη would reflect the Hebrew *imperfect* תכלינה rather than the more commonly proposed "prophetic perfect" which presumably lies behind examples of the futuristic aorist. It is often concluded that the future referring aorist indicates more certainty (Gewißheit)[52] due to an assumed temporal, rhetorical shift. However, 1) this is overly dependent on a temporal conception of the aorist; 2) it ignores the default nature of the aorist tense; 3) any notion of certainly belongs to the authority of the angelic voice, not the aorist tense form.[53] If the aorist grammaticalizes verbal aspect, this usage of the aorist to refer to a future process, however rare, is not anomalous.

Rev 11.2: ὅτι **ἐδόθη** τοῖς ἔθνεσιν

Though few commentaries discuss this example, Thompson and Fanning list it as a future referring aorist, as does Aune, who follows Fanning.[54] Since John is commanded by the guiding angel to perform the action of measuring the temple, while excluding the outer court, an action that obviously John has not done at the point of the angel's instructions, the act of giving (ἐδόθη) it over to the gentiles has not taken place yet: it is still future. This may find confirmation from the future tense form (πατήσουσιν) which follows. More specifically Fanning labels this an "aorist of 'divine decree' which views a future event as certain because of God's predestination of it in eternity past or else portrays a course of action just determined in the councils of heaven but not yet worked out on earth: the aorist refers to the future working out, but it is seen as certain in the light of God's decree."[55] However, Fanning's treatment

---

[50] Cf. BDF § 356. See the parallel construction in Mark 13.4. Cf. Beale, *Revelation*, 541; Charles, *Revelation, I*, 265; Osborne, *Revelation*, 400.

[51] Theod has συντελεσθῆναι. For the Danielic influence in 10.5–7 see Beale, *Revelation*, 537–546.

[52] Giesen, *Offenbarung*, 235–236.

[53] Contra Osborne, *Revelation*, 400 n. 13, citing Wallace, *Greek Grammar*, 564.

[54] Thompson, *Semitic Syntax*, 40; Fanning, *Verbal Aspect*, 274; Aune, *Revelation 1–5*, clxxxvii. *Contra* Mussies, *Morphology*, 339.

[55] Fanning, *Verbal Aspect*, 247. Fanning lists other NT texts as exemplary of this function: Rom 8.30, and perhaps Mark 11.24; 13.20; 1 Thes 2.16. This option is entertained by Aune, *Revelation 6–16*, 578.

is based on his theological conclusion rather than grammatically on the semantics of the aorist tense form. Any notion of certainty stems from the nature of the voice speaking, and has little, if anything, to do with the aorist aspect.

However, the aorist ἐδόθη should probably be taken as past time referring here. It refers to the act of giving over, which will then be followed by the trampling (πατήσουσιν) recorded in the future tense form. So this usage should probably be removed from the category of future-referring aorists.

Rev 14.8: **ἔπεσεν ἔπεσεν** Βαβυλὼν ἡ μεγάλη

That the aorists in Rev 14.8 are future referring is fairly standard among commentaries and grammars.[56] Like other instances of this use of the aorist, usually the occurrences of the aorists here are explained as examples of a proleptic aorist reflecting the Hebrew "prophetic perfect." The destruction of Babylon is seen as if it has already transpired, a *fait accompli*.[57] Beale summarizes this persistent perspective when he concludes that the aorists function as a prophetic perfect, "expressing the occurrence of Babylon's fall as though it had already occurred,"[58] with the usual added connotation of "a vivid, certain vision of a future occurrence as though already fulfilled."[59] However, this assessment of the aorists in 14.8 once again assumes past time value as a semantically constituent feature of the aorist tense form. Rev 14.8 occurs as the pronouncement of the second angel in a series of three angelic pronouncements (14.6–11).[60] Structurally, all three angelic pronouncements contain messages of future judgment, as can be seen by the warning of God's coming wrath in v. 10 for those who worship the beast and the future tense form βασανισθήσεται. Furthermore, Babylon does not fall

---

[56] Fanning, *Verbal Aspect*, 274; Porter, *Idioms*, 37–38; Beale, *Revelation*,754; David E. Aune, *Revelation 6–16* (WBC 52b; Nashville: Thomas Nelson, 1998) 829; Simon J. Kistemaker, *Revelation* (NTC; Grand Rapids: Baker, 2001) 410; Osborne, *Revelation*, 537; Smalley, *Revelation*, 363; Blount, *Revelation*, 274. Cf. Thompson, *Semitic Syntax*, 41: "Babylon the Great is falling, is falling."

[57] Resseguie, *Revelation*, 198. The action is seen "comme déjà realize" (Pierre Prigent, *l'Apocalypse de Saint Jean* [CNT XIV, Lansanne: Delachaux & Niestlé, 1981], 226).

[58] Beale, *Revelation*, 754. Cf. Aune, *Revelation 6–16*, 829: the aorists "emphasize the certainly of the fall of Babylon, which from the standpoint of the speaker, is an event that has not yet occurred."

[59] Fanning, *Verbal Aspect*, 274.

[60] See Osborne, *Revelation*, 533–547.

until 16.19; 18, so the announcement in 14.8 is clearly anticipatory.[61]
Thus the repeated aorist ἔπεσεν is apparently future referring.

Moreover, 14.8 is an intertextual allusion to Isa 21.9 where John apparently follows the Hebrew text (נפלה נפלה בבל) since the LXX has the
perfect πέπτωκεν (ms B has the doubling πέπτωκεν πέπτωκεν).[62] Since
John is dependent on the Hebrew text, his choice of the aorist could
reflect translation Greek (Isa 21.9). Therefore, those that think this is an
example of the aorist reflecting a "prophetic perfect" may be on firmer
footing here, though this is due, I would suggest, to the fact that the aorist
overlaps in meaning and temporal reference with the Hebrew perfect
at this point, rather than reflecting any kind of Semitic intrusion upon
John's use of the aorist tense form. Thus, since the aorist conceives of the
action as a complete whole and can be used in various temporal contexts,
including future, it is a suitable translation equivalent for the Hebrew perfect here.[63]

It may also be possible to take 14.8 as present referring in this context.
While in his later work Porter classifies them as future referring ("great
Babylon is going to fall, is going to fall!"), in his earlier work he seems
to translate them as present referring ("it has fallen").[64] The focus would
be on the giving of the angelic pronouncement as a verdict rendered on
Babylon, a decree of judgment given in advance of the act of judgment
itself executed later in 16.19; 18.2 (on 18.2 see the next Ch. on 18.4–20).[65]
Therefore, *from the standpoint of the angelic pronouncement* the verdict
is past or present: "the destruction of Babylon has been decided."[66] But
since the statement clearly anticipates the fall of Babylon which does not
transpire until Ch. 18, it is probably better to take it as future-referring. In
any case, the aorists in 14.8 should not be understood as past referring,
or as some temporal, rhetorical transfer (the action is seen from a past
time standpoint as though it has already occurred). Rather, verbal aspect

---

[61] See Jan Fekkes, *Isaiah and Prophetic Traditions in the Book of Revelation* (JSNTSS 93;
Sheffield: JSOT Press, 1994) 88.

[62] For the textual issues relating to Rev 14.8 see Aune, *Revelation 6–16*, 786.

[63] Therefore, it is doubtful that Ian Boxall's statement is correct: "The angel's opening
words ... evoke Isa. 21:9, although Revelation's preference for the Greek aorist over
Isaiah's perfect tense accentuates the completed nature—proleptically described—of the
city's fall" (*The Revelation of Saint John* [BNTC; Peabody, MA: Hendrickson, 2006] 207).

[64] Cf. *Idioms*, 37–38; *Verbal Aspect*, 226 respectively.

[65] Cf. also Mussies, *Morphology*, 338, whose translation "has now been decided" is
patently temporally past.

[66] Mussies, *Morphology*, 338.

can adequately explain this usage. Neither is it likely that the future-referring aorist stresses any greater certainty or confidence (so-called *perfectum confidentiae*).[67] Not only does this reflect an overdependence on a temporal approach to the aorist (seeing the event as already past), in addition it is difficult to see how the aorists ἔπεσεν ἔπεσεν in 14.8 are any more certain or vivid than the judgments referred to in the future (βασανισθήσεται) or the present (πίεται; cf. v. 11) forms which surround it. Something similar could be said about 11.2, where the aorist ἐδόθη is followed by a future πατήσουσιν. Are we to understand the aorist as more certain than the future? Instead, as previously mentioned, any notion of certainty comes from the authority of the voice of the speaker (angelic being, God) rather than the aorist tense form. Rather than explaining this *usage of the aorist* in terms of certainty, it should be explained in terms of verbal aspect. The author wishes to view a future process as a complete, undifferentiated whole.

15.1: ὅτι ἐν αὐταῖς **ἐτελέσθη** ὁ θυμὸς θεοῦ

The aorist ἐτελέσθη found in 15.1 is often understood as future referring ("is about to be completed").[68] At this point in the narrative the angel who holds the bowls full of God's wrath clearly has not poured them out yet (Ch. 16).[69] Alternatively, however, it may be preferable to interpret ἐτελέσθη as temporally past from the standpoint of the vision; that is, following the καὶ εἶδον that begins this section John is narrating *what he saw*; ἐτελέσθη as an explanation of the bowls belongs within this temporal framework. Unlike the other examples treated in this section, 15.1 is *not part of a speech*, but part of the narration of what John saw. Falling within the ὅτι clause, it describes the seven plagues possessed by the angel. Thus the aorist ἐτελέσθη would be assessed as an aorist in narration and could be translated, "in them *were completed* the wrath of God." That is, in his vision he saw the wrath of God completed in the pouring out of the bowls.

---

[67] Mussies, *Morphology*, 339; Fanning, *Verbal Aspect*, 270: "The aorist gives a vivid picture of the occurrence or emphasizes its certainty or imminence." Cf. Aune, *Revelation 6–16*, 829; Beale, *Revelation*, 754. Osborne cites Porter on the future use of the aorist, but reiterates the common notion of the "absolute certainty" of the fall due to the aorist tense form (*Revelation*, 537).

[68] Cf. Porter, *Idioms*, 38. Porter concludes that "there may be many more examples in Revelation" (38). Prigent suggests that the action in 15.1 is seen "comme déjà accompli" (*L'Apocalypse*, 238); Bousset, *Offenbarung*, 392.

[69] Fanning, *Verbal Aspect*, 274. Dougherty, "Syntax," 423; Kistemaker, *Revelation*, 430: "God's wrath is finished at the end of the seven plagues."

In this sense 15.1 would function as a summary statement for the rest of the chapter and is then further explicated in the following verses. Such an interpretation is not to revert to a temporal (past) conception of the aorist; the aorist only grammaticalizes perfective aspect. Any notion of past time is contextually determined through deictic and other indicators. Other possible future-referring aorists are 11.10–13 (on which see below); 18.17–19 (on which see below); 21.23 (ἐφώτισεν followed by a future in v. 24), though these all have alternative explanations.[70] All of the above discussed examples resist analysis based on a strictly temporal conception of the aorist tense form. Rather, they fit nicely within an aspectual model for understanding the aorist, with future time, however uncommon (I only found two unambiguous examples), as one of its possible temporal implicatures.

Aorist as Perfect

Some scholars have postulated the use of the aorist in Revelation with the force of the perfect tense (stative), a usage that is not usually attributed to Semitic influence. Charles lists numerous examples of aorists that require translation into English with the present perfect tense (cf. ἀφῆκας in 2.4; εἶδες in 1.19), though it is not clear if they should be treated semantically as perfects.[71] Aune highlights several uses of the aorist with perfect value (ἠγάπησα in 3.9—"I have loved;" cf. 4.11; 11.17; 14.18; 18.3;[72] Mussies includes 14.7 [ἦλθεν]; 19.7 [ἦλθεν][73]), while Dougherty claims that this usage occurs 99 times in Revelation.[74] Smalley asserts that ἐπλούτησαν ("have become rich") in 18.3 is an aorist with the sense of a perfect.[75] However, when examined more closely the apparent perfective force of the aorist can usually be accounted for by the lexical meaning of the verb (ἐγένετο in 11.17), or by contextual factors that might indicate a resultant state (ἔκτισας in 4.11). But this is not the same as concluding

---

[70] See Mussies, *Morphology*, 339–340. Of 21.23 Mussies says that ἐφώτισεν could be an ordinary past tense, but we would expect the imperfect (*Morphology*, 340), but it is not clear why this is the case.

[71] See Charles, *Revelation, I*, cxxv for a complete listing of verbs.

[72] Aune, *Revelation 1–5*, clxxxvii.

[73] Mussies, *Morphology*, 339.

[74] Dougherty, "Syntax," 420–422. However, Dougherty thinks that the aorist is appropriate in these instances since the focus is on the action and not the resultant state. So it is not clear whether he thinks they still function as true aorists.

[75] Smalley, *Revelation*, 445.

that the aorist tense takes on stative force and confuses semantics and pragmatics. Moreover, in most of the cases the perceived perfect force is more often the result of idiomatic English translation (e.g. ἠγάπησας in 3.9—"I have loved;" ἐπλούτησαν in 18.3—"have become rich"), even as Charles appears to recognize, rather than the semantics of the aspect. Yet just because the force of a verb comes across as "perfect (stative) in force" in our English translation (or any other target language) does not justify attributing that meaning to the aorist tense form. As McKay wisely counseled, "Idiomatic English translations must use English categories, but this does not imply that those categories can be directly transferred to the explanation of Greek idiom."[76] Therefore, it is doubtful whether any of these aorists should be construed as containing the force of the perfect; rather, they can all be seen as true aorists aspectually—they view the simple action in its entirety. As such they are to be distinguished semantically from the perfect tense.

Based on the analysis of the above examples, it appears, then, that the use of the aorist in different temporal spheres throughout Revelation, recognized by Thompson and others, fits well with its temporal distribution in the rest of the New Testament as amply demonstrated by Porter's analysis of the aorist (past, present, future, omnitemporal, timeless).[77] All of these usages, including the function of the aorist referring to processes which are temporally future, can be explained in light of verbal aspect. Yet what might account for the common insistence that the aorist often reflects the Hebrew perfect? Thompson certainly needs more than the 95 instances of the Hebrew perfect in the Old Testament that he examines to prove his point.[78] Further, Thompson's appeal to the translation of the Hebrew *qatal* in the LXX with the aorist tense form is unjustified since, except for cases where John may be alluding to the Hebrew text of the Old Testament, Revelation is not a translation document.[79] But perhaps the observations of Thompson and other scholars can be explained by the fact that the reason for the overlap of the aorist and the Hebrew perfect

---

[76] McKay, *New Syntax*, 28. Cf. also Porter, *Verbal Aspect*, 265. James H. Moulton also warns against reliance on English translation for the presence of perfective aorists (*A Grammar of New Testament Greek, Prolegomena, Vol. 1* [ed. James H. Moulton; Edinburgh: T. & T. Clark, 1908] 136).

[77] Porter, *Verbal Aspect*, 182–239; *Idioms*, 35–40.

[78] Thompson, *Semitic Syntax*, 37. See his table of statistics.

[79] For this criticism see also Porter, "Language of the Apocalypse," 589. Recall the three levels of Semitic influence as articulated by Porter (cf. *Verbal Aspect*, 118).

is not due to interference from the Hebrew verb system, but the similar meaning and temporal functions of the two forms. The Hebrew tense system itself appears to be an aspectual one, rather than temporal.[80] As stated above, if some of John's usage of the aorist do reflect the Hebrew perfect or at least appear similar to it in function, it is because the semantics of the Greek aorist and its range of temporal functions overlap with that of the Hebrew perfect.

In conclusion, there is nothing unusual or un-Greek (or necessarily Semitic) about the function of the aorist tense within the discourse of Revelation. Though the aorist in Revelation most frequently refers to past time narration, when seen as grammaticalizing verbal aspect rather than *Aktionsart* or absolute temporal reference (past time), all the various temporal realizations of the aorist tense form can adequately be accounted for. Even possible future uses of the aorist in Revelation, however uncommon, are explicable in light of verbal aspect. Consistent with an aspectual approach, in all cases, the aorist tense can be seen to grammaticalize the author's perspective (perfective) on the process.

The Present Tense

There are 175 occurrences of the present indicative form in Revelation, excluding examples of the aspectually vague εἰμί.[81] As seen above, in contrast to the aorist, the present tense is used by an author to view an action internally, as it develops and unfolds.[82] The Greek present tense form occurs throughout the Apocalypse primarily in the following temporal contexts: 1) present, 2) future, 3) past, and 4) temporally unrestricted. As with the aorist tense form, attempts to account for the temporal and contextual distribution of this form throughout Revelation have usually commenced with an exclusively temporal point of departure.

---

[80] On the Hebrew tense system as aspectual cf. Gary A. Long, *Grammatical Concepts 101 for Biblical Hebrew* (Peabody: Hendrickson, 2005) 92–98; Bruce K. Waltke and M. O'Conner, *An Introduction to Biblical Hebrew Syntax* (Winona Lake: Eisenbrauns, 1990) 347–348.

[81] For other aspectually vague verbs, see: εἰμί, κεῖμαι, φημί, νεόμαι, κάθημαι. Cf. Porter, *Verbal Aspect*, 443; "Aspect Theory and Lexicography," 212.

[82] In Porter's words, "its internal structure is seen as unfolding" (*Idioms*, 21). The typical explanations of the present in terms of "continuous," "durative," or "ongoing," as seen in the previous chapter, reflect *Aktionsart*.

Present Time

Consistent with what is usually deemed the most common pragmatic function of the present tense, the present tense form used in present-time contexts in Revelation hardly requires justification, and there is no need to belabor this point with a list of numerous examples.[83] Most of the examples of this use of the present are found in the speeches and hymnic forms throughout Revelation. There are numerous apparent examples in Chs. 2–3: e.g. λέγω/λέγει (2.1, 7, 8, 11, 12, 17, 18, 24, 29; 3.1, 6, 7, 13, 14, 17, 22); δύνῃ (2.2); ἔχω/-εις (2.3, 4, 6, 14, 15, 20; 3.1, 4, 11); μισεῖς (2.6); κατοικεῖς (2.13); ἀφεῖς (2.20); θέλει (2.21); τήρει (3.3); συμβουλεύω (3.18); κρούω (3.20) among others.[84]

Future Time

Thompson observes the "strange yet obvious future sense expressed by certain present indicative Greek verbs."[85] However, except for his strong temporal starting point, it is unclear why he thinks this is so strange since Greek grammarians (some of which Thompson himself notes) have long recognized this function as a legitimate use of the present tense, however infrequent its occurrence.[86] Often this usage is lexically determined. As most grammarians recognize, a number of these usages occur with ἔρχομαι and other verbs of 'coming' and 'going' (cf. ὑπάγω).[87] There have been numerous attempts to explain this usage in Revelation. Several scholars point to Semitic influence for this function of the present tense form. Thus Thompson, as he did with the aorist tense form, appeals to examples from the LXX to demonstrate the present with a future sense used in numerous cases to translate the Hebrew participle (*futurum instans*).

---

[83] As Porter correctly laments, "While tense names in a language are based on some typical function, this function is usually not the only function of the form concerned, and a speaker risks causing considerable confusion if he fails to make clear that the name often only reflects one of several functions" (*Verbal Aspect*, 80). Hence, deviation from the typical functions of tenses are not to be construed as exceptional.

[84] Dougherty only finds three examples of what he calls the "simple present"—2.24; 3.18, 20. See "Syntax," 406.

[85] Thompson, *Semitic Syntax*, 29.

[86] Outside of the grammars that Thompson discusses, cf. Burton, *Syntax*, 9–10; Robertson, *Grammar*, 869–870; Moule, *Idiom Book*, 7; Smyth, *Grammar*, 421–422. See Moulton, *Prolegomena*, 120.

[87] Cf. McKay, *New Syntax*, 41; cf. Dougherty, "Syntax," 405–406.

Furthermore, Thompson admits that this is an example of an "over-working of a Greek construction" due to the future use of the participle in Hebrew rather than a grammatical innovation, removing this from being strictly considered a true Semitism. This future sense of the present tense, according to him, has developed in the New Testament independently of Hellenistic literature.[88] For Revelation, Thompson divides the uses of the futuristic present into two categories: those preceded by ἰδού (2.16, 22; 3.9, 11; 9.12; 16.15; 21.5) reflecting the הנה of Hebrew, and those not preceded by ἰδού (1.11; 2.27; 3.7, 9; 5.10; 7.15, 17; 9.6; 11.5, 9, 10, 15; 13.10; 14.9, 10, 11; 17.11, 12; 19.3, 11; 22.5).[89] While Thompson attributed this "over-working" of the future-referring present to the Hebrew *participle*, Charles postulated that the Hebrew *imperfect* with a future sense accounts for its usage in Revelation.[90] (Is this another example of semantic overlap between a Hebrew and Greek tense form?). This disagreement demonstrates the difficulty of formulating a theory apart from consistent criteria due to the fact that Revelation is not a translation document.

Furthermore, the future-referring present tense is customarily seen as reflecting the assumed present time value of the present tense. Thus it is perceived as more vivid, more confident in its assertion.[91] What apparently renders it more vivid or assured is the temporal transfer that takes place: it is seen as if present from the standpoint of the speaker/hearer. Mussies finds the "futural present" used 39 times in Revelation.[92] But Mussies contends that these uses of the present merely serve as an intermediate stage for a shift to future verbs which clearly portray the predictive, prophetic character of the visions. Otherwise, the present tense throughout Revelation indicates "what he [John] is seeing again before his eyes, and as such these present indicatives give the idea of lively representation."[93]

---

[88] Thompson, *Semitic Syntax*, 31–32.

[89] Thompson, *Semitic Syntax*, 32–33. Thompson also notes a number of usages that contain a textual variant with a future tense. Thus in Rev 2.22 א[a] 046 P 325 *al* have βαλῶ instead of βάλλω. Cf. Aune, *Revelation 1–5*, 198 for a discussion of the textual evidence. Cf. also 3.7 where some copyists changed the present ἀνοίγει to the future ἀνοίξει. On this change see Aune, *Revelation 1–5*, 229.

[90] Charles, *Revelation, I*, cxxiii ("due to a Hebraism"); Lancellotti, *Sintassi ebraica*, 67.

[91] Cf. BDF § 323, who recognizes this usage is not unknown in Classical Greek. See Fanning, *Verbal Aspect*, 225, who refers to this use of the present in prophetic or oracular pronouncements. He cites Rev 9.6 as an example.

[92] Mussies, *Morphology*, 333.

[93] Mussies, *Morphology*, 334.

However, the common denominator in all of these treatments of the futuristic use of the present semantically is a temporal point of departure for the present tense. This apparently explains the propensity of Charles, Thompson and others to exploit Semitic influence from the Hebrew imperfect or participle to explain the apparently strange or deviant usages. Dougherty thinks that the present is often used with the simple time-value of the future, and unnecessarily classifies this as a distinct use of the future referring present.[94] According to him, in these cases the present tense is equivalent to a future, yet he goes on to admit that "[t]his future nuance of the present comes from the meaning of the verb and/or from the context."[95] However, identical temporal function does not entail lack of semantic differentiation. Hence, the future and present tenses should be kept distinct semantically.

Porter has adduced numerous examples of precisely this use of the present in Hellenistic (including the New Testament) Greek, rendering any appeal to direct Semitic influence unnecessary and unwarranted.[96] As several grammarians have recognized, the futuristic present was known in prophetic and oracular literature (cf. Hdt 7.140, 141), which is suggestive of its prevalent usage in Revelation.[97] Furthermore, as already noted grammarians have pointed out that the future force of the present is often lexically determined since it is "mostly found with verbs of coming and going" such as ἔρχομαι and ὑπάγω.[98] At other times the futuristic use of the present is determined by other contextual or deictic indicators (cf. 1 Cor 15.32: αὔριον γὰρ ἀποθνῄσκομεν). Porter provides an explanation that accounts for this usage in the New Testament and Revelation based on verbal aspect: "The speaker conceives of the process as in progress and this progress may very well carry over into what he sees as the future."[99] Or according to McKay, "an activity whose completion is still in the future may be represented as simply in process."[100]

---

[94] Dougherty, "Syntax," 405: "Sometimes the present tense is simply equivalent to the future."

[95] Dougherty, "Syntax," 405. But equivalency of temporal reference does not suggest equivalency of meaning. The distinction remains a semantic one.

[96] Porter, *Verbal Aspect*, 230–232.

[97] Cf. Turner, *Syntax*, 63; BDF § 323; Porter, *Verbal Aspect*, 232; Fanning, *Verbal Aspect*, 225; Aune, *Revelation 1–5*, clxxxv.

[98] McKay, *New Syntax*, 41. Cf. BDF § 323; Turner, *Syntax*, 63; Porter, *Verbal Aspect*, 232; Fanning, *Verbal Aspect*, 222, 225; Dougherty, "Syntax," 405–406.

[99] Porter, *Verbal Aspect*, 231. At least in one place Fanning correctly notes that this use of the present is not due to a rhetorical transfer of time, but the aspect value of the present tense form (*Verbal Aspect*, 222).

[100] McKay, *New Syntax*, 41.

In Revelation, one encounters a number of presents used with this future sense which are based lexically on ἔρχομαι (1.7; 2.5, 16; 3.11; 9.12; 11.14; 16.15; 22.7, 12, 20). Several of these occur with ἰδού preceding it (1.7; 9.12; 11.14; 16.15; 22.7, 12).[101] Three instances of ἔρχεται occur alongside of future tense forms, accentuating their future-referring temporal function: 1.7: ἔρχεται … ὄψεται … κόψονται; 2.5: ἔρχομαι … κινήσω; 2.16: ἔρχομαι … πολεμήσω.

The usages of ἔρχομαι can be divided up further into those instances that refer to the coming of Christ (1.7; 2.5, 16; 3.11; 16.15; 22.7, 12, 20), and two instances that refer to the coming of two woes (9.12; 11.14). With reference to the coming of Christ, two of the examples of ἰδοὺ ἔρχομαι constitute rather clear instances of a quotation or an allusion. Rev 1.7 constitutes a combined citation of two Old Testament texts: Dan 7.13 and Zech 12.10–12, and so could fall under Porter's first category of "direct translation."[102] The relevant part of the citation for our purposes comes from Dan 7.13:

> Rev 1.7: Ἰδοὺ ἔρχεται μετὰ τῶν νεφελῶν
> Dan 7.13 (MT): וארו עם־ענני שמיא … אתה הוא
> Dan 7.13 (LXX): καὶ ἰδοὺ ἐπὶ τῶν νεφελῶν τοῦ οὐρανοῦ … ἤρχετο
> Dan 7.13 (Theod): καὶ ἰδοὺ … ἐρχόμενος
> Cf. Matt 24.30: τὸν υἱὸν τοῦ ἀνθρώπου ἐρχόμενον ἐπὶ τῶν νεφελῶν τοῦ οὐρανοῦ

Though Thompson thinks that ἰδού and the futuristic present reflect the Semitic הנה + participle, it is interesting that in the text to which John alludes neither the LXX nor Theod translate the Semitic participle with the present indicative form. John's Ἰδοὺ ἔρχεται may be an independent translation of אתה הוא. However, both Matthew 24.30 and Revelation change Dan 7.13 from a narrative account of a vision to prophetic

---

[101] Thompson, *Semitic Syntax*, 32–33. He states that "while recognizing that the present ἔρχομαι alone has no special Semitic flavour, even when its sense is future, we have demonstrated that when preceded by ἰδού the resulting biblical Greek construction can represent the literal rendering of Hebrew *hinnê* plus participle." The use of ἰδού as a discourse marker of emphasis, or to draw attention, is not uncommon elsewhere in the New Testament, even outside of the Gospels where it occurs with the most frequency, and is found used similarly outside of the New Testament. LSJ, 819 provide several examples from extra-biblical Greek of ἰδού meaning "lo, behold" with nouns and verbs. So once again it can hardly be concluded that ἰδού + verb is a strict Semitism.

[102] Porter, "Language of the Apocalypse," 587. These same two texts are combined, but in the reverse order, in Matt 24.30. Both Matthew and Revelation have turned the past narration of a vision in Dan 7.13 to a prophecy predicting the coming of the Son of Man.

prediction, suggesting a common tradition rather than direct dependence, so that Revelation may also be dependent on Synoptic tradition
at this point, though John is still unique in his use of the present ἔρχεται.[103]

In Rev 16.15 the author may be alluding to the logion of Jesus found
in Matt 24.43; Luke 12.39–40 (cf. 1 Thess 5.2, 4; 2 Pet 3.10).

> Rev 16.15: Ἰδοὺ ἔρχομαι ὡς κλέπτης
> Matt 24.43: ὁ κλέπτης ἔρχεται
> Luke 12.39–40: ὁ κλέπτης ἔρχεται ... ὁ υἱὸς τοῦ ἀνθρώπου ἔρχεται
> (1 Thess 5.2: ὡς κλέπτης ... οὕτως ἔρχεται)[104]

However, the addition of ἰδού to Rev 16.15, lacking in the Jesus logion,
still reflects the Dan 7.13 text. In any case, it appears that Dan 7.13 as well
as the coming of the Son of Man tradition in Christian eschatological
expectation together have influenced John's use of ἰδοὺ ἔρχομαι to refer
to a future process.

It is also likely, then, that the other uses of ἔρχομαι (with or without
ἰδού) to refer to Christ's coming in Revelation 2.5, 16; 3.11; 16.15; 22.7,
12, 20 also reflect Dan 7.13 as Aune has argued, and probably also
Christian tradition.[105] Thus, given the reliance on Dan 7.13, one could
argue that Revelation's ἰδοὺ ἔρχομαι reflects Semitic influence at the
level of translation. Yet the presence of the ἰδού elsewhere in the New
Testament and extra-biblical Greek, the use of ἔρχομαι in Christian
tradition to refer to the (future) coming of the Son of Man, and the
attested use of the futuristic present in first century Greek clearly suggest
that this construction is not un-Greek.[106] In any case ἔρχομαι clearly has
future implicature throughout Revelation due to the lexical meaning of
the verb.[107] Beale thinks that ἔρχεται refers to the conditional coming of
Christ in judgment which will climax with the Parousia of Christ, as part

---

[103] Matthew has ἐρχόμενον. The other differences between Rev 1.7 and Matt 24.30
suggest dependence on a common tradition rather than direct literary influence. Richard
J. Bauckham, *The Climax of Prophecy* (Edinburgh: T. & T. Clark, 1993) 319–322.

[104] Cf. 2 Pet 3.10 which, however, has ἥξει.

[105] Aune, *Revelation 1–5*, 54.

[106] This is not to conclude that everywhere in Revelation ἰδού is devoid of Semitic
influence. The places where ἰδού introduces a vision, or segment within a vision, it
is possible that it reflects the Hebrew הנה, creating a resonance with Old Testament
prophecy. Cf. Ezek 1.4. Cf. H. Kraft, *Die Offenbarung des Johannes* (HNT 16a; Tübingen:
Mohr, 1974) 34. But again this must be understood as an enhancement, since there is
nothing un-Greek about this construction.

[107] Fanning, *Verbal Aspect*, 221–222. Italics his. Cf. Porter, *Verbal Aspect*, 231.

of the "already-not yet" tension in Christian eschatology.[108] Though this may be valid theologically, it does not necessarily provide a grammatical explanation for ἔρχομαι.[109]

The remaining instances of ἔρχομαι refer to the coming of the woes, which are clearly future in the narrative. In 9.12 the two woes are in the process of coming (ἰδοὺ ἔρχεται). Then in 11.14 the author announces the (future) coming of the third woe (ἰδοὺ ... ἔρχεται). Thus the futuristic present is not always eschatological, but may refer to what will transpire in later sections of the vision.

The verb ὑπάγω, lexically another verb of motion,[110] also occurs with future time reference in Revelation. It occurs 3 times in the indicative mood, all with apparent future implication.[111] In 13.10, which constitutes a call for endurance in the midst of a visionary segment, ὑπάγει is part of a conditional sentence, and clearly has future force.

> εἴ τις εἰς αἰχμαλωσίαν, εἰς αἰχμαλωσίαν **ὑπάγει**.

This example, however, has the present tense in the apodosis of a conditional sentence, and so it should be taken as logically future, dependent on the fulfillment of the protasis.[112] It occurs twice more in Revelation 17.8, 11 to refer to the future destruction of the beast (ἀπώλειαν ὑπάγει), possibly as a deliberate contrast to the future coming (ἔρχομαι) of the Lamb (see below).

Perhaps the clearest examples of the futuristic use of the present tense occur where the present tense form is used alongside of future tense forms, clearly indicating future temporal implicature. The following examples are sufficient to demonstrate this usage.[113]

> 2.22–23: ἰδοὺ **βάλλω** αὐτὴν εἰς κλίνην ... καὶ τὰ τέκνα αὐτῆς ἀποκτενῶ
>
> 9.6: ἐν ταῖς ἡμέρεις ἐκείναις ζητήσουσιν ... καὶ οὐ μὴ εὑρήσουσιν ... καὶ ἐπιθυμήσουσιν ... καὶ **φεύγει** ὁ θάνατοκς ...[114]

---

[108] Beale, *Revelation*, 199.

[109] Cf. Osborne, *Revelation*, 69 n. 27.

[110] Semantic Domain 15 in Louw and Nida, *Greek-English Lexicon*.

[111] It occurs twice as an imperative (10.8; 16.1) and once in the subjunctive mood (14.4).

[112] Cf. Porter, *Verbal Aspect*, 230–231 for this usage of the present tense in conditional type sentences.

[113] Cf. also Dougherty, "Syntax," 404–405. The λατρεύουσιν from 7.15–17 could be included here as well, especially since it is followed by a string of future tense forms, but I have included it in a different category of "timeless-descriptive" (see below). So I have excluded it from consideration here.

[114] Cf. the future φεύξεται in 1611[1854 2329] 2351 Byzantine lat cop.

11.7–9: *νικήσει* ... *καὶ ἀποκτενεῖ* ... *καὶ* **βλέπουσιν** ... **ἀφίουσιν**[115]

14.10–11: **πίεται** ... *καὶ βασανισθήσεται* ... *καὶ ὁ καπνὸς* ... **ἀναβαί-νει** ... *καὶ* **ἔχουσιν**[116]

17.12–14: ... **λαμβάνουσιν** ... **ἔχουσιν** ... **διδόασιν** ... *πολεμήσουσιν* ... *νικήσει*

21.24: *καὶ περιπατήσουσιν τὰ ἔθνη* ... *καὶ οἱ βασιλεῦς τῆς γῆς* **φέρουσιν** *τὴν δόξαν* ....

22.5: καὶ νὺξ ἔσται ἔτι, καὶ οὐκ **ἔχουσιν** χρείαν φωτὸς λύχνου καί φῶς ἡλίου, ὅτι κύριος ὁ θεὸς *φωτίσει ἐπ᾽* αὐτούς, καὶ *βασιλεύσουσιν* ....[117]

It is possible that the present tense form in 21.5: Ἰδοὺ καινὰ **ποιῶ** πάντα, should be included here as well, though it may be due to a direct allusion to the LXX of Isa 43.19: Ἰδοὺ **ποιῶ** καινά.[118] Though Thompson postulates Semitic influence in such instances,[119] future time is a temporal implicature of the use of the present tense form, which communicates aspect, in these contexts. By using the present tense form the author is able to communicate aspectual information (action viewed in its internal makeup) which is not available in the aspectually vague future tense form. The future tense form would emphasize what could be expected to occur (see below), while the present tense depicts future processes as developing or unfolding. Robertson is close to the truth when he says "It affirms and not merely predicts."[120] Semantically, aspect is still the *primary feature* of future referring presents rather than time.

In conclusion, there is no need to look outside of the normal semantics of the present tense form in order to explain its future referring function. While some examples may clearly reflect influence of an underlying Old Testament text, the need to find Semitic influence on John's use of the present for temporally future events is misguided and often stems from the assumption that the present must indicate a process in the present time. However, if the Greek verbal system grammaticalizes verbal aspect and not absolute time, then John's use of the present to depict

---

[115] Cf. the future ἀφήσουσι in Oecumenius[2053] Andr d f[2023 2073] h i[2042] 94 Byzantine it[gig] vg cop.

[116] 14.10–11 is not John's narrative comment, but is part of the proclamation of the angel (Aune, *Revelation 6–16*, 797–798; Osborne, *Revelation*, 539). Thus I have classified the present tenses here, along with the future βασανισθήσεται, as future referring rather than past referring (narrative).

[117] Cf. ἔξουσιν in A fam 1006[1006 1841] fam 1611[2050 2329] Oecumenius[2053 2062] it[gig] vg cop[sa]. David E. Aune, *Revelation 17–22* (WBC 52c; Nashville: Thomas Nelson, 1998) 1140.

[118] See Beale, *Revelation*, 1054.

[119] Thompson, *Semitic Syntax*, 34–35.

[120] Robertson, *Grammar*, 870.

future events is not odd or deviant, but is clearly in line with acceptable Greek usage and the semantics of the present tense form. Therefore, there should be no difficulty in seeing the present aspect used in future time contexts. Semantically, the present tense form in Revelation can be used when the author sees a process in progress in the future.[121] However, the most important thing about presents used in future time contexts is not the temporal information they convey (future), but the semantic information. Thus the main distinction between the present and future to refer to future time is not a temporal but a semantic one. In distinction to the future (see below) the use of the present tense in future time contexts allows the author to grammaticalize verbal aspect. Finally, this also means that any notion of certainty derives from the context or speaker, not from the present tense form temporally conceived, especially since this effect is often attributed to the aorist as well.[122]

Past Time

The present tense is clearly used in Revelation to refer temporally to narrated past-time events, mainly in the narration of visions. Aune counts 43 such instances in Revelation, many of these with the verb λέγω to introduce speech.[123] Grammarians have long recognized the fact that the present tense can be used in past-time contexts in narrative, the narrative present.[124] Frequently this usage of the present is explained temporally.[125] As Fanning concludes, the present tense presents "a clearly past occurrence *as though it were simultaneous* with the writer/reader which produces the vivid or immediate effect."[126] Porter has surveyed and evaluated

---

[121] Porter, *Idioms*, 32. Cf. *Verbal Aspect*, 231.

[122] That notions of certainty come from the speaker and not the tense form can be seen from the fact that grammarians attribute certainly to both the future referring aorist and the future referring present, though for different reasons.

[123] Aune, *Revelation 1–5*, clxxxiv. By comparison, Mark has it around 151×, Matthew 78×, and Luke 12× (Acts 13×). Dougherty only lists 16 occurrences of the historical present, with some of the texts included by Aune placed by Dougherty in different categories (Timeless; Descriptive).

[124] As explained in the previous chapter, this terminology is preferable over "historical present," since "narrative present" is more functionally descriptive, while "historical present" could be misconstrued as temporal.

[125] Cf. Robertson, *Grammar*, 880; BDF § 321; Turner, *Syntax*, 60–62; Wallace, *Greek Grammar*, 526–532. See also Moulton, *Prolegomena*, 120–121. Moulton finds this usage present in the papyri as well (121).

[126] Fanning, *Verbal Aspect*, 228. Italics mine. Fanning gives examples in English of narrating a series of events with the English present tense. However, this phenomenon

the numerous proposals for the present tense in past time contexts, so discussion of the various approaches will not be rehearsed here.[127] Given the starting point of verbal aspect, that is the author's desire to conceive of the action in a particular way, the past-time use of the present tense form is a normal pragmatic manifestation. The present tense used in past-time narration depicts a past-time action as an action in progress, as developing or unfolding.[128] As discussed in the previous chapter, the function of the present tense form used of past-time events is to add vividness or descriptive color and to draw attention to certain events, characters, or speeches in narrative.[129] While the aorist tense propels the narrative forward, the present (and imperfect) dwells on or describes and focuses attention on selected processes.

As with the other tense forms and their functions, discussion of the present tense in Revelation has gotten bogged down in temporal concerns or questions of Semitic influence. Mussies construes the present tenses in Revelation's vision from a temporal standpoint, and sees them as depicting what is "again before his eyes, and as such these present indicatives give the idea of lively representation."[130] Mussies' conception exhibits the following weaknesses, however. His understanding of the present tense is exclusively dependent on temporal notions (present time). Yet if the Greek verb tense form primarily grammaticalizes verbal aspect there is no need to appeal to a temporal shift (John and his readers relive what John saw) to account for its usage in Revelation. Furthermore,

---

does not provide a precise parallel to what happens in ancient Greek narration. In the English examples that Fanning gives (and others that I have seen), the present tense form occurs in continuous strings, whereas in ancient Greek narrative the present is alternated with aorists and imperfects.

[127] Porter, *Verbal Aspect*, 189–196.

[128] Therefore, Wallace is incorrect when he states that "The *aspectual* value of the historical present is normally, if not always, reduced to zero" (*Greek Grammar*, 527). However, this clearly confuses aspect with *Aktionsart*. That is, Wallace assumes a *durative* value to the present which he does not see in some of its past-time usages. Campbell explains that the present tense looks at only part of the action. Using the same parade illustration used by Porter (*Verbal Aspect*), Campbell says that "Not only is the parade unfolding in front of him, but there is a focus on the *part of the parade* that is closest to him" (Campbell, *Verbal Aspect*, 50, italics mine [see his diagram on p. 51]). However, this would only work with events which are temporally present, as with many past events the present tense looks at the entire process rather than just the part that is before the author.

[129] Porter, *Verbal Aspect*, 196; Decker, *Temporal Deixis*, 104. Decker denies the notion of "vividness" and he is correct if it is tied to an assumed rhetorical, temporal transfer. But the category is still useful if it is tied to verbal aspect. That is, it is the aspect of the present, which looks at the action as in progress, which adds the notion of vividness.

[130] Mussies, *Morphology*, 334. Cf. Bousset, *Offenbarung*, 168.

Mussies does not ask the question of why certain processes are selected for "lively representation" and not others. His view does not account for the shifting tenses, a problem that we will turn to in the next chapter. That is, he has difficulty accounting for the shift to the present tense and then back to the aorist. Though possible, it is unlikely that the readers would be meant to constantly shift temporal spheres of reference in such a rapid manner.

Thompson divides the narrative use of the present tense forms into two categories: 1) historic present with verbs of saying; 2) other present verbs with past sense.[131] Under the first category there are a number of examples of verbs of saying (λέγω, ᾄδω, κράζω) which function in the Apocalypse to introduce the speech of various figures. Since this usage is recognized as an acceptable Greek idiom, being found in a wide range of periods in the Greek language, Thompson concludes that there is nothing unusual or Semitic about this construction.[132] As Porter notes, "the use of the historic Present is a thoroughly Greek phenomenon."[133]

For the second category of usage, however, Thompson prefers Semitic influence as the explanation for the numerous past-referring present tense forms. That is, the Semitic participle, which could refer to past, present, or future time, accounts for this use of the present indicative. Thompson does not provide extensive documentation from LXX examples, but concludes that the "Hebrew participle with past durative sense is obviously responsible for the LXX translation with a present tense verb at this point."[134] He then gives examples of the use of the present tense in Revelation to refer to past time but concludes that this use of the present is "anomalous" and that the "only reasonable explanation is that they here represent a Semitic participle with past sense."[135]

Yet there are numerous problems with Thompson's analysis. Like Mussies, he is overly dependent on a temporal understanding of the present tense: it must refer to present time. The past-referring use of the present can only be seen as an anomaly if the starting point is a purely temporal

---

[131] Thompson, *Semitic Syntax*, 35–36.

[132] Thompson, *Semitic Syntax*, 35. Here Thompson follows the assessment of the historic present with verbs of saying in Matthew Black, *An Aramaic Approach to the Gospels and Acts* (3rd edn; Oxford: University Press, 1967) 130.

[133] Porter, *Verbal Aspect*, 135. Porter thinks that the only Semitic influence on Revelation would be enhancement, but thinks that this is unlikely since the use of the narrative present varies highly among non-biblical Greek writers.

[134] Thompson, *Semitic Syntax*, 36.

[135] Thompson, *Semitic Syntax*, 36.

one (present time), compelling Thompson to look outside of Koine Greek for an adequate explanation. Given the narrative use of the present tense form in biblical and extra-biblical Greek with verbs outside of verbs of saying, one wonders how Thompson can claim that this use is anomalous.[136] And like Mussies, Thompson does not address the question of why some verbs appear to be so semitically affected and not others. Moreover, Thompson's assessment of the past-referring present at this point depends on a rather weak cumulative argumentation.[137] Yet if his general approach can be called into question, his cumulative argument loses much of its force. Thompson incorrectly places the burden of proof on those who would argue for a Greek usage. Rather, as Porter has argued, the burden of proof should lie with those who argue for Semitic influence.[138]

The narrative use of the present tense form in Revelation is explicable in light of verbal aspect. Therefore, it should not be surprising to find numerous usages of the present tense form in past-referring contexts once verbal aspect is recognized as our starting point rather than absolute temporal reference. The present aspect sometimes occurs pragmatically in past-time contexts in Revelation.

Verbs of Speaking

There are a number of present tense forms used with verbs of 'speaking' (the most common are λέγω, ᾄδω, κράζω) to introduce significant speeches of various groups or figures throughout the Apocalypse, sometimes against the background of aorist tense forms used in narration (cf. 5.5, 9; 6.16; 7.10; 10.9, 11; 14.3; 15.3; 17.15; 19.9, 10; 21.5; 22.9, 10, 20). The use of the present tense in discourse is contextually appropriate since speech has the effect of slowing down the discourse. According to Campbell, "This pausing of the narrative sequence creates the effect of taking the reader *inside* the narrative, and unfolding the communication-

---

[136] Porter provides an example of the widespread use of the historical present with verbs other than those of "saying" in Apollodorus 3.11.1–15.4 ("Language of the Apocalypse," 588).

[137] For a similar criticism see Porter, "Language of the Apocalypse." Thompson's logic can be seen in the following sentences: "It cannot be denied that the Greek historic present could be used to express a similar sense in *Koine* Greek, although it was never used on a large scale. But in such a text as the Apc., which is noted for its Semitic constructions, this use of the present tense can be described as yet another point of contact with Semitic verbal syntax" (*Semitic Syntax*, 36–37).

[138] Cf. Porter, "Language of the Apocalypse," 587.

event before the view of the reader."[139] Though Campbell's terminology adds a temporal perspective ("unfolding the communication-event
before the reader"), as the aspect which looks at the action imperfectively,
the present tense form has the effect of pausing to consider the speech in
more detail. While at times the rationale for the use of the present does
not clearly emerge (λέγει, 21.5),[140] it is likely that the author chooses
the present in order to draw attention to or highlight the speech being
referred to.

In 5.5 John's λέγει serves to introduce the speech of one of the elders
who provides a solution to John's predicament (there is no one to open
the scroll). The seer's inability to find someone able or worthy to open
the scroll (ἐδύνατο) and his response (ἔκλαιον) set the stage by using the
more remote imperfect tense form, while the solution given by the elder
uses the more marked present λέγει. In 5.9, 14.3, and 15.3 the present
of ᾄδω is used to introduce and highlight the new song sung by the
living creatures, the voice from the throne, and the Song of Moses sung
by the victorious saints. The present of a verb of speaking is also used
to introduce and highlight other important or climactic speeches (6.16;
7.10; 10.9, 11; 19.9, 10; 22.9, 10).

One common use of the present tense with verbs of saying outside of
the indicative mood form is the appearance of the present participle to
introduce a speech (e.g. λέγων/-οντες). This construction occurs numerous times in the Apocalypse to introduce the speech of an angel or heavenly voice, or hymnic material sung by various groups. (cf. e.g. 1.11, 17;
4.8, 10; 5.2, 9, 12, 13; 6.1 ff.; 7.10, 12, 13; 10.8; 11.15, 17; 12.10; 14.13; 15.3;
16.5, 7; 18.2, 4, 10, 16, 19, 21; 19.1, 4, 5, 6; 21.3, 9).[141] Thompson claims
that the use of the participle λέγων/-οντες in Revelation to introduce
speeches represents the Hebrew infinitive absolute לאמר.[142] According
to him this construction is translated in the LXX with the participle λέ-
γων/λέγοντες/λέγουσα. In Porter's estimation, the infinitive construct
לאמור occurs roughly 870 times in the Old Testament and is translated
in the LXX approximately 770 times with a form of the present participle

---

[139] Campbell, *Verbal Aspect*, 54.

[140] Here the author alternates the present λέγει with the suppletive aorist form εἶπεν.

[141] For other examples cf. 7.3; 8.13; 9.14; 10.4, 8, 9; 11.1, 12; 13.4, 5, 14; 14.7, 8, 9, 13,
15, 18; 16.1, 17; 17.1; 18.18; 19.17.

[142] Thompson, *Semitic Syntax*, 69–70. Actually, as noted by Porter (*Verbal Aspect*,
138), Thompson incorrectly identifies this as an infinitive absolute; this is the infinitive
construct, not absolute.

of λέγω.[143] This has led Thompson and others to argue for Semitic influence on this construction in Revelation.[144] Moreover, he also claims that λέγων/-οντες occurs in Revelation with the same two meanings found in Biblical Hebrew: 1) "to say;" 2) redundantly as "thus."[145] However, Porter has noted a number of instances of the present participle λέγων/-οντες in extra-biblical Greek.[146] Cf. Hdt 1.88.2: ὁ δὲ αὐτὸν εἰρῶτα λέγων.[147] And Turner also recognizes its attestation in Classical Greek and in the papyri, though like Thompson he thinks that the wide-spread usage in the New Testament points to a specialized Semitic background.[148]

The usage of this participial construction in extra-biblical Greek suggests that at the most the "density" of the use of this construction in the Apocalypse can only be given the status of Semitic enhancement, according to Porter's threefold classification.[149] Further, although the necessity of dividing the usages of λέγων into "to say" and "thus" could be questioned, Porter has at least demonstrated that the two-fold division can apply to the extra-biblical examples.[150] Thus the author of Revelation has used an accepted Greek construction to introduce numerous speeches throughout his work, perhaps enhanced by its use in the LXX to translate לאמור. The choice of the present participle is significant, since the assumed underlying Hebrew infinitive *did not grammaticalize aspect*. If this is the case, perhaps this acceptable Greek construction which is aspectually imperfective influenced its usage in the LXX to translate the non-aspectual Hebrew infinitive.[151] Therefore, there is nothing distinctly Semitic about John's use of this construction. As such, John used it to introduce speeches throughout his work, focusing on the content of what was said.

---

[143] Porter, *Verbal Aspect*, 138. For the LXX see F.C. Conybeare and St. George Stock, *Grammar of Septuagint Greek* (Peabody: Hendrickson, 1995, reprint from the original edn published by Boston: Gin and Co., 1905) 96.

[144] Cf. Charles, *Revelation, I*, cxxvii, who labels this a Hebraism; Beale, *Revelation*, 365, who sees this as one of the possibilities for this construction in Revelation 5; Turner, *Syntax*, 155; Bousset, *Offenbarung*, 243.

[145] Thompson, *Semitic Syntax*, 69–70.

[146] Porter, *Verbal Aspect*, 139; "Language of the Apocalypse," 590.

[147] Cf. Thuc 2.65.1; Plato *Apol* 29C; *Gorg* 512 C1; Jos, *JW* 1.515; P. Fay 123.15–16; Her 1.118.1; 1.125; Epict 4.8.26; BGU 624.15.

[148] Turner, *Syntax*, 155–156. Turner lists Hdt (ἔφη λέγων; εἰρῶτα λέγων; ἔλεγε φάς); UPZ 1.6.30; P. Giss 36.10; BGU 624.15; 523.6; P. Par 51.23; 35.30, though he does not consider the latter four examples pleonastic. Cf. BDF § 420.

[149] Cf. also Aune, *Revelation 1–5*, 66.

[150] Porter, *Verbal Aspect*, 138–139.

[151] Porter, *Verbal Aspect*, 139.

Non-speech Instances

The narrative present occurs with verbs other than verbs of saying in the Apocalypse. Beginning with the narration of the vision in 4.1, at least the following usages can be categorized as examples of present indicative verbs used in narration (what John saw) to refer temporally to past time events:[152] 4.5 (ἐκπορεύονται), 8 (γέμουσιν, ἔχουσιν); 9.10, 11 (ἔχουσιν [2×], ἔχει), 17 (ἐκπορεύεται), 19 (ἀδικοῦσιν); 12.2 (κράζει), 4 (σύρει), 6 (ἔχει), 14 (τρέφεται); 13.12 (ποιεῖ [2×]), 13 (ποιεῖ), 14 (πλανᾷ), 16 (ποιεῖ); 16.14 (ἐκπορεύεται), 21 (καταβαίνει); 19.15 (ἐκπορεύεται); 21.23 (ἔχει).[153] This list could be very slightly expanded, but the number of narrative presents would not vary significantly. As I will suggest below, some of these usages could fall under a different category: timeless-descriptive (4.5, 8; 9.17, 19; 19.15; 21.23), which would not refer to specific past time events, but are temporally unrestricted. Aune proposes the following three functions of the narrative use of the present in Revelation: 1) it allows the writer to assume the role of eyewitness; 2) it draws attention to decisive actions in the narrative; 3) it is used to enumerate a series of actions.[154] But Aune's first category seems to be dependent on a temporal, rhetorical shift that takes place in the mind of the writer (it is as if the writer is present during the events he is describing). But this problematically requires the hearers to shift rapidly between temporal spheres of reference, since the present tense often occurs interspersed within aorists or imperfects.

Campbell has argued that the present tense in narration can be accounted for in two ways. First, the present tense in past time contexts is primarily the result of "spill" from the imperfective, proximate context in which they occur, namely discourse (by which he means speech). Therefore, "the imperfective-proximate context [created by discourse] may impose itself on verbal distribution ... by *attracting* verb forms that are able to convey both imperfectivity and proximity."[155] In this way

---

[152] Once again, this list of present tense forms is exclusive of the aspectually vague εἰμί.

[153] For a similar list of references cf. Aune, *Revelation 1–5*, clxxxiv, though our lists differ slightly. In addition to other texts which I have excluded, Aune also includes three verbs from 18.11 (κλαίουσιν, πενθοῦσιν, ἀγοράζει). However, these belong to the speech of a heavenly voice, and are not properly narrative. So I have excluded them from discussion here. There are a number of examples from Revelation 11.1–13 that could have been included, but I have not included them here based on the uncertainty regarding whether 11.1–13 is a narration of a vision or a prophesy. See on Ch. 11 below.

[154] Aune, *Revelation 1–5*, clxxxiv.

[155] Campbell, *Verbal Aspect*, 55–56.

Campbell claims that the present tense in narrative is primarily limited to discourse within narrative. This is because the imperfective-proximate context of the discourse "spills" over into the verbs which introduce the discourse, and perhaps to other verbs. Consequently, Campbell finds little significance in the use of the present tense. The second way that the present tense is used is with verbs of propulsion, verbs of coming and going, giving and taking, etc.[156] That is, verbs that indicate the movement from one point to another occur in the present tense to accent the "heightened transition."[157] Thus, according to Campbell, "the present tense-form is used either in connection with discourse or to convey propulsion when outside the scope of discourse."[158]

Campbell's association of the present tense with discourse is helpful in understanding its function as slowing down the discourse. And there are numerous usages of the present tense in Revelation to introduce discourse (speech) or which are found within speech. However, the presence of verbs of speaking to introduce discourse in the aorist tense (εἶπον) suggests that the present tense is explicable by more than just attraction to an imperfective-proximate context. When one examines the distribution of the present tense form in Revelation it is evident that the present tense occurs regularly outside of discourse. Campbell's explanation of the remaining verbs occurring in the present tense outside of discourse as due to "spill" or verbs of propulsion also requires significant qualification. Campbell does not address the issue of why the so-called "spill" has only affected some verbs and not others, especially since present forms continue to alternate with aorist forms. Why the "spill" only onto some verbs and not others? Furthermore, it is likewise not the case that the remaining present tense forms can be accounted for at least in Revelation by the category of "verbs of propulsion." Much of Campbell's discussion of verbs of propulsion problematically depends on the classificatory system of Vendler.[159] But many of Campbell's instances which he cites could easily be understood as something other than propulsion, since as Fanning recognizes, "no verb is entirely uniform in its actional

---

[156] Campbell, *Verbal Aspect*, 46–49, 52, 68.

[157] Campbell, *Verbal Aspect*, 68. "The highlighting of this transition from one point to another is achieved by depicting the action as in front of the author/speaker, and thereby causing the author/speaker to take account of such a transition in a more heightened way …." (52).

[158] Campbell, *Verbal Aspect*, 48.

[159] Campbell, *Verbal Aspect*, 46–49. See also Fanning, *Verbal Aspect*, 144–145.

behavior."[160] Other instances can only be understood as verbs of propulsion given a rather broad and vague definition of "propulsion."[161] Different results may obtain by using the *Greek-English Lexicon Based on Semantic Domains* by J.P. Louw and E.A. Nida.[162]

In the following section I have analyzed as a starting point the above listed present tense forms which I have categorized as having past time implicature from Revelation to test whether the present tense forms in them can be accounted for primarily by the fact that they are verbs of propulsion. I have focused on present tense verbs in narrative, and have not included verbs which clearly introduce discourse, or which are included within discourse (speech), since these could fit within Campbell's criteria. Rather than Vendler's more philosophically oriented classification, I have chosen to use Louw and Nida's classification of verbs based on Semantic Domains. Louw and Nida include what seems to me to be the closest to Campbell's "verbs of propulsion" in two semantic domains: 15 (Linear Movement); 16 (Non-linear Movement). Thus I will indicate those verbs which are found in Louw and Nida's domains 15 and 16 for verbs that could fall into Campbell's category of verbs of "propulsion." The following tabulation focuses at this point only on indicative verbs.

> 4.5: ἐκπορεύεται—Propulsion (L & N domain 15)
> 4.8: γέμουσιν—Non-propulsion (L & N domain 59) ἔχουσιν—Non-propulsion (L & N domain 57)
> 9.10: ἔχουσιν—Non-propulsion (L & N domain 57)
> 9.11: ἔχουσιν; ἔχει—Non-propulsion (L & N domain 57)
> 9.17: ἐκπορεύεται—Propulsion (L & N domain 15)
> 9.19: ἀδικοῦσιν—Non-propulsion (L & N domain 20)
> 12.2: κράζει—Introduces discourse (L & N domain 33)[163]
> 12.4: σύρει—Propulsion (L & N Domain 15)
> 12.6: ἔχει—Non-propulsion (L & N domain 57)
> 12.14: τρέφεται—Non-propulsion (L & N domain 35)
> 13.12–13: ποιεῖ (3×)—Non-propulsion (L & N domain 42)
> 13.14: πλανᾷ—Non-propulsion (L & N domain 31)

---

[160] Fanning, *Verbal Aspect*, 127–128.

[161] For example, Campbell accounts for the occurrence of διαφθείρω (slay, destroy) in Thucydides 1.105.6 by classifying it as a verb of propulsion. Yet his explanation seems forced: "The activity of slaying someone or destroying something may be understood in terms of bringing one to their death, or dashing an object into ruin" (*Verbal Aspect*, 47).

[162] J.P. Louw and E.A. Nida, *A Greek-English Lexicon of the New Testament Based on Semantic Domains* (2 vols.; New York: United Bible Societies, 1988).

[163] Domain 33 is the semantic domain of "Communication." Therefore, it fits Campbell's category of present tenses in association with discourse.

13.16: ποιεῖ—Non-propulsion (L & N domain 42)

16.21: καταβαίνει—Propulsion (L & N domain 15)

19.15: ἐκπορεύεται—Propulsion (L & N domain 15); πατεῖ—Non-propulsion (L & N domain 19)[164]

19.16: ἔχει—Non-propulsion (L & N domain 57)

21.23: ἔχει—Non-propulsion (L & N domain 57)

It appears, then, that only a handful of verbs, particularly ἐκπορεύομαι, which fall within Louw and Nida's Semantic Domain 15, can be accounted for by Campbell's category of verbs of propulsion. However, the above comparison shows that at least for Revelation the present tense form occurs quite regularly in narrative outside of the two categories of speech and propulsion. So propulsion or discourse "spill" cannot account for most of them. And given Campbell's description of verbs of propulsion as "heightened transition," their significance in foregrounding the processes still cannot be overlooked.

The narrative present, by viewing the action aspectually as in progress or unfolding, then, can be used with past time implication.[165] More specifically, this use of the present in Revelation serves to add descriptive color to the vision and to highlight or foreground certain activities.[166] As Porter notes, "Often further analysis of what are held to be arbitrary choices yields appreciation for development of the argument."[167]

In 4.5, 8 the present tense, then, functions to highlight significant features of the throne room scene: the thunder and lightening which comes from (ἐκπορεύονται) the throne (which plays an important role in judgment in the rest of the book) and the eyes which cover the creatures (γέμουσιν). At the conclusion of the fifth trumpet in 9.10–11 two present tense forms, ἔχουσιν … ἔχουσιν describe specific features of the locusts. In the previous verses (8, 9) John employs the imperfect of ἔχω twice: εἶχον. As the more heavily marked forms (the imperfects grammaticalize remoteness; see below), the two present forms draw attention to the power to harm humanity (v. 10) and the fact that these locusts advance as an army under a demonic leader (v. 11). The present tense ἐκπορεύεται

---

[164] Cf. Louw and Nida, *Greek-English Lexicon*, 228, though one of the possible meanings of this term, "step," is placed within Semantic Domain 15.

[165] Porter, *Verbal Aspect*, 196; *Idioms*, 31.

[166] As noted in the previous chapter, this descriptive color or vividness is not due to an assumed temporal transfer (the writer is writing as if present at the time of the events). Rather, it is due to the aspect of the present, which views the action in progress, as developing or unfolding. This could lend itself to descriptive color or vividness when certain events are focused upon rather than summarized as a whole (aorist).

[167] Porter, *Verbal Aspect*, 197.

in v. 17 climaxes the description of the locusts in preparation for the description of the harm they inflict on humanity with the three plagues that proceed from their mouths (vv. 18–19). The conclusion of the plague of the sixth angel ends with a present tense form, ἀδικοῦσιν (v. 19), foregrounding the destructive power of the horses as the climax of this plague, though this may be a timeless-descriptive usage (see below).

The present aspect is also used in 12.2, 4 to highlight the woman's pain (κράζει) and the contrasting power of the dragon (σύρει), while in vv. 6, 14 it is used to draw attention to the preservation of the woman (ἔχει; τρέφεται; cf. the present subjunctive τρέφωσιν in v. 6) in the face of the dragon's attempt to exterminate her. The repetition of the present tense of ποιεῖ in 13.12–13, 16 and the present πλανᾷ serve to emphasize the beast's ability to carry out the authority of the first beast and dragon, particularly through deception. (For details on the present tense in Ch. 13 see the next chapter). In 16.14 the present ἐκπορεύεται functions to draw attention to the main function of the demonic beings which John saw: they came out to gather the kings for battle (cf. v. 16), and in v. 21 the present tense form καταβαίνει is used because the hail in v. 21 is climactic, but it still does not elicit a response of repentance.[168] In 19.15–16 the present (ἐκπορεύεται) describes and highlights an important feature of the rider on the white horse in order to prepare for the battle/judgment scene in vv. 17–21.[169]

One verb which characteristically occurs in the present tense form is ἔχω. In Revelation the present indicative of this verb is found 33 times.[170] This might suggest that the writer's semantic choice aspectually was constrained, since there are no aorist forms attested in Revelation, though it is attested elsewhere in the New Testament, and that we should therefore not attach any semantic significance to occurrences of ἔχω. However, ἔχω does occur once in the future tense form (2.10, ἕξετε)[171]

---

[168] Cf. Beale, *Revelation*, 844–845; Porter, *Verbal Aspect*, 197.

[169] I have not included a discussion of κεῖται in Rev 21.16 (καὶ ἡ πόλις τετράγωνος κεῖται) since it is aspectually vague, that is, it does not offer a contrasting aorist tense form. However, it does offer a choice in the imperfect. Cf. Porter, *Verbal* Aspect, 443. See under Imperfect Tense.

[170] It is found throughout Revelation another 61 times as a present participle.

[171] For the correctness of the future reading ἕξετε see Aune, *Revelation 1–5*, 158, over against the present subjunctive form ἔχητε attested in A 025 fam 1611[1854 2344] 254 598 2019 2038 et al. It appears that the present subjunctive reading came about as a result of reading ἕξετε with the ἵνα. However, it is also possible to take it grammatically as parallel to the μέλλει βάλλειν, which is future in force. This is the way the UBSGNT 4th edn has punctuated this verse.

and five times in the imperfect tense form in narration (6.9; 9.8, 9; 13.11; 21.15). Moreover, it is found in the aorist and perfect tenses elsewhere in the New Testament, and develops across a full range of tense forms outside of the New Testament.[172] At the very least John did have a choice at the level of +/-remoteness. Most likely John chooses the present tense because ἔχω tends to be highly descriptive of various characters and features of the visions, making the present of ἔχω aspectually appropriate for its descriptive function. That is, the descriptive character of his vision has influenced his aspectual choice. But as just mentioned, John does have a choice between +/- remoteness. As such, in 9.8–11 both forms are used, the more remote imperfect form (εἶχον) to depict certain features of the locusts, while the non-remote present form (ἔχουσιν) is reserved for their ability to harm humanity.

Another notable lexical item which is not as frequent, but which characteristically occurs throughout Revelation in the present tense, is ἐκπο-ρεύομαι (cf. 4.5; 9.17; 11.5; 16.14; 19.15).[173] Due to the fact that it occurs only in the present tense form in Revelation, it might be wise to refrain from making specific semantic judgments concerning its function. This may be due to "an idiomatic predilection to use the historical present more commonly with some verbs."[174] However, as noted above, it is possible to account for the predominance of the present tense of this verb based on the fact that it is a verb of motion or propulsion. Such verbs lend themselves to present tense forms (imperfective) "because they accentuate the movement from one point to another."[175] Perhaps the author wishes to draw attention to these movements within his discourse, since the present tense with such verbs accentuates the movement from one point to another in a heightened transition. Except for the participle form in 22.1 (ἐκπορευόμενον) all of the occurrences of ἐκπορεύομαι are used to refer to judgment or destruction. Moreover, except for 4.5 they refer to something proceeding from someone's mouth (ἐκ τοῦ στόματος) in judgment: 9.17; 11.5; 16.14; 19.15. The author presumably could have chosen the aorist form, ἐξῆλθον. After using the present ἐκπορεύεται to

---

[172] See LSJ, 749. See also Porter, "Aspect Theory and Lexicography," 209–215 on aspects and verb frequency, and the need to not confine our observations of a given lexical item's aspect distribution to only the New Testament. On verb tense frequency cf. also Stanley E. Porter and Matthew B. O'Donnell, "The Greek Verbal Network from a Probabalistic Standpoint: An Exercise in Hallidayan Linguistics," *FN* 14 (2001) 3–41.

[173] ἐκπορεύομαι also occurs three times in present participle form: 1.16; 9.18; 22.1.

[174] Fanning, *Verbal Aspect*, 235.

[175] Campbell, *Verbal Aspect*, 52.

refer to the sword coming out of the rider's mouth in 19.15(cf. 1.16), in
19.21 the author used the aorist participle to refer to the identical phenomenon (τῇ ῥομφαίᾳ ... **τῇ ἐξελθούσα** ἐκ τοῦ στόματος αὐτοῦ). It
appears, then, that the closely related aorist ἐξῆλθον could function as
the aorist choice for ἐκπορεύομαι. By using the more heavily marked
present tense the author descriptively highlights the destructive nature
of judgment and destruction which issues both from God, the Lamb and
his followers, as well as the demonic beings. In 16.14 ἐκπορεύεται climaxes the description of the three frogs that come from the mouth of the
dragon to gather the kings for battle. In contrast to the scenes of judgment starting in 4.5 the present participle ἐκπορευόμενον in 22.1 highlights the life of the New Creation that issues from the throne (cf. 4.5)
now that judgment is past.

Timeless-Descriptive

In the Apocalypse there are also a number of examples of the present
tense that I have labeled "timeless-descriptive."[176] That is, the present
tense is used not to refer to specific actions or a series of events in
the visions, but to describe various characteristic activities or features
of objects in John's vision which are temporally unrestricted.[177] It is
sometimes difficult to distinguish many of these from the past referring
"narrative" presents (see previous category), but due to their descriptive
nature and the fact that they do not appear to refer to specific past processes, I have placed them in the category I call "timeless-descriptive."
Dougherty's explanation of the "Descriptive Present" as "though the
visions were present now in their description" assumes the present carries the temporal value of present time.[178] Within the narration of John's
vision, this usage of the present aspect functions to draw attention to
the activity or characteristic of certain objects in the vision. For example, the present tense γέμουσιν in 4.8, while it may be a past referring
present, may describe an important feature of the living creatures and

---

[176] This is a combination of two categories from Dougherty, "Syntax," 402–403. But
the texts that I place in this category are very different from Dougherty. Furthermore,
there seems to be no clear rationale why he has included the texts that he has in the
two categories "Descriptive Present" and "Historical Present," which he sees as somewhat
similar.

[177] On this category of usage in the New Testament see Porter, *Verbal Aspect*, 237–238.
"The event described is seen to be outside of temporal considerations" (*Idioms*, 33).

[178] Dougherty, "Syntax," 403.

is temporally unrestricted. The present tense form λατρεύουσιν in 7.15, while it could function to indicate future time since it is followed by a string of future tense forms, is probably timeless-descriptive, that is, it describes a characteristic activity of those before the throne: they worship day and night.[179] The two usages of ἔχουσιν in 9.3, 4 do not seem to refer to a sequence of events but describe the locusts and those whom they harm. The reference to harming, ἀδικοῦσιν, in v. 19 may also be timeless-descriptive (but see above); it does not describe a specific activity, but is descriptive of what the locusts are capable of doing. Two other possible examples appear to be explanatory comments which intrude upon the narrative: 8.11 (λέγεται); 11.8 (καλεῖται).

Probably also timeless and descriptive is the usage of the present tense forms found in 19.11, 15–16. In verse 11 the two present tense verbs κρίνει and πολεμεῖ are descriptive of the rider, telling us what is true about the rider seated on the horse: when he dispenses justice he always does what is right. Aune labels them gnomic or general uses of the present tense.[180] That is, rather than referring to any specific instances of judgment or warfare, the author, in describing what he saw, makes timeless, descriptive assertions about the rider on the white horse. Regarding the verbs in vv. 15–16 (ἐκπορεύεται, πατεῖ, ἔχει), Aune classifies them as past referring, though he translates πατεῖ as future and ἔχει as present later on.[181] However, the present tense forms in vv. 15–16 may all be taken as timeless-descriptive, depicting what is also true about the one seated on the horse. In other words, these verses are still describing the Messianic warrior rather than referring to specific events: fire comes from his mouth, he tramples the winepress of God's wrath, and he has a name written on him.[182] As such they are temporally unrestricted. The actual battle itself is then narrated in vv. 17–21 (see below). In 20.6, as part of a makarism (μακάριος), those who will have part in the first resurrection are described with the timeless statement: ἐπὶ τούτων ὁ δεύτερος θάνατος οὐκ ἔχει ἐξουσίαν, a statement that

---

[179] For the function of the present in this text see the following chapter.

[180] Aune, Revelation 17-22, 1053. Cf. Smalley, Revelation, 488, who also labels them as gnomic. According to H.B. Swete the present tense form "is used because the writer is stating the normal characteristic of Divine judgments and wars" (The Apocalypse of St. John [3rd edn; London: Macmillan, 1911] 247). The omnitemporal nature of the actions may also be suggested by the fact that this description picks up an important OT theme (Ps. 7.11; 9.4; 50.6; 67.4; 72.2; 96.13; 98.9). See Beale, Revelation, 951.

[181] Aune, Revelation 1-5, clxxxiv; Revelation 17-22, 1041.

[182] The use of the future ποιμανεῖ αὐτοὺς ἐν ῥάβδῳ σιδηρᾷ may be due to an allusion to Ps. 2.9: LXX ποιμανεῖς αὐτοὺς ἐν ῥάβδῳ σιδηρᾷ.

is true about all who have a part in the first resurrection: "The second death is powerless."[183] Cf. also 6.13; 10.3; 11.6–7; 19.3 (though this latter text could also be future referring: ἀναβαίνει). Two of these contain the present tense in proverbial ("gnomic") type statements: 6.13 (ὡς συκῆ βάλλει τοὺς ὀλύνθους) and 10.3 (ὥσπερ λέων μυκᾶται).[184] In all of these examples verbal aspect provides an adequate explanation for this usage. While some of these examples could be disputed, my point is that traditional time-based explanations or appeals to Semitic influence are inadequate and unnecessary to explain these usages.[185]

Participles

One non-indicative form to consider is the disproportionate number of present participles which punctuates John's visionary drama. As seen above, there are 295 present participle forms (excluding the aspectually vague εἰμί) scattered throughout Revelation, which is over half of its present tense forms.[186] As with the indicative mood form, the present participle semantically encodes imperfective aspect.[187] Consistent with its aspectual force, I would propose that John uses the present participle primarily for descriptive purposes. In depicting his graphic vision, the author employs the present participle form to describe various static features or characteristic activities of the objects of his vision. One or two brief examples will suffice. In 4.4–7 the present participle is used to describe various features of the elders and living creatures: καθημένους, καιόμεναι, γέμοντα, ἔχων, πετομένῳ.[188] While the first four participles depict static features of the vision, the final participle (πετομένῳ) depicts an activity which characterizes the creatures. 21.10–12 depicts the New Jerusalem with a string of present participles which describe important features of the celestial city: καταβαίνουσαν, ἔχουσαν, κρυσταλλίζοντι, ἔχουσα (2×). At other times the present participle occurs across the entire stretch of discourse in Revelation to refer to a characteristic feature

---

[183] Osborne (*Revelation*, 709) translates it this way.

[184] For the difference between timeless and omnitemporal statements see Porter, *Verbal Aspect*.

[185] Furthermore, of all the verbs treated in this previous section of timeless-descriptive verbs, only ἐκπορεύομαι falls within Campbell's category of Propulsion (L & N Domain 15). Two other verbs, λέγεται and καλεῖται could fit his category of verbs in Discourse and others are associated with discourse (7.15; 11.5–6; 18.17; 19.3; 20.6).

[186] By contrast there are only 12 aorist participles in the Apocalypse.

[187] See Porter, *Idioms*, 188; Campbell, *Non-Indicative Verbs*, 22.

[188] Though κάθημαι is probably aspectually vague.

of a person or group (e.g. οἱ κατοικοῦντες).[189] This descriptive function accounts for the author's preferential choice of present participle forms. For other examples see 7.2; 17.1–6.

Conclusion

Once again, overall there is no need to appeal to direct Semitic influence, as Thompson has done, to explain the use of the present tense form to refer to actions that are temporally non-present referring in the Apocalypse. The present tense indicative form manifests pragmatically a range of temporal functions: past, present, future, and timeless. When the present tense is seen as grammaticalizing verbal aspect, that is, depicting a process as developing or unfolding rather than absolute temporal reference, then the phenomenon of the present tense form in Revelation is in line with normal usage in Koine Greek.

The Imperfect Tense

There are 40 imperfect tense forms in Revelation. But this number, for the purpose of analyzing verbal aspect, can be reduced by bracketing the 17 instances of the imperfect form of the aspectually vague εἰμί. That leaves 23 imperfect forms in Revelation. For further breakdown and statistics see Aune.[190] The most common function of the imperfect is alongside of the aorist form in narration. The imperfect form gramaticalizes aspectually the internal perspective of an action in progress and the semantic feature of +remoteness, and in narration is the more marked form in opposition to the aorist.[191] Bousset claims that the imperfect is used primarily in secondary clauses (1.12; 2.14; 6.9).[192] But this is not its only function. The imperfect frequently functions in opposition to the aorist in narrative to provide descriptive details. "The imperfect, semantically more heavily marked than the Aorist, is aspectually imperfective ..., also often occurring in past contexts as the foreground narrative tense."[193]

---

[189] For οἱ κατοικοῦντες ("those who dwell [on the earth]"), see 3.10; 6.10; 8.13; 11.10 (2×); 13.8, 12, 14 (2×); 17.2, 8. On this phrase in Revelation see particularly Bauckham, *Climax*, 239–242. Cf. also οἱ προσκουνοῦντες.

[190] Aune, *Revelation 1–5*, clxxxv.

[191] Cf. Porter, *Verbal Aspect*, 199; Campbell, *Verbal Aspect*, 84–85.

[192] Bousset, *Offenbarung*, 169.

[193] Porter, *Verbal Aspect*, 199. Cf. McKay, "Time and Aspect," 221; Aune, *Revelation 1–5*, clxxxvi, who is dependent on Porter and McKay.

Thus the imperfect ἔλεγον in 5.14 is used of the speech of the living creatures ("Amen"), while the aorists are reserved for the summary response of the elders (ἔπεσαν, προσεκύνησαν). In 6.8 the imperfect ἠκολούθει highlights the sinister nature of this horse through in association with Hades, and in 6.9 εἶχον describes the reason for the beheading of the saints. Furthermore, in 13.11 the two imperfects εἶχεν and ἐλάλει introduce the beast and highlight the association of this beast with the dragon from Ch. 12. The imperfect in 16.10, ἐμασῶντο, highlights the results of the fifth bowl which still did not lead to repentance (v. 10). The imperfect is also used to depict the response (ἔκραζον) of the onlookers to the destruction of Babylon in 18.18–19. According to Decker, the more remote imperfect can be used to record events simultaneous with other events.[194] Thus in 1.12 the implication may be that John turned while the voice was in the process of speaking (ἐλάλει) with him.

However, the imperfect is also used side-by-side in contexts with the present, both grammaticalizing imperfective aspect. According to Porter, "it [imperfect] is used in contexts where the action is seen as more remote than the action described by the (non-remote) Present."[195] In 5.3–4 the more remote imperfect form (ἔκλαιον) is used to describe the seer's response to the dilemma and set the stage for the solution to the dilemma, whereas the present (λέγει) is used of the solution announced by the angel. In 9.8–9 the imperfect is used to describe certain features of the locusts (εἶχον), while the present tense is reserved for their ability to harm humans under their leader (ἔχουσιν) in vv. 10–11. Within the context of perfects and presents, the imperfect form describes the armies that follow the warrior messiah in 19.14 (ἠκολούθει), perhaps because the focus is on the description of the warrior. In 21.15 the imperfect, over against aorists, draws attention to the instrument of measurement (εἶχεν), while the more marked present is used of the shape of the city (κεῖται, v. 16). Though κεῖται is aspectually vague, it still offers a semantic choice at the level of +/- remoteness (cf. ἔκειτο in 4.2).[196] In conclusion, the imperfect tense presents few challenges

---

[194] Decker, *Temporal Deixis*, 107. Moulton refers to the use of the imperfect for "pictoral narrative" in contrast to the summary aorist (*Prolegomena*, 128).

[195] Porter, *Verbal Aspect*, 207.

[196] Therefore, verbs such as κεῖμαι that do not offer a full aspectual paradigm may still offer a semantic choice (though not aspectual, and perhaps not as semantically significant) in terms of +/- remoteness. As Porter says, the imperfect "is used in contexts where the action is seen as more remote than the action described by the (non-remote) Present" (*Verbal Aspect*, 207).

for understanding its function in Revelation. As Decker observes, "That past time predominates in the imperfect is not surprising given that this would be the most common type of remoteness in narrative literature."[197]

The Perfect Tense

The Force of the Perfect in Revelation

The perfect indicative form is attested in the Apocalypse 34 times, but is far more frequent in participle constructions (especially in the passive voice), being found 83 times. This section will consider primarily the perfect tense forms of the indicative mood. According to our earlier discussion the perfect tense form in Revelation can be seen as grammaticalizing the semantic feature of state of affairs.[198] Yet there has been much discussion of the perfect tense form in Revelation by grammarians and commentators. The primary debate seems to revolve around whether the perfect aspect should be given its full semantic force in English translation and in exegesis. In his commentary Bousset referred to the "vulgar mixing" (vulgäre Vermischung) of the perfect and the aorist throughout Revelation.[199] A standard observation is that the perfect functions alongside of aorist tense forms with no more than "aoristic" meaning, resulting in the observation that John confused the aorist and perfect forms, or that the perfect's force is frequently neutralized, giving rise to the grammatical category of "aoristic perfect."[200] The most obvious culprits in this regard are εἴληφα and εἴρηκα (cf. 3.3; 5.7; 7.14; 8.5; 11.17; 19.3).[201] Though Moulton questions the extent of the so-called aoristic perfect, he does find texts such as Rev 5.7; 7.14; 8.5; 19.3 succumbing to this usage.[202]

---

[197] Decker, *Temporal Deixis*, 107.

[198] This may or may not include an anterior activity that produced the state, which is contextually determined. Cf. Porter, *Verbal Aspect*, 259; McKay, *New Syntax*, 31; *contra* Fanning, *Verbal Aspect*, 112–120.

[199] Bousset, *Offenbarung*, 169.

[200] Regarding the confusion of aorist and perfect tense forms in the NT, Wallace says that "The Seer of the Apocalypse is especially susceptible of this charge" (*Greek Grammar*, 578), though he does not explain why this is the case.

[201] F. Blass, *Grammatik der Neutestamentlichen Griechisch* (Göttingen: Vandenhoeck und Ruprecht, 1902) 204; Mussies, *Morphology*, 348; Turner, *Syntax*, 69; BDF § 343; Fanning, *Verbal Aspect*, 303; Wallace, *Greek Grammar*, 579. See also the comments of commentaries on Rev 3.3; 5.7; 7.14; 8.5; 11.17; 19.3.

[202] Moulton, *Prolegomena*, 145. His primary reason for this is the lack of reduplication in εἴληφα and εἴρηκα.

Thompson also notices several instances of the perfect tense form where "the sense of the perfect seems not to fit at all," though in some cases he thinks the perfect is used in its "proper sense."[203] This comment betrays a common misconception of the perfect tense form: a past action with present results. To account for this apparent abandonment of the sense of the perfect Thompson appeals to "an underlying Semitic verb of derived conjugation."[204] He draws attention to examples in the LXX where the perfect tense is used to translate derived conjugations in the Hebrew tense system, such as the *niphal, piel, pual,* and *hiphal.* Furthermore, the puzzling mix of the perfect form of ἵστημι with presents (3.20; 8.2; 12.4) according to Thompson "was influenced by the Hebrew nāsab."[205] Thompson then concludes that in exegesis there is no need to account for the meaning of the perfect in Revelation since its Semitic underlay explains its presence.

The overriding assumption in these treatments is that the normal temporally-governed sense of the perfect (completed action with present results) does not seem to fit in the contexts in which it occurs in Revelation and cannot be easily brought out in English translation; particularly in contexts where it occurs in conjunction with other aorist tense forms it is better translated as an aorist tense.[206] This is often augmented with the observation that the perfect tense is dying out in Koine Greek and is being confused with the aorist (e.g. the introduction of "weak" aorist endings into the perfect paradigm).[207] However, McKay and Porter have argued for the validity of the perfect as a distinct semantically-based form in the New Testament.[208]

---

[203] Thompson, *Semitic Syntax,* 42.

[204] Thompson, *Semitic Syntax,* 42.

[205] Thompson, *Semitic Syntax,* 45. In the OT nāsab "in the niphal conjugation mean[s] 'to stand'" (45).

[206] However, Fanning does qualify his statements on the perfect used aoristically (with no sense of "present result" according to him): "It must be emphasized that the aoristic use of the perfect is rather rare in the NT" (*Verbal Aspect,* 303).

[207] See further Turner, *Syntax,* 81–82. Fanning summarizes: "Some have noted that the aoristic sense for the perfect may be due in part to confusion in morphology. For example, perfect actives could be confused with the 'alpha' endings of the first aorist, especially with the third plural -αν for -ασι(ν), and perfects with indistinct reduplication such as εἴληφα and εἴρηκα could be misread for aorists. Alternatively, idiomatic frequency of some perfects in Hellenistic Greek may have led to their over-extension" (*Verbal Aspect,* 303).

[208] McKay, "Perfect Use," who argues that the transition of the perfect being confused with the aorist did not take place until after the writing of the New Testament; Porter,

The view that the ostensible meaning of perfect tense verbs in Revelation is semantically neutralized so that they have lost the perfect force or possess only an aoristic sense needs to be seriously questioned in light of a number of observations. First, much discussion of this use of the perfect reflects a misconception of the semantics of the perfect tense form perpetuated in most grammars. Usually, discussion of the perfect tense in Revelation proceeds from a definition of the perfect along temporal lines. Thus "it denotes the *continuance* of *completed action*."[209] Under this conception the perfect is regarded as sort of a combination of the aorist and present.[210]

(Completed Action) → (Continuing Results)

When Thompson and others are convinced that the meaning of the perfect tense does not fit in numerous instances in Revelation, they usually have in mind the above temporal conception of *a past action with results continuing into the present*, the latter which is apparently absent in some contexts. So Fanning explains this use of the so-called "Aoristic Perfect" "as a simple narrative tense to report past occurrences without attention paid to their present consequences."[211] However, as

---

Verbal Aspect, 271–273. Cf. also Campbell, *Verbal Aspect*, 165–166. See also for the most part Moulton, *Prolegomena*, 142–145.

[209] BDF § 340. Italics theirs. This is a fairly common conception of the perfect tense form in grammars from basic to advanced levels. Cf. Moule, *Idiom Book*, 13; Smyth, *Grammar*, 434; H.E. Dana and J.R. Mantey, *A Manual Grammar of the Green New Testament* (New York: Macmillan, 1955) 200; James W. Voelz, *Fundamental Greek Grammar* (St. Louis: Concordia, 1986) 162; Wallace, *Greek Grammar*, 573 (though Wallace is rightly careful to avoid the notion of "abiding results" [574]). Fanning reiterates this perspective in a slightly more sophisticated way as "a condition resulting from an anterior occurrence" (*Verbal Aspect*, 291).

[210] Cf. Blass, *Grammatik*, 203.

[211] Fanning, *Verbal Aspect*, 299–300. However, Fanning does conclude that this use of the perfect tense is rare in the NT and that the perfect used alongside of aorists does not always lose its "present results" (303). There is some confusion in nomenclature and function here. Grammarians typically discuss an "Aoristic" use of the perfect, which is usually conceived of as the use of the perfect tense form without the usual notion of "existing results" (Fanning, *Verbal Aspect*, 299–300; Robertson, *Grammar*, 898–899; BDF § 343; Turner, *Syntax*, 69). However, other grammars discuss what is often labeled a "Dramatic use of the Perfect" (Robertson, *Grammar*, 896; James A. Brooks and Carlton L. Winbery, *Syntax of New Testament Greek* [Lanham: University Press of America, 1979] 106; Dana and Mantey, *Manual Grammar*, 204) and distinguish this from the "Aoristic Perfect." This use supposedly involves the use of the perfect in past time contexts in a dramatic and vivid fashion as if the events are present for the readers. In this case the so-called "present results" are still in force and are apparently what give this use of the

argued above, the perfect tense form semantically grammaticalizes a state of affairs, and not a temporal sphere of reference. If this is the case, then the perfect tense form can be used with its stative meaning in a variety of temporal contexts, including along with aorists to refer to past time.[212] This only creates a difficulty with conceptions of the perfect that postulate some notion of abiding results. In fact, the common notion of "present consequences" or "abiding results" for the perfect simply does not neatly fit in numerous contexts in Revelation. In 5.7, Christ's reception of the scroll can hardly be seen to indicate continuing results (as if Christ still holds the scroll as John writes), especially since he apparently gives the scroll up in Ch. 10. In 8.5 the angel's act of taking the censer can hardly be said to have present consequences or continuing results, since the possession of the censer is for the purpose of pouring out its contents. Moreover, the speech of John in 7.14 and the voice in 19.3 do not indicate ongoing results existing at the present time. So it is only such a misunderstanding of the perfect that leads H. Giesen to claim of the perfect ἐνδεδυμένοι in 19.14 that "haben die Christen dieses Gewand für immer erhalten."[213] The perfect tense says nothing about the duration of the state.

Second, and related to the previous observation, conclusions regarding the aoristic sense of the perfect in Revelation often seem to be governed

---

perfect its vividness and dramatic effect (*otherwise there would be nothing vivid about it*). See Robertson, *Grammar*, 896; Brooks and Winbery, *Syntax*, 106; Dana and Mantey, *Manual Grammar*, 204. However, the confusion comes with Wallace's apparent conflation of these two ostensible functions. He labels this use of the perfect as an "Aoristic Perfect," yet also calls it a "Dramatic or Historical Perfect." He even cites with approval Fanning who says that it is used as a simple past tense and *lacks present consequences*. Yet Wallace then describes this usage of the perfect as highly vivid (*Greek Grammar*, 578). However, this is all problematic from two standpoints. First, while Wallace sees this use of the perfect as not having present consequences, most other grammars who use the category of "Dramatic Perfect" for the sake of vividness do find the present results still in force, because this is apparently what gives it is vividness (Brooks and Winbery divide the two functions into separate categories: Dramatic and Aoristic [*Syntax*, 106–107]). Second, if the perfect has lost its present results and functions just like an aorist, it is difficult to see how, under the traditional approach, it can be vivid or dramatic at all apart from some notion of present results. Wallace cannot have it both ways. Probably both labels are better abandoned since they rely on a misunderstanding of the perfect tense which is overly dependent on a temporal model. One wonders whether such labels would have even been necessary apart from an inadequate understanding of the perfect tense form.

[212] See Porter, *Idioms*, 40–42 for the different temporal contexts in which the perfect tense form is utilized in the New Testament.

[213] Giesen, *Offenbarung*, 423. The perfect tense, however, says nothing about the continuance of the state.

more by English translation than by the semantics of the Greek tense form. That is, in many cases it is somewhat awkward to attempt to bring out the feature of existing results or temporally present consequences in translation, and usually an "aoristic" sense fits better.[214] However, it is methodologically unsound to base our understanding of the semantics of a Greek tense form on translation equivalence. The failure to capture the meaning of the perfect in our English translation, or any other target language, does not entail a lack of semantic distinction.[215] McKay is appropriately sensitive to the problems: "Idiomatic English translations must use English categories, but this does not imply that those categories can be directly transferred to the explanation of Greek idiom."[216]

Third, "The mere fact of the use of aorists and perfects side by side does not prove confusion of tenses."[217] That is, just because the two forms are juxtaposed in identical temporal contexts (perfect and aorist for past time) does not imply confusion or identical semantics of the two forms.[218] As part of a verbal system of choices, the perfect tense form may have been chosen in contrast to other tense forms because it communicates the author's perspective on a process. As M. Zerwick observes, "the choice between aorist and perfect is not determined by the objective facts, but by the writer's wish to connote the special nuance of the perfect; if this be not required, the aorist will be used."[219] Further, it is

---

[214] See Swete's awkward attempt to bring out the force of the perfect (temporally understood) of εἴληφεν in 5.7: "And I saw him go, and *now he has taken* [the book] out of the hand …." (*Apocalypse*, 78).

[215] Cf. Porter, *Verbal Aspect*, 265 ("Failure to make a translational distinction does not minimize semantic value or contrast."); McKay, *New Syntax*, 28–29.

[216] McKay, *New Syntax*, 28. Earlier in the same work McKay cautions that "most allegations of confusion between the perfect and aorist of ancient Greek are the result of paying too much attention to idiomatic translation into English or another language, and not enough to the context and the alternatives available to the ancient Greek writer" (xi). The principle difficulty is that there is little semantic overlap between the English and ancient Greek tense systems, making reliance upon translational sense even more questionable.

[217] Robertson, *Grammar*, 901. Robertson goes further and suggests that the use of perfects and aorists side-by-side, rather than proving the confusion of tenses "argues the other way." Cf. Porter, *Verbal Aspect*, 264–265.

[218] In the midst of his discussion on the aoristic use of the perfect Fanning does admit that "Even when perfects are used in close connection with aorists, they normally preserve a distinctive sense in that they refer not only to a past occurrence but also to some present result of the action" (*Verbal Aspect*, 303). While Fanning's description of the perfect here is inexact and time-bound, he is correct that the perfect carries its force when utilized in the midst of aorist tense forms.

[219] Zerwick, *Biblical Greek*, 97.

not just that the perfect is used alongside aorist forms in Revelation, but sometimes aorist forms of the same verb (e.g. εἴληφα, ἔλαβον), making it unlikely that the forms were confused. Rather, the juxtaposition of the forms argues just as readily for semantic differentiation. Perhaps the unexpected nature of the perfect in the midst of narrative aorists is explicable in light of the highly marked nature of the perfect tense form.

Fourth, if the above three observations hold, then it is unnecessary to postulate Semitic influence for the use of the perfect tense form in Revelation. Thompson's conclusions seem solely to be necessitated by the fact that his (temporal) understanding of the perfect does not fit in most contexts in Revelation, as well as a sort of argument by inference (if the other tense forms are Semitically influenced, so then must be the perfect). But when divorced from strictly temporal conceptions of the perfect, the difficulty of bringing out this force of the perfect in English translation, and the assumption that similarity of usage implies identical semantics with the aorist, the perfect tense form in Revelation does not need a Semitic explanation and can be seen as having its full stative force. T.V. Evans has recently called into question Thompson's assessment of the perfect tense.[220] He rightly criticizes Thompson for only examining a handful of examples. Furthermore, Evans shows that in every one of these examples cited by Thompson the semantics of the perfect tense form fits admirably when divorced from an outmoded, traditional conception of the perfect upon which Thompson so heavily depends. Evans' own (limited) study demonstrates that in the LXX of Genesis the perfect tense form is used for a variety of verb stem types, calling into question Thompson's theory.[221] And Thompson needs much clearer criteria by which to differentiate perfects, which according to him are used in their proper sense, and those that do not seem to fit at all.

Instead, one should start with the assumption that semantically the perfect tense will manifest its full stative meaning within the various contexts in which it occurs in Revelation, and then examine its usage in each context to determine its possible pragmatic function. As the more heavily marked tense which can indicate frontgrounded actions in a discourse,

---

[220] See Evans, *Verbal Syntax*, 156–158, for a refutation of Thompson's view of Semitic interference into the Greek perfect tense form. Though Evans does not see stativity as an aspect, he still apparently sees it as grammaticalized in the tense endings.
[221] Evans, *Verbal Syntax*, 157.

the perfect may be used to establish prominence in narration. That is, the more heavily weighted form of the perfect 'disrupts' the discourse, perhaps accounting for why some scholars think it is often so unusual. Therefore, in the instances where the perfect occurs alongside of aorist tense forms the perfect is the more heavily marked form, establishing the more significant process. Thus Rev 2.3 juxtaposes the aorist ἐβάστασας and perfect κεκοπίακες. Rather than referring to two events belonging to distinct temporal spheres, the aorist simply summarizes the response ("they bear up"), while the more marked perfect indicates more specifically how they have born up by indicating the state which they have avoided: they have not grown weary in doing so.[222]

The Function of the Perfect in Revelation

There are a number of noteworthy occurrences of perfect indicative verbs throughout Revelation by which to test this theory. The perfect indicative form εἴληφα (-ας/-εν) occurs five times in Revelation with reference to important characters taking or receiving something (2.28; 3.3; 5.7; 8.5; 11.17).[223] Perhaps more than any other verb in the perfect tense, this perfect form is deemed to have only aoristic force, and is often considered to be influenced Semitically.[224] However, when divorced from a strictly temporal understanding, and when seen as aspectually indicating a state of affairs, the perfect tense form can be seen to function in significant ways within Revelation's discourse. In 2.28 εἴληφα is used of Christ's reception of the Morning Star (he is in the state of possessing it), perhaps to highlight his authority to give the star to the readers (δώσω αὐτῷ). In 3.3 the readers are exhorted to recall that they were in the state of

---

[222] Swete's explanation is unnecessarily temporal and the effect is dubious: the perfect "indicates a condition which continued when the endurance (ἐβάστασας) was at an end" (*Apocalypse*, 26), followed by Smalley, *Revelation*, 61. Aune also opts for an exclusively temporal explanation for the tense shift: the present tense ἔχεις indicates their present situation, the aorist ἐβάστασας indicates their past behavior, and the perfect κεκοπίακες indicates they have been faithful up to the present time (*Revelation 1–5*, 146). Rather, all three processes refer generally to the same time. Aune is unable to leave behind temporally-based schemes for the Greek tenses.

[223] Cf. Dougherty, "Syntax," 468. The verb λαμβάνω occurs 12 times in the indicative mood in Revelation. Five of these are the perfect (εἴληφα), three occur in the present tense, and the remaining four are aorist forms. It also occurs a number of times in aorist non-indicative forms and once as a present participle.

[224] Cf. BDF § 343; Turner, *Syntax*, 69; Fanning, *Verbal Aspect*, 303; Thompson, *Semitic Syntax*, 42–43; Charles, *Revelation I*, 144. See the commentaries on 3.3; 5.7; 8.5; 11.17.

having received (εἴληφας) the truth to emphasize the basis for their need to repent. The perfect εἴληφεν in 8.5 refers to the angel's possession of the censure full of fire. In this case εἴληφεν occurs in the midst of narrative aorists, and probably has past time implicature.[225] Scholars typically regard 8.5 as an example of an aoristic perfect for the reasons mentioned above.[226] Smalley draws the unsupported and unnecessary conclusion that it might suggest that the angel previously laid down the censer and now picks it up again![227] Instead, semantically εἴληφεν should be given its full stative meaning, depicting a state of affairs in this case with past time implicature (John narrates what he saw, εἶδον). Over against the aorist, with the choice of the more heavily marked perfect form John is drawing attention to (frontgrounding) the reception of this important item in the visionary narrative in preparation for pouring out the trumpet judgments. Rev 11.17 is part of a hymnic piece sung by the twenty four elders (vv. 17–18). Εἴληφας refers here to God's reception of great power, highlighting that which makes the reign of God possible, recorded in the less heavily marked aorist (ἐβασίλευσας).

The use of εἴληφεν in 5.7 has attracted particular attention as an example of confusion with the aorist, perhaps reflecting Semitic influence.

5.7: καὶ ἦλθεν καὶ **εἴληφεν** ἐκ τῆς δεξιᾶς τοῦ καθημένου ἐπὶ τοῦ θρόνου.

BDF, followed by several others, call this an unquestionable example of the aoristic use of the Greek perfect.[228] Here εἴληφεν clearly occurs in the midst of aorist tense forms of narration (ἦλθεν, ἔλαβεν, ἔπεσαν). That εἴληφεν is not to be confused with the aorist, though, is suggested by the presence of the aorist form ἔλαβεν in the very next verse to refer to the identical act of receiving, as well as the occurrence of the aorist form twice more in infinitive form (λαβεῖν), all referring to the same

---

[225] Verses 3–5: ... ἦλθεν ... ἐστάθη ... ἐδόθη ... ἀνέβη ... **εἴληφεν** ... ἐγέμισεν ... ἔβαλεν ... ἐγένοντο.

[226] Cf. Burton, *Moods and Tenses*, § 80; Fanning, *Verbal Aspect*, 302–303; Osborne, *Revelation*, 346 n. 13; Smalley, *Revelation*, 217. Cf. the uncertainty in Beale (*Revelation*, 460). The fact that the aorist form of λαμβάνω does occur elsewhere in Revelation argues against this. Rather, the perfect tense tends to "stick out" in the midst of the more usual aorists of narration.

[227] Smalley, *Revelation*, 217.

[228] BDF § 343. Cf. Mussies, *Morphology*, 348; Thompson, *Semitic Syntax*, 44; Zerwick, *Biblical Greek*, 290; Fanning, *Verbal Aspect*, 303; Wallace, *Greek Grammar*, 579; Charles, *Revelation, I*, 144; E. Lohmeyer, *Die Offenbarung des Johannes* (HNT 16; Tübingen: Mohr, 1970) 55 ("aoristisch gebrauchte Perfekt"); Beale, *Revelation*, 357. Cf. the uncertainty in Osborne, *Revelation*, 267.

event (vv. 9, 12).[229] Along with the aorist, it probably connotes past time implicature (John narrates what he saw).[230] The alteration with the aorist tense suggests that the author wished to draw attention to this process with the more heavily marked form as important in the visionary narrative where the climactic transition of the scroll from the hand of the one seated on the throne to the Lamb takes place.[231]

Other efforts to explain the perfect εἴληφεν here in 5.7 have attempted to give it its full perfect force, but usually conceived of in temporal terms. Stephen S. Smalley thinks that the perfect εἴληφεν indicates realistic action, apparently due to a rhetorical temporal transfer of the present results of the perfect tense form.[232] Robertson labels the perfect in 5.7 with the temporally awkward and confusing label "Dramatic Historical Present Perfect" which indicates "an action completed in the past … conceived in terms of the present time for the sake of vividness."[233] H. Giesen suggests that εἴληφεν should be understood as indicating "bleibende Gabe."[234] But such a notion overemphasizes a temporal dimension for the perfect (present, continuing results), which if present at all must be contextually and theologically determined and is not part of the semantics grammaticalized in the perfect tense form. These explanations, however, rightly detect a change in the status of the discourse created by the perfect (dramatic, vividness), though they incorrectly attribute it to a temporal, rhetorical transfer of the assumed force of the perfect

---

[229] Robertson correctly denies that εἴληφεν is equivalent to ἔλαβεν (*Grammar*, 897).

[230] Cf. Porter, *Idioms*, 41.

[231] Virtually the only commentary that recognizes a deliberate choice of the perfect in terms of aspect is Aune, *Revelation 1–5*, 354. Cf. Osborne, *Revelation*, 267, who, along with treating the perfect here as aoristic, entertains the possibility of a 'frontgrounding' feature for the perfect in 5.7 following Porter.

[232] Smalley, *Revelation*, 133. Cf. also Swete, *Apocalypse*, 78. See his awkward-sounding translation: "And I saw Him go (aor.), and *now he has taken* [the book] out of the hand of Him who sits on the Throne." Cf. Robert H. Mounce, *Revelation* (NICNT; Grand Rapids: Eerdmans, 1977) 146.

[233] Robertson, *Grammar*, 896. This seems also to be the approach of Brooks and Winbery, *Syntax*, who label the perfect in 5.7 as a Dramatic Perfect which functions "to bring a past event vividly and dramatically into the present" (106). Cf. Young, *Intermediate*, 128.

[234] Giesen, *Offenbarung*, 169. Cf. Bousset, *Offenbarung*, 259: "Das Perf. Steht hier nach dem vorhergehenden Aor. mit Absicht. Christus empfängt die Offenbarung der Zukunftsgeheimnisse als *bleibenden Besitz*." Italics mine. Smalley also entertains this notion (*Revelation*, 133). However, any notion of 'continuing results', if present at all, is contextually and theologically dependent, rather than grammatically. But under this conception should Christ be seen as presently possessing the scroll as John was writing? This is highly unlikely and goes beyond the semantics of the perfect tense form.

tense form. Rather than grammaticalizing temporal reference, however, the perfect tense form grammaticalizes a state of affairs. The fact that it is the most heavily marked tense form which can be used to front-ground certain actions in contrast to the aorist can account for its presence here. That is, verbal aspect accounts for the perceived change of status in the discourse at this point (for a more detailed treatment of this verse see the next chapter). In addition to the earlier noted cautions against too quickly dismissing the full semantic force of the perfect εἴληφα, it is highly unlikely that the perfect form of this lexeme has only aoristic force in Revelation since the aorist form of λαμβάνω occurs several times elsewhere in Revelation in both indicative and non-indicative moods (cf. e.g. 3.11; 4.11; 6.4; 10.8, 9, 10; 17.12; 18.4; 20.4; 22.17).[235]

Something similar could be said concerning the perfect form εἴρηκα (7.14; 19.3). Charles, followed by a number of others, thinks that εἴρηκα is a clear example of a perfect used aoristically as a true preterit.[236] Thompson agrees, but thinks that it reflects the *piel* of the Hebrew דבר, which could have past, present, or future sense depending on the context.[237] Fanning proposed that the lack of reduplication in εἴρηκα could have accounted for its confusion as an aorist.[238] A further rationale for treating εἴρηκα as an aorist, like εἴληφας, is that it is used in past time contexts, and in juxtaposition with aorist forms (cf. εἶπεν and εἴρηκα in 7.14).[239] However much merit these observations may have, it is unlikely that the author has misread εἴρηκα as an aorist or that its full aspectual force should be semantically neutralized. The fact that it is juxtaposed with the suppletive aorist form εἶπεν in 7.14 suggests that the choice of εἴρηκα was intentional and carries its full stative force, however difficult

---

[235] The present indicative of λαμβάνω also occurs three times in Revelation: 14.9, 11; 17.12 (it occurs once as a present participle in 2.17). This state of affairs for λαμβάνω suggests a conscious semantic choice for the perfect on the part of the author rather than semantic confusion.

[236] Charles, *Revelation, I*, 212; Moulton, *Prolegomena*, 145; BDF § 343; Fanning, *Verbal Aspect*, 303; Mussies, *Morphology*, 348; Mounce, *Revelation*, 192; Aune, *Revelation 6–16*, 472; Beale, *Revelation*, 929; Osborne, *Revelation*, 323 n. 10. Robertson is less certain (*Grammar*, 902).

[237] Thompson, *Semitic Syntax*, 45.

[238] Fanning, *Verbal Aspect*, 303 asserts that "perfects with indistinct reduplication such as εἴληφεν and εἴρηκα could be misread for aorists. Alternatively, idiomatic frequency of some perfects in Hellenistic Greek may have led to their over-extension." Cf. also BDF § 343.

[239] Aune, *Revelation 6–16*, 472.

it may be to capture its full force in English translation. Therefore, starting from the standpoint of verbal aspect there is no need to posit confusion with the aorist nor to appeal to Semitic influence to account for its use in past time contexts.[240] It should be given its full semantic (stative) weight in Revelation and can be shown to be semantically motivated in its occurrences.

εἴρηκα could have been used for simple stylistic variation with εἶπεν. Yet a closer examination of the two contexts suggests that the perfect tense form here played more than just a stylistic role. In 7.9–17 a series of speeches are introduced which come from various voices (saints, angels) using a present or aorist tense verb followed by the participle λέγων/-οντες. Though at times a heavenly being offers an explanation of a vision (cf. 1.19–20; 17.7–18), remarkably here one of the elders questions John concerning the identity of what he has seen (τίνες). In reply to the question of the elder, the seer responds using εἴρηκα (v. 14). The use of the perfect, then, functions to highlight John's response, perhaps due to his surprise at the question of the elder (see below),[241] and throws the question back on the interrogating elder. The elder's response is then simply summarized with the less marked aorist form (εἶπεν). In 19.3 the εἴρηκα is again used to introduce a speech in a series of speeches from heavenly voices introduced by a form of the present participle λέγων (vv. 1, 4, 5, 6). Here εἴρηκα seems to be used to highlight what is spoken, while the speeches introduce what was heard (vv. 1, 6). Verse 3 draws attention to the finality and totality of God's judgment of Babylon, with vv. 4 and 5 providing the response to it.[242]

A noteworthy, and often much discussed, occurrence of the perfect tense form in Revelation is ἵστημι. The verb ἵστημι occurs nine times in the indicative mood, with three of these occurring in the perfect tense form. It is also found in the aorist, future and pluperfect tense forms.[243] Moreover, it also appears frequently as a perfect (stative) participle (11×). The aspectual distribution of indicative forms for ἵστημι in Revelation is as follows:

---

[240] *Contra* Thompson, *Semitic Syntax*, 45.

[241] Porter, *Verbal Aspect*, 279.

[242] Cf. Beale, *Revelation*, 929–930; Aune, *Revelation 17–22*, 1026, though they apparently opt for an "aoristic" reading of the perfect here reflecting the persistence of temporal approaches to the perfect.

[243] My count of ἵστημι also revealed one (1) aorist infinitive form (6.17, σταθῆναι).

Perfect – 3× (3.20; 8.2; 12.4) (11 × as a participle)
Aorist – 4× (8.3; 11.11; 12.18; 18.17)
Future – 1× (18.15)
Pluperfect – 1× (7.11)[244]

Mussies claims that the perfective value of ἕστηκα was evidently disappearing, and was giving way to the present form στήκω.[245] Thompson notes that the author of the Apocalypse is fond of the perfect tense form of ἵστημι, finding it odd that it would be used along with a present tense (3.20) or in places where one might expect another tense form (8.2; 12.4). Thompson then claims that it has perhaps been influenced by the Hebrew *niphal* of נצב (to stand).[246] However, the fact that ἵστημι elsewhere in Revelation exhibits aorist and future tense forms argues against suggestions that the "perfect" meaning of this verb has disappeared or has been muted due to confusion with the aorist or due to Semitic influence. Moreover, Thompson's reticence to see the perfect tense form ἕστηκα functioning in an "acceptable" way seems to reflect his misconception (temporal) of the perfect tense. Thus it is not clear, for example, why for him the mixing of the perfect ἕστηκα and the present κρούω in 3.20 is so "puzzling."[247] Dougherty thinks that the perfect of ἵστημι (he also includes οἶδα) is equivalent to a present three times (3.20; 8.2; 12.4).[248] Yet his explanation confuses the semantics of the tense forms and their temporal pragmatic manifestations. He then inconsistently describes these so-called "Present Sense" perfects as expressing a present state.

Beale and others construe the perfect ἕστηκα in 3.20 as equivalent to the present tense, as having a "durative" sense equivalent to the present κρούω that follows it.[249] However, this confuses semantics and pragmatics and incorrectly assumes that identical (temporal) contexts imply identical semantics. Thus, Smalley goes well beyond the evidence when he concludes that Christ has been standing at the door for some time.[250] But why should this be the case? The perfect ἕστηκα indicates a state,

---

[244] For treatment of the pluperfect form εἱστήκεισαν in 7.11 (the only occurrence of the pluperfect form in the Apocalypse) see the analysis of Revelation 7 in the following chapter.

[245] Mussies, *Morphology*, 347.

[246] Thompson, *Semitic Syntax*, 44–45. He cites LXX Exod 17.9 as an example of the translation of נצב with ἕστηκα.

[247] Thompson, *Semitic Syntax*, 44.

[248] Dougherty, "Syntax," 401, 424. Cf. Osborne, *Revelation*, 342 n. 1 on Rev 8.2.

[249] Beale, *Revelation*, 309; Osborne, *Revelation*, 212; Smalley, *Revelation*, 101; Kistemaker, *Revelation*, 177. Cf. Robertson, *Grammar*, 895.

[250] Smalley, *Revelation*, 101.

probably temporally present in this instance, but grammatically indicates nothing about the duration of the state: Christ is in the state of standing at the door, with the more heavily marked perfect receiving the attention over the present κρούω. In this instance it functions to highlight (front-ground) Christ's climactic, present invitation to the readers as a powerful motivation to repent (v. 19). In 8.2 the perfect ἑστήκασιν is used to high-light the angels as in the state of standing before God as they are given (ἐδόθησαν) the trumpets and prepare to blow them. The fact that the aorist ἐστάθη is used in the very next verse (v. 3) argues for an aspectual distinction here. Likewise, the perfect ἕστηκαν occurs in 12.4 to draw attention to the dragon's stance before the woman in a diabolical attempt to devour her child. The persecution of the people of God finds its ulti-mate source in the dragon's attempt to exterminate the Messiah.[251] The aorist ἐστάθη appears later in 12.18 to depict the dragon standing on the sea shore, again suggesting an intentional and semantically motivated selection of the perfect in 12.4.

The perfect participle form of ἵστημι (11×) is also usually significant in its function. It often functions to introduce key figures in the vision-ary narrative and places them in different locations (e.g. 5.6; 7.1, 9; 10.5; 11.4; 14.1; 15.2; 18.10). The first instance of the participle form occurs as a reference to Christ who stands (ἑστηκός) in the midst of the throne as slain. In 14.1 the Lamb stands on Mt. Zion. But other groups are also located in heaven: angelic beings (7.1; 10.5); the people of God (7.9; 11.4; 15.2). The function of the perfect participle is to draw attention to the heavenly location of these various groups and persons. This may be to highlight the priestly function of the various persons or groups. But addi-tionally, according to Blount "standing," especially in Revelation, "has a provocative implication of resistance."[252] So the posture of standing as applied to God's people in particular suggests and highlights an impor-tant theme in Revelation: the victory of the saints. Moreover, as the Lamb overcame, though in the posture of being slain (5.6), so his followers will likewise overcome even in the face of death (cf. esp. 7.9; 14.1). Yet the Serpent stands in provocative defiance and resistance to God's people in his attempt to devour them (12.4). The appearance of the perfect par-ticiple in 18.10 (ἑστηκότες) to refer to the posture of the kings of the earth who mourn at Babylon's demise may also be deliberate. The fact that they are depicted as in the state of standing from afar (μακρόθεν) may

---

[251] Cf. Beale, *Revelation*, 637.
[252] Blount, *Revelation*, 111.

be a heightened contrast with the saints who stand (overcome) before the throne in heaven. That is, the kings of the earth are separated locationally from the source of their well being. So the perfect of ἵστημι also functions to add cohesion across the various visionary segments, by comparing/contrasting the posture of various groups and persons.

It is possible that the repeated occurrence of the perfect of ἵστημι throughout Revelation is the result of Semitic influence by means of imitation of Old Testament prophetic texts. The following comparison reveals the usage of ἵστημι in the three books from the prophetic corpus which have had the most profound and recognizable intertextual impact on Revelation: Isaiah, Ezekiel, Daniel.[253] The following count indicates indicative forms. The range of aspectual usage of ἵστημι throughout these texts covers aorist, perfect, pluperfect, and future tense forms.

> Isaiah – 17 (aorist – 7; future – 9; pluperfect – 1)
> Ezekiel – 25 (aorist – 11; future – 6; pluperfect – 8)
> Daniel – 38 (aorist – 24; future – 11; perfect – 1; pluperfect – 2)

Given the intertextual influence of these works on Revelation, it is likely that John's usage of ἵστημι is Old Testament-based. However, given the distribution of the Greek tense forms in the LXX of the above three texts, and given the tense distribution of this lexeme in Revelation, it appears that the influence from the Old Testament is lexical, rather than aspectual. Thus, John's usage of ἵστημι in the perfect tense form betrays an intentional aspectual choice on the part of the author.

One other notable perfect form, γέγονεν/-αν, occurs at two key junctures in John's visionary construct (16.17; 21.6). In both cases it functions to draw attention to climactic pronouncements of God's judgment (16.17) and salvation (21.6).[254] Both pronouncements structurally are then followed by visionary expansions of the judgment of Babylon (Chs. 17–18) and the New Jerusalem (21.1–22.5). As Aune rightly concludes regarding 16.17, "γέγονεν … suggests a contrast with the previous use of aorist tenses and points to the climactic end of the series of plagues that God has inflicted on the world."[255]

---

[253] For the extensive influence of these three books at a broad structural and more detailed verbal level cf. Beale, *Revelation*; Fekkes, *Isaiah and Prophetic Traditions*; Steve Moyise, *The Old Testament in the Book of Revelation* (JSNTSS 115; Sheffield: Academic Press, 1995).

[254] Cf. Beale, *Revelation*, 1054–1055; Bousset, *Offenbarung*, 169.

[255] Aune, *Revelation 6–16*, 899.

The perfect tense form of other verbs may also be used in other places in Revelation to highlight key processes in the text (cf. e.g. 2.5; 3.2, 8, 17; 14.8; 18.3; 19.13). For example, the perfect πέπτωκας in 2.5 highlights the need for repentance. The problem of the church in Sardis is also frontgrounded by the perfects εὕρηκα and πεπληρωμένα (3.2). In 3.8 the perfect δέδωκα is used to make focally prominent what Christ who holds the keys of David (v. 7) has given to his church (cf. the perfect participle ἠνεῳγμένην), in contrast to what he has given to those who call themselves Jews (v. 9), using the less marked present tense form (διδῶ). Moreover, the incorrect self-evaluation of the Laodicean church is highlighted with the perfect πεπλούτηκα and stands in stark contrast with Christ's evaluation of their condition (vv. 15–16).²⁵⁶ In 14.8 the perfect form πεπότικεν focuses attention on the reason for Babylon's judgment. In its expansion in Revelation 18, which 14.8 anticipates, the reason for Babylon's fall is once again depicted with a perfect tense form πεπότικεν in 18.3, emphasizing the complicity of the nations in the idolatrous practices of Babylon. (On 19.13 see the next chapter.)

Assessments of the Greek perfect in Revelation have often proceeded from the assumption that the perfect tense form semantically has lost its force and taken on aoristic meaning. A common assessment in this regard is to assume that some level of Semitic influence is at work when the assumed force of the Greek perfect does not contextually fit.²⁵⁷ Rather, I have argued that the perfect tense in Revelation indicates the verbal aspectual quality of stative viewpoint, depicting a state of affairs. Verbal aspect can adequately account for the perfect's range of usage in Revelation. Consequently, this means that the perfect tense form cannot be ignored by the exegete (*contra* Thompson). The perfect tense form grammaticalizes the author's conception of a process as a state of affairs and as the more heavily marked tense form in the verbal system it can also function in narrative to give prominence to certain features within the discourse.

Far more frequent in the Apocalypse is the use of the perfect tense with participles. As noted above the perfect participle occurs 83 times in Revelation. Though the perfect middle/passive participle is sometimes

---

²⁵⁶ Cf. Beale, *Revelation*, 304.

²⁵⁷ Thompson, *Semitic Syntax*, 45. Thompson's assessment has significant exegetical implications: "This would remove the need for exegetes to account for the 'perfect' or 'completed' nature of the action of verbs where this is not evident" (p. 45). But this statement incorrectly assumes a temporal understanding of the perfect tense form that understandably does not work in numerous contexts.

seen as assuming only the strength of an adjective, this confuses form and function.[258] The following will argue for its stative meaning in Revelation.[259] As Thompson remarks, "the perfect passive participle occurs with surprising frequency in the Apc."[260] While he recognizes that the construction is acceptable Greek, he remarks that "it was not considered as correct as a relative clause among classical authors."[261] He then proposed that the perfect passive participle in Revelation reflects *qal* passive participles, but also *niphal, pual,* and *hophal* participles. As with other verbal constructions, he finds a parallel in the LXX's handling of Semitic participles. Thompson understands this as implying a close connection between the subject and an external action, for which, he claims, Classical Greek would have used an aorist. Three difficulties with these proposals are evident. First, he measures Koine Greek against the standard of Classical Greek. Second, he compares Revelation with the LXX, which is translation Greek. Third, his conception of the perfect tense is skewed. The perfect aspect grammaticalizes a perspective on the process as state of affairs;[262] an external action may or may not be implied and derives from the lexical meaning of the verb or from the context if present at all. Dougherty perpetuates a well-warn definition of the perfect tense with participles: "The perfect refers to a present state or condition resulting from a past action."[263] His temporally-based definition is inconsistent with the recognition even by traditional approaches to Greek verb tenses that absolute time does not play a role outside of the indicative mood.[264] Rather, the perfect participle grammaticalizes stative aspect.[265]

At times the author's employment of a perfect participle reflects his Old Testament intertexts, where the LXX has an identical construction. Though John's use of the Old Testament no doubt reflects dependence

---

[258] Though even if one sees it as functioning as an adjective, the selection of the perfect aspect is still semantically significant.

[259] Cf. Turner, *Syntax*, 81 who asserts that the perfect middle participle assumed the strength of an adjective. For the participle retaining its full aspectual force see Campbell, *Non-Indicative Verbs*, 14–47; Porter, *Verbal Aspect*, chap. 8. Cf. Dougherty, "Syntax," 518, though he confuses aspect with *Aktionsart* when he refers to the aspect expressed by the present participle as "continuous, repeated, habitual, or characteristic action."

[260] Thompson, *Semitic Syntax*, 71.

[261] Thompson, *Semitic Syntax*, 71.

[262] Cf. Porter, *Verbal Aspect*, 394–400.

[263] Dougherty, "Syntax," 524.

[264] In his introduction to participles Dougherty asserts that like "the indicative mood the tenses of the participle have a temporal and an aspectual meaning" (Dougherty, "Syntax," 517).

[265] Porter, *Verbal Aspect*, 394–400.

on the Hebrew Bible, at other times the LXX is his primary intertextual quarry. The following usages in Revelation probably reflect LXX dependence and function to draw attention to the Old Testament antecedent.

1.13: ἐνδεδυμένον (LXX Dan 10.5, ἐνδεδυμένος)
  περιεζωσμένος (LXX Dan 10.5, περιεζωσμένος;[266] cf. Ezek 9.2
  ἐνδεδυκώς).
5.1: γεγραμμένον (LXX Ezek 2.10, γεγραμμένα)
  κατεσφραγισμένον (Theod Dan 12.9, σφραγισμένον)
17.4: κεχρυσωμένη (LXX Exod 26.32, κεχρυσωμένων)
17.16: ἠρημωμένην (LXX Ezek 29.12, ἠρημωμένης)

But this does not justify finding Semitic influence or interference in relation to the perfect participle in Revelation. Nor does it demand restraint in finding significant patterns of usage or a prominence function. A more careful examination of the perfect participle constructions throughout Revelation reveals a common pattern, even when Old Testament texts can account for John's usage. The author of Revelation frequently clusters two or more participles around new or significant persons or objects introduced in his vision, often referring to their dress and/or posture (standing). The following are the most important.

1.13, 15: The Son of Man (ἐνδεδυμένον, περιεζωσμένον, πεπυρωμένης)
5.1: The scroll (γεγραμμένον, κατεσφραγισμένον)
5.6: The Lamb (ἑστηκός, ἐσφαγμένον, ἀπεσταλμένοι)
7.4–8: The 144,000 (ἐσφραγισμένων, -οι [4×])
7.9: The great multitude (ἑστῶτες, περιβεβλημένους [cf. v. 13])
11.3–4: The two witnesses (περιβεβλημένοι, ἑστῶτες)
12.1, 4: The woman with twelve stars (περιβεβλημένη)
14.1–3: The victorious saints (ἑστός, γεγραμμένον, ἠγορασμένοι)
15.2: The overcomers by the sea (μεμιγμένην, ἑστῶτας)
15.6–7: The angels who deliver the last plagues (περιεζωσμένοι,
  ἐνδεδυμένοι)
17.4 (cf. 18.16): The harlot/Babylon (περιβεβλημένη, κεχρυσωμένη)
19.12–16: The warrior Messiah (γεγραμμένον, βεβλημένος, βεβαμμένον, γεγραμμένον)
21.2: The bride/New Jerusalem (ἡτοιμασμένην, κεκοσμημένην)

Thus the author of Revelation apparently deliberately clusters perfect participles around key objects or persons and scenes, when they are first introduced or when they play a key role. The focus of attention is not on the participles themselves but on the visional objects that they attach to and introduce. Though his conception of the perfect participle as

---

[266] Cf. LXX Ps. 64.7, περιεζωσμένον.

indicating imperfective aspect with heightened proximity can be questioned, Campbell has suggested that the perfect participle is "prominent or intensified."[267] In this case the clustering of prominent and frontgrounding perfect participles served the purpose of introducing and focusing attention on key objects and persons in the author's visionary narrative.

The Future Tense

As discussed above, the future tense form should probably not be treated as entering into aspectual relationship with the other tense forms. Whether it is a modal form or a true tense, it grammaticalizes the semantic feature of expectation often referring to future time.[268] As Porter summarizes, with the future form "future temporal implicature is dependent on deictic indicators and grows naturally out of the semantic function of expectation."[269] It occurs frequently throughout the book of Revelation, though as we have seen future time can be indicated by other tense forms (present, aorist).[270] The difference is the semantic feature grammaticalized by the tense forms, the present and aorist grammaticalizing verbal aspect. The future indicative form occurs 106 times in Revelation, "reflecting the typical Hellenistic Greek uses of the future tense."[271] Bousset thought that the future tense in Revelation should be characterized as "ein Aus-der-Rolle-fallen."[272] Mussies treats the future tense form in Revelation in a rather straightforward manner, seeing it as indicating the predictive, prophetic character of John's visions while representing the Mishnaic Hebrew and Aramaic *yiqtol* tense which was non-durative and futural-modal in value.[273]

Instances of the future tense used to refer to future time (often referred to as the "prospective" use of the future) need not be extensively documented or argued. The extensive occurrence of the future tense form in John's vision can be explained by the fact that, as a prophecy (cf. 1.3; 22.18–19), John's narration of what he saw or heard often includes pro-

---

[267] Campbell, *Non-Indicative Verbs*, 28–29.
[268] Cf. Porter, *Verbal Aspect*, ch. 9; Fanning, *Verbal Aspect*, 120–124.
[269] Porter, *Verbal Aspect*, 426.
[270] Cf. Charles, *Revelation, I*, cxxiii–iv.
[271] Aune, *Revelation 1–5*, clxxxvi.
[272] Bousset, *Offenbarung*, 169.
[273] Mussies, *Morphology*, 340–341. "That the Apc. is full of future indicatives which have a futural value needs hardly any illustration" (341).

cesses which can be expected to take place in the future. The feature of expectation naturally entails events which are expected to take place in the future. This would account for the high number of occurrences in Revelation of future tense forms. A number of examples occur in Chs. 2–3 in the form of promises of eschatological reward, often with δώσω (2.5, 7, 10, 16, 17, 23, 25, 26, 27, 28; 3.3, 4, 5, 9, 10, 12, 20, 21). Other examples in later visionary and auditory segments include: καὶ ὄψεται ... καὶ **κόψονται** (1.7); οὐ **πεινάσουσιν** ἔτι οὐδὲ **διψήσουσιν** ἔτι ... ὅτι τὸ ἀρνίον ... **ποιμανεῖ** ... καὶ **ὁδηγήσει** ... καὶ **ἐξαλείψει** ... (7.16–17); **πατήσουσιν** ... καὶ **δώσω** ... καὶ **προφητεύσουσιν** (11.2–3); καὶ **νικήσει** ... καὶ **ἀποκτενεῖ** ... (11.7); καὶ **βασανισθήσεται** ἐν πυρί ... (14.10); καὶ ..., **μισήσουιν** ... καὶ ... **ποιήσουσιν** ... καὶ ... **κατακαύσουσιν** ... **τελεσθήσονται** ... (17.16–17); **κλαύσουσιν** καὶ **κόψονται** ... (18.9); **βληθήσεται** Βαβυλὼν ἡ μεγάλη πόλις (18.21); ἀλλ᾽ **ἔσονται** ἱερεῖς ... καὶ **βασιλεύσουσιν** (20.6); ὁ διάβολος ... καὶ τὸ θηρίον καὶ ψευδοπροφήτης, καὶ **βασανισθησονται** (20.10); ὁ νικῶν **κληρονομήσει** ταῦτα (21.7); καὶ **περιπατήσουσιν** τὰ ἔθνη ... (21.24). Some of the uses of the future may be the result of John's allusion to/quotation of Old Testament texts. It is possible that 1.7 is John's translation of the Hebrew text of Zech 12.10 (וספדו ... והביטו). In contrast to John's ὄψεται ... κόψονται the LXX has ἐπιβλέψονται ... κόψονται, while Matt 24.30 is similar to Rev 1.7 but contains the order κόψονται ... ὄψονται. As seen above on the present tense, it is possible that Rev 1.7 is recalling Christian tradition (Matt 24.30), though John has followed the order of the verbs in Zech 12.10. In any case, the use of the future has been influenced by an allusion to Zech 12.10 and depicts the events of seeing and mourning as that which can be expected to occur in the future. Likewise, the futures in Rev 7.16–17 may reflect the OT texts upon which John draws (Isa 49.10 [LXX οὐ πεινάσουσιν οὐδε διψήσουσιν]; Ezek 34.23 [LXX ποιμανεῖ]; Isa 25.8 [cf. Rev 21.4]). On this text see the following chapter. In the narration of his vision John also records events that can be expected to take place.

Though the future tense form is frequently used of future time reference, this does not seem to account for all its occurrences in Revelation. The future tense form occurs in 1) conditional constructions and 2) following ἵνα in subordinate clauses in place of a subjunctive. In conditional statements, the semantic feature of expectation indicated in future verb forms functions to indicate what will take place when the protasis is fulfilled. Thus in 2.5, following the protasis (εἰ δὲ μή), a future tense verb, κινήσω, follows a (future-referring) present (ἔρχομαι), where the

author indicates what Christ is going to do and can be expected to do
if the conditional is fulfilled. In 14.10, the future βασανισθήσεται follows three present tense verbs (προσκυνεῖ, λαμβάνει, πίεται). The first
two presents occur in the protasis of a first class conditional sentence (εἰ,
v. 9). The present πίεται then asserts the logical conclusion and the future
βασανισθήσεται indicates the punishment that can logically be expected
as a result. This is what will happen if the condition of the protasis is fulfilled.[274] In a conditional-like construction, 11.7 utilizes the future form
to indicate what the beast can be expected to do (νικήσει, ἀποκτενεῖ)
whenever (ὅταν) the witness of the two witnesses is completed (see below
on 4.9–10). In 22.18–19, following the use of aorist subjunctives (ἐπιθῇ,
ἀφέλῃ) in 3rd class conditional statements (with ἐάν), the author used
the future forms of corresponding verbs (ἐπιθήσει, ἀφελεῖ) in the protasis to indicate what God is going to do if the hypothetical apodoses are
fulfilled.[275]

The future form also occurs where one might expect the subjunctive
mood form, particularly following ἵνα.[276] Grammarians and commentaries have long noted the apparent confusion of the aorist subjunctive
and future tense forms in this construction in Revelation.[277] Thus in 3.9
ἵνα is followed by two future tense forms: ἥξουσιν καὶ προσκυνήσουσιν. In 9.4 the locusts are commanded not to harm the vegetation ἵνα
ἀδικήσουσιν, while in 9.5 they are not allowed to kill humanity but only
to torture them with ἵνα μὴ ἀποκτείνωσιν ... ἀλλ᾽ ἵνα **βασανισθήσονται** .... Moreover, in 9.20 ἵνα μὴ προσκυνήσουσιν indicates what would
have happened if the recipients of the plagues had converted, which they
did not.[278] According to Porter, "where a choice is offered between the
Subjunctive and the Future, the Future is more heavily marked semantically."[279] In 3.9, then, the future is used of what can be expected of those
who are not of the synagogue of Satan, who call themselves Jews. In

---

[274] On the future tense in conditional constructions see Porter, *Verbal Aspect*, 421.
He classifies them as timeless in implicature. For other usages of this in Revelation see
Dougherty, "Syntax," 414.

[275] On the conditional construction of these verses and the future tense forms found
and their temporal functions see Porter, *Verbal Aspect*, 437.

[276] For a listing of examples of ἵνα followed by a future tense form see Dougherty,
"Syntax," 415–416.

[277] See the discussion in Porter, *Verbal Aspect*, 414–416; Robertson, *Grammar*, 960–
961; BDF §§ 369, 378; Mussies, *Morphology*, 242; Aune, *Revelation 1–5*, clxxxvi. For the
LXX cf. Conybeare and Stock, *Grammar*, 93.

[278] See Dougherty, "Syntax," 417.

[279] Porter, *Verbal Aspect*, 414.

Revelation 9 the future with ἵνα is used for the limitations of the harmful effects of the locusts (v. 4), and in v. 5 in contrast to the aorist subjunctive (ἀποκτείνωσιν) it emphasizes what can be expected to take place, though it is the more terrifying of the two options (see the following chapter for further treatment). Cf. 2.10; 6.4, 11; 8.3; 13.12; 14.13; 22.14.

As discussed above, the future tense frequently occurs alongside the present and/or aorist tense forms (for details see above). The primary distinction is a semantic one. For example, in the message to Thyatira 2.22–23 begins with a present form βάλλω referring to future time, but then switches to the future form ἀποκτενῶ and γνώσονται. The future emphasizes the more serious consequence (death) of the followers of Jezebel's behavior if they do not repent: her followers can expect to be punished; and all the churches will know of the power of God's judgment.[280] Also, in 3.9 the present διδῶ is followed by a string of future forms, ποιήσω ... ἵνα ἥξουσιν καὶ προσκυνήσουσιν ..., the future forms emphasizing what can be expected to happen to those who call themselves Jews. As Beale recognizes, 3.9 is an ironic reversal of an Old Testament allusion, which originally applied to Gentiles.[281] Now those who call themselves Jews can expect to come and worship before the feet of Gentiles.

In 9.6 a string of future tense verbs (ζητήσουσιν, εὑρήσουσιν, ἐπιθυμήσουσιν) is capped off with a present (φεύγει, referring to future time). Here the deictic indicator ἐν ταῖς ἡμέραις suggests that the verb forms indicate what will take place in the future when the events of the fifth trumpet transpire (9.1–5). The future verbs emphasize what people will do during this time, while the present (φεύγει) records what death will do. In 11.10 a sequence of present forms (χαίρουσιν, εὐφραίνονται) is capped by a future (πέμψουσιν), indicating the climax of the world's rejoicing. Another example of the future occurring at the end of a string of present and/or aorist verb tense forms is 17.12–14. The aorist ἔλαβον summarizes the reception of authority by the ten horns. The present tense forms λαμβάνουσιν, ἔχουσιν, and διδόασιν then describe the coalition between the beast and the horns. The future tense is reserved to emphasize the result that can be expected from this: they will make war (πολεμήσουιν) with the Lamb but the Lamb will defeat (νικήσει) them. In the next segment (v. 16) the present φάγονται occurs in the midst of futures

---

[280] Osborne, *Revelation*, 161.
[281] Beale, *Revelation*, 288–289. Cf. Isa 45.14; 49.23; 60.14; Ps. 86.9.

(μισήσουσιν, ποιήσουσιν, κατακαύσουσιν) to depict a particularly gruesome detail of the downfall of the prostitute. It appears that when either the present or future is used within or at the end of a cluster of the other (i.e. a future with presents or vice versa) the "deviant" form is the one that stands out. The main function of the future in John's visions appears to be to add the notion of certainty and expectation, and contextually indicates the future referring nature of the visions. With the aorist and present tense forms used for the future the author is able to grammaticalize verbal aspect (action viewed as a complete whole or in progress). With the future form the author indicates the semantic feature of expectation. As a prophecy, in recording what John saw and heard, the author then indicates actions that can be expected to take place. In view of this analysis, it is unlikely that Bousset is correct that John's use of the future is inconsistent or mistaken ("Aus-der-Rolle-fallen").[282]

There has been some discussion regarding the alleged "past" usage of the future tense in Revelation. The passage that receives the most attention in this regard is 4.9–10. Thompson, therefore, considers 4.9–10, along with a number of other texts, as past usages of the future tense (5.10; 11.15; 17.8; 18.8; 21.3).[283] According to Thompson, this can be accounted for by reading the future with a past sense as a representation of the Hebrew imperfect. He points to a handful of passages where the LXX renders the Hebrew imperfect with a future tense form in Greek, though he admits that this is very rare.[284] In 4.9–10, then, the future tense should be treated as past in sense. Thus the past sense of the future in 4.9–10 is a "true Semitism" since there are apparently no non-biblical Greek parallels.[285] Turner sees the futures in 4.9–10 as entirely due to Semitic influence. According to him the futures in vv. 9–10 are a "literal rendering of the Heb. impf. which can be future under some circumstances."[286] Dougherty has labeled these as "timeless" uses of the future tense. That is 4.9–10 "seems not to be about a particular future event, but to be part of the description of the elders and the creatures."[287]

---

[282] Bousset, *Offenbarung*, 169. According to Bousset exceptions are 7.16–17; 13.10; 14.10; 17.14–16.
[283] Thompson, *Semitic Syntax*, 45–47. Cf. Charles, *Revelation I*, lxxiv; Zerwick, *Biblical Greek*, 95; Turner, *Syntax*, 86.
[284] Thompson, *Semitic Syntax*, 46.
[285] Thompson, *Semitic Syntax*, 47.
[286] Turner, *Syntax*, 86.
[287] Dougherty, "Syntax," 418.

In my judgment Mussies' assessment of the so-called past sense of the future in 4.9–10 is on target: "The evaluation of these futures as past tenses is due to the exegesis of the whole chapter" rather than the semantics of the future tenses.[288] That is, Thompson seems to assume that the future tense forms in vv. 9–10 refer to something *in Ch. 4* (the Trisagion, v. 8?). If this were the case it would require attaching a past time value to the future in this 4.9–10. However, it is doubtful whether the reference of the future forms in vv. 9–10 can be limited to v. 8. Rather, Mussies has argued that the only time the activity in vv. 9–10 is accomplished is in 5.13 ("Blessing and honor and glory and strength forever and ever").[289] Beale and Aune argue that the ὅταν refers to a unique event, and like Mussies identify it with 5.13–14, though, as Beale correctly argues, based on verbal parallels it should also include 5.8–12.[290] If this is the case, the future tense forms are not past- time referring (*contra* Thompson), though they still refer to a specific contextually derived event.

Following ὅταν, the future form δώσουσιν, grammaticalizing expectation, indicates what will take place. The following future forms πεσοῦνται, προσκυνήσουσιν, and βαλοῦσιν in v. 10 refer not to a specific future actions, but processes that take place at the same time as δώσουσιν, since the elders and four living creatures worship together (5.8–14).[291] In other words, the construction should be understood as a conditional-like construction. The future forms in 4.10 indicate what can be expected to take place when the condition of v. 9 is fulfilled (the four living creatures give glory to God). In this case the futures may be understood as temporally unrestricted, though logically they are future from the standpoint of the fulfillment of the ὅταν clause. However, it is likely that the reference of 4.9–10 is not limited in scope to just 5.8–14, but includes other instances of the elders falling down and worshipping God at key manifestations of God's salvation and judgment (7.11; 19.4; cf. 11.16, though there is no mention of the four living creatures). If this is correct, the future verbs indicate what will happen whenever the conditions in the ὅταν clause

---

[288] Mussies, *Morphology*, 344.

[289] Mussies wonders where honor, glory, and blessing are given to God in Revelation. He finds the answer in 5.13 (*Morphology*, 345).

[290] Beale, *Revelation*, 333–334; Aune, *Revelation 1–5*, 307. On the use of the future tense where one would expect to find a verb in the subjunctive mood in Revelation cf. Mussies, *Morphology*, 322, 342; Aune, *Revelation 1–5*, clxxxvi.

[291] "The two actions are coordinated as simultaneous" (Swete, *Apocalypse*, 72). For the deliberative use of the future see Porter, *Verbal Aspect*, 324–326.

present themselves.[292] Consequently, it is highly doubtful that the future tense form refers to past time as a reflection of the Semitic imperfect, as Thompson and others have claimed.

In conclusion, while in a few instances the future tense may be the result of John's translation from the Hebrew or dependence on the LXX, John's use of the future tense expresses actions that will occur, and adds the feature of expectation and certainty to John's visions. It is commonly used of future referring actions and its nature as indicating expectation is suited for these contexts. In some instances in Revelation the future may even be timeless, especially when it occurs in conditional sentences and after ἵνα. As with the aorist, present, and perfect tense forms, there is no need to posit Semitic influence for the future tense form in John's Apocalypse. Thus, the semantic feature of expectation can account for its range of functions.

Conclusion

In this chapter I have focused attention on and examined the main tense forms (aorist, present, imperfect, perfect, future) utilized in Revelation in the indicative mood and have sampled some of their respective functions, temporally and otherwise, within the book. I have not attempted to be exhaustive, but the examples that have been analyzed should be sufficient to establish the importance of the semantic category of verbal aspect for understanding the verb tenses in Revelation and their range of pragmatic functions. Virtually all previous approaches to the question of verb tenses in the Apocalypse have been entrenched in temporal models, which required explanation of the many apparent "deviations" from this model. The most common solution to the seemingly "irregular" or "inconsistent" use of tenses was to posit some sort of underlying Semitic influence over John's use of tense forms (esp. Thompson).[293] At other times the tenses are seen as retaining their true temporal force, or sometimes as

---

[292] Porter recognizes the use of the future tense form to refer to omnitemporal action (*Verbal Aspect*, 423–424). Is this what Beale means (*Revelation*, 333)? Smalley incorrectly wonders whether vv. 9–10 take place in the eschaton due to the future tense of the verbs (*Revelation*, 123).

[293] Again, I am not suggesting that there is a necessary correlation between a temporal view of the Greek tenses and finding Semitic influence. It is just that those who argue for Semitic influence seem to start with a strong temporal orientation to Greek verbs and then look to the Semitic verbal system to explain deviation from this temporal "norm."

semantically neutralized in certain contexts. However, I have tried to show that verbal aspect, particularly as advocated by Porter, where in each of the major tense forms the author grammaticalizes his conception of the process rather than time or *Aktionsart*, has the explanatory power to account for the various pragmatic manifestations of the various tense forms throughout Revelation. Though at times John's use of a given tense form may reveal Semitic enhancement, or may be the result of allusion to the LXX, the use of the major verb tenses in the indicative mood throughout Revelation is explicable in light of verbal aspect and reflects the aspectual system of first century Koine Greek and the rest of the New Testament. It remains to examine the function of shifting aspects across larger segments of visionary discourse in Revelation.

CHAPTER FOUR

SHIFTING TENSES IN THE APOCALYPSE

Introduction

One of the conspicuous features of the Apocalypse is the manner in which the author shifts back and forth between all the major Greek tense forms in the indicative mood in the visionary (and auditory) segments, a shift which Bousset characterized as "das regellose Schwanken."[1] Revelation's visionary material exhibits these tense shifts while usually referring to the same temporal sphere, normally a narrative account of what John saw. This shifting of tense forms would appear to present a problem for strictly temporal approaches to the Greek verbal system. Consequently, scholars have attempted to account for this phenomenon. Lancellotti thought that the shifting of tenses revealed confusion on the part of the author based on the underlying Hebrew tense system. Mussies, however, contends that the shifting tenses in Revelation must be understood temporally from the standpoint of John's visionary experience. According to Mussies in many cases the tenses reveal distinct groupings, where there is a group of past tenses (aorist) followed by a group of present tenses followed by a group of futures.[2] This accounts for the following three perspectives corresponding to the groupings of tense forms:

a) the past time when the visions were actually seen, or are pretended to have been seen (aorist);
b) the life pictures of events and situations (present);
c) the prophetic character of the visions (future).[3]

Thus Mussies does give the varying tense forms in Revelation's visions their full temporal values.

---

[1] Bousset, *Offenbarung*, 168.
[2] Mussies, *Morphology*, 340.
[3] Mussies, *Morphology*, 340.

However, Mussies' treatment of this issue suffers from overdependence on a temporal orientation toward the Greek tense forms. As seen above, along with the rest of the New Testament, John's Greek grammaticalizes verbal aspect in the formal tense endings. Moreover, while some visions often exhibit a grouping of tense forms, the tenses commonly appear distributed throughout the visions, rendering much of Mussies' proposal tenuous and of limited value. For example, though not strictly a vision (see below) in 11.1–13 aorist tense forms begin (ἐδόϑη) and end (εἰσῆλϑεν, ἔστησαν, ἔπεσεν, ἤκουσαν, ἀνέβησαν, ἐϑεώρησαν, ἐγένετο, ἔπεσεν, ἀπεκτάνϑησαν, ἐγένετο) the narrative, and carry the main story line throughout. The present tense also occurs distributed throughout this segment (v. 5, ϑέλει, ἐκπορεύεται; v. 6, ἔχουσιν; v. 8, καλεῖται; v. 10, χαίρουσιν, εὐφραίνονται), as does the future (v. 2, πατήσουσιν; v. 3, προφητεύσουσιν; v. 7, ποιήσει, νικήσει, ἀποκτενεῖ; v. 10, πέμψουσιν). Likewise, in Ch. 13 the aorist tense predominates throughout, and present tenses (v. 4, δύναται; v. 10, ὑπάγει; v. 12, ποιεῖ; v. 14, πλανᾷ, ἔχει; ποιεῖ), two imperfect forms (v. 11, εἶχεν, ἐλάλει) one perfect (v. 8, γέγραπται), and future tense forms are scattered throughout the vision (v. 8, προσκυνήσουσιν; v. 12, προσκυνήσουσιν). In view of the fact that the tenses shift back and forth throughout the vision, one wonders how likely it was that the readers were meant to shift temporal spheres back and forth so rapidly while hearing/reading the visionary narratives.

The more predominant approach to the issue is to find Semitic influence of some kind behind John's seemingly odd (non-temporal) use of tense forms.[4] One of the most recent, thorough treatments from this perspective is that of Thompson, who postulates a Semitic pattern for the tense shifts found in Revelation's visions.[5] Thompson notes the "sudden and seemingly inexplicable shifts among aorist/present/future tenses of verbs in connected narrative, without a corresponding shift in the time during which the action being described actually takes place."[6] While he admits that this phenomenon of shifting tenses can be found elsewhere

[4] Lancellotti, Charles. While Mussies sees Semitic influence behind John's use of verb tenses (from Aramaic and Mishnaic Hebrew), he nevertheless does not find the Greek tenses used in an un-Greek manner (*Morphology*), though he invests them with their "normal" temporal values.

[5] Thompson, *Semitic Syntax*.

[6] Thompson, *Semitic Syntax*, 47. Thompson states that his starting point for examining shifting tenses is his previous argument that Semitic influence must account for the irregular usage of aorist, present, and future tenses. I would also include the perfect tense form, though it occurs much less frequently in Revelation.

in the New Testament to a limited degree, according to him it is far more pronounced in the Apocalypse.[7] After rejecting Mussies' temporal explanation, Thompson suggests that the shifting tenses in Revelation can be accounted for by Semitic influence by way of similar shifts in prophetic literature.[8] As with his treatment of the individual verb tenses, he appeals to the LXX to illustrate shifting Greek verb tenses that reflect a corresponding shift in the underlying Hebrew. Thompson provides examples from Dan (Theod) 4.31–32, 35; 7.26–27; Hos 4.10; 9.3. In each of these instances he finds the shifts in Greek tense forms corresponding to shifts in the underlying Hebrew. Based on the OT examples that he adduces, he discovers the following pattern in both the LXX (Theod) and the texts which he examines in Revelation (6.15–17; 7.16, 17; 14.2b–3; 20.7–10):

Aorist	=	Semitic Perfect
Present	=	Semitic Participle
Future	=	Semitic Imperfect[9]

Thompson concludes that this shifting of tenses in Greek in these examples (and presumably others), which reveals a corresponding shift in the underlying Hebrew text, explains the verb tense alternations in Revelation.

Thompson's solution to the shifting tenses in Revelation, however, creates a number of difficulties. First, Thompson, like Mussies, assumes a strict temporal model for Greek verb tenses. Second, some of his argument for an underlying Hebrew tense shift depends on the validity of his argument more generally that John's use of tenses is semitically influenced. Yet if his treatment of the individual tense forms can be called into question as the previous chapter has attempted to do, then there is less reason to appeal to Semitic influence for the shifting tenses as well.[10] Much of his cumulative argument loses its force at this point.

---

[7] Thompson does not tell us what New Testament texts he has in mind or to what degree he finds tense shifting more pronounced in the Apocalypse.

[8] Thompson, *Semitic Syntax*, 48. He calls the tense shifts "strange yet acceptable phenomena" (48). But his criteria for labeling a given tense usage "strange" is clearly whether it manifests its assumed temporal values.

[9] Thompson, *Semitic Syntax*, 48–49. Curiously, the underlying Hebrew verbs that Thompson provides are not the ones that are actually found in the MT of Dan 4.31–32. Instead he appeals to the Aramaic imperfect as corresponding to the futures in v. 32.

[10] As with many of his arguments for Semitic influence of individual verb forms in Revelation examined in the previous chapter, Thompson's argument is cumulative. Based on his argument that individual verb tenses reveal Semitic influence, he looks to Semitic

Third, like many of his arguments for the individual tense forms, he depends on the Greek translation (LXX) of the Old Testament to confirm his point. While John's use of tenses may reflect an underlying Semitic tense shift when he is deliberately quoting from or alluding to the Old Testament (even the LXX), unlike the LXX, Revelation as a whole is not translation Greek based on an underlying Hebrew text.[11] Thompson seems to have in mind that John is either consciously imitating the LXX or has unconsciously been influenced by its translation procedure.[12] Both the LXX and John would presumably share a semitized Greek. The one clear example that Thompson cites comes from Rev 7.16, 17. But this is an obvious case of translation Greek, where John cites Old Testament texts (Isa 49.10; 25.8).[13] But this is hardly sufficient to establish a pattern. Fourth, Thompson's examples are not extensive enough, nor does he tell us by what criteria he has chosen these examples. He cites only three or four such examples, not nearly enough to establish his case, and they only cover a span of a verse or two. He would need to consider much more extensive and lengthier textual samples, since what we encounter in Revelation are tense shifts that take place over an extended discourse.

More problematic is that his examples come from sections that are generically prophetic or are speeches, but do not narrate a vision per se. Dan 7.31–32 records a voice from heaven which decrees that the dream which Nebuchadnezzar relates in 4.4–18 will now be fulfilled. V. 35 is actually part of a hymn that Nebuchadnezzar sings to the most high (vv. 33–35). The text from Hos 4.10 that Thompson cites is part of a charge that God brings against his people (4.1). Thus, along with other prophetic texts, it would have been more helpful for Thompson also to examine more extended Old Testament texts which purport to narrate a vision.[14]

---

influence in the shift in tense form as well. "If the Seer could produce such strange yet acceptable phenomena, then surely there must have been some precedent for it" (*Semitic Syntax*, 48).

[11] Even where John is quoting from or alluding to the Hebrew text, he must still choose a Greek tense form from the verb tense system.

[12] See Schmidt, "Septuagintalisms," which may also describe what Thompson thinks is taking place with John's use of tenses, though Thompson sees explicit underlying Semitic influence and not just imitations of "Septuagintalisms."

[13] Cf. Beale, *Revelation*, 441–443.

[14] Cf. Isa 6.1–8; Dan 7.1–14; Ezek 1.4–28; 40.1–27; 43.1–11, all upon which John draws extensively.

More recently Dougherty has also broached the question of shifting tenses in the Apocalypse which he characterizes as often inconsistent.[15] According to Dougherty, the tense usage in various sections of Revelation can be categorized according to 1) consistency; 2) apparent inconsistency; 3) inconsistency. In examining this issue he claims that the "same tense is normally used throughout a given passage for all the verbs that refer to action occurring at the same time."[16] The following chart illustrates the criteria by which Dougherty judges tense usage in Revelation:

Narration	*Description*	*Prediction*
Aorist	Present	Future
Imperfect	Perfect (present perfect)	
Perfect (past perfect)		

Thus, in the Narration, the predominant tenses are aorist and imperfect, with the perfect occasionally being used in a past sense. The present and the perfect with a present sense indicate Descriptive material, and the future tense indicates Predictive material. Deviations from this scheme that cannot be explained are "inconsistent" according to Dougherty.

Thus visions where this principle holds are labeled "consistent," e.g. 1.9–12, 17: ἐγενόμην … ἐγενόμην … ἐπέστρεψα … εἶδον … καὶ ὅτε εἶδον … ἔπεσα … ἔθηκεν.. "Apparent inconsistency" occurs in visions where tenses may be mixed for various reasons, but they do not violate the above principle. Dougherty points to examples where the perfect and aorist tense are congruent, e.g., 8.5: εἴληφεν … ἐγέμισεν, or where the present occurs alongside of the future, e.g. 2.5: ἔρχομαι … πολεμήσω. He treats the final category, "Inconsistency," at much more length. According to Dougherty, there are 21 examples of tense shifting in Revelation that appear to violate the above principle of consistency. He thinks that this may be due to a shift in perspective, or mixed modes of writing (future tense—prediction; past tense—narration; present tense—description). But many tense shifts simply have no explanation.[17]

For example, Dougherty is confused by ᾄδουσιν in 5.8–9, since one might expect an aorist in narration. Yet he explains this as the continuation of a description of the elders and living creatures begun in the previous clause; in other words, it is not narration. In 9.1–6, 7–11 Dougherty

---

[15] "Syntax," 426–447.
[16] Dougherty, "Syntax," 426.
[17] Dougherty, "Syntax," 428.

detects inconsistency in the shift from aorist tense forms to future forms
in vv. 1–6, and from the imperfect to present forms in vv. 7–11. In 11.3–
13 he seems perplexed with the alternating between future, present, and
aorist forms. He concludes that "there is in this section a narrative begun
and continued in the future, then continued in the present tense, and
after a brief return to the future continued and concluded in the aorist."[18]
Likewise, in 12.1–6 he seems surprised to find a present tense used in
narration in v. 4, since one would expect a past tense (note the temporal language). Given his principle, he concludes that "either a present
time verb is narrative, or an aorist verb is descriptive."[19] And in 13.11–
17 he notices descriptive elements in the past (imperfect) tense: εἶχεν,
ἐλάλει, where one might expect present tense forms. With 18.4–20, an
extended speech, Dougherty is once again confused by the shifting of
tenses between future, present, and aorist. Problematic for him are the
aorist tense forms found in vv. 17a–19, which he describes as "interjec-
tions of narrative material into the predictive statements of the voice in
v. 4."[20] In 19.11–16 Dougherty explains the interjection of a future tense
verb into the present tense vision in v. 15 (ποιμανεῖ) as possible part of
a ἵνα clause, not narration. The perfect κέκληται can be explained as a
"present perfect," and the imperfect, ἠκολούθει, is narrative, not descriptive.

Thus, Dougherty seems to operate with the assumption that *future
tenses* are used in prediction, *present tenses* (and *present perfects*) in
descriptive material, and *aorists* and *imperfects* in narration. The difficulty emerges when one encounters the tenses outside of this scheme, as
appears to be the case in a number of instances. But, like Mussies and
Thompson, Dougherty ultimately utilizes a temporal template to interpret the tense forms in Revelation. That is, his perplexity stems from finding verb tenses outside of their assumed (temporal) functions in Revelation. This is the criterion by which he judges whether the use of tenses in
the visions fall into the categories of "Consistency," "Apparent Inconsistency," and "Inconsistency." Dougherty has highlighted, I think, a common pattern in Revelation: aorist and imperfect in narrative, present in
descriptive material; future in predictive sections (e.g. speech). But this
is not the whole story, for present, perfect, and future forms are found

---

[18] Dougherty, "Syntax," 436.
[19] Dougherty, "Syntax," 437.
[20] Dougherty, "Syntax," 443.

within narrative material. While Dougherty begins his work by saying that the term "tense" is a misnomer as applied to Greek verb tenses, since they indicate aspect rather than time, his analysis demonstrates time and again that he is ultimately not able to divest himself of a temporal conception for the Greek tense system.

Analysis of Selected Texts

In the rest of this chapter I will examine selected segments from Revelation, particularly those sections that have been noted for their apparently "inconsistent" or "irregular" use of tenses, in order to consider the phenomenon of shifting tense forms from the standpoint of verbal aspect: Rev 5; 7.9–17; 9; 11.1–13; 12–13; 17; 18.4–20; 19.11–21. These sections provide a cross-sampling of material in Revelation which exhibits striking tense shifts in sections representing different literary character (vision and audition). The shifting of tense forms in Revelation's visions provide fertile ground for the application of aspect theory in terms of how the aspects function to indicate the author's perspective on processes and to structure the discourse, as well as perhaps to indicate levels of discourse prominence. Thus I will utilize verbal aspect theory as a working hypothesis in exploring the tense shifts in Revelation's visionary segments. Again, the primary focus of this work is on the aspects in indicative mood forms, though I will make reference at times to the aspects of some of the non-indicative mood forms in Revelation's visionary material as well.

Revelation 5

Though Ch. 5 is structurally a continuation of the throne scene in Ch. 4, Ch. 5 nevertheless introduces several novel features: the scroll, the slain Lamb, the reception of the scroll by the Lamb.[21] David E. Aune has demonstrated that this dramatic scene in Rev 5 depicts the investiture of the Lamb, where the Lamb is invested with authority to open the sealed

---

[21] Cf. Boxall, *Revelation*, 93. Beale says "The scene in ch. 4 continues uninterrupted in 5.1. The 'One sitting on the throne', the recipient of praise in 4:9–11, is now portrayed again with the additional feature that he is holding a book in his hand" (*Revelation*, 337).

scroll and divulge its contents (5.7, 11–14).[22] In depicting the processes that make up the visionary narrative the author employs a full array of Greek tense forms.[23]

Rev 5.1 commences the vision with εἶδον which functions to introduce the vision and the first item for consideration: the scroll.[24] As Aune has noted καὶ εἶδον functions in three important ways throughout Revelation as an introduction to a new vision narrative, as an introduction to a major scene within a continuing visionary narrative, or to focus on a new or important figure or activity within the vision.[25] εἶδον occurs three additional times in Ch. 5 to indicate a change in the scene or focus in the vision: vv. 2, 6, 11 (along with ἤκουσα), providing the basic structure of the vision. In vv. 2 and 6 it introduces additional, important figures in the visionary scene: the angel (vv. 2–5) and the Lamb (vv. 5–10). It then introduces a large throng of angels who respond to the song sung by the elders and living creatures (vv. 11–14).[26]

5.1–2: The introduction of the first novel element, the βιβλίον, is achieved through two participles in the stative aspect γεγραμμένον and κατεσφραγισμένον. The effect of the more heavily marked perfects is to draw attention to this new element in the vision (see above). The two perfect passive participles probably reflect Old Testament influence and may function to draw attention to the Old Testament background. In LXX Ezek 2.10 the author describes a book γεγραμμένα. Further, in both Isa 29.11; Dan 12.9 a book is described as ἐσφραγισμένου/α (LXX). Perhaps John found the perfect tense forms from the Old Testament precursors appropriate not only for identifying the Old Testament background, but as the most heavily marked aspect for drawing attention to the βιβλίον in his own vision. The fact that he clusters them around the book in 5.1 suggests that John wants to draw attention to this feature.

5:2–5: The next section marked off by καὶ εἶδον describes the appearance of a new actor, an angel, who will function to introduce the basic dilemma of the vision: who is worthy to open the scroll? In contrast to the βιβλίον, the preaching of the angel is described with the present par-

---

[22] Aune, *Revelation 1–5*, 336–338. Cf. also Beale, *Revelation*, 350–366. Cf. Daniel 7; Ezekiel 1–2.

[23] For further details see David Mathewson, "Verbal Aspect in the Book of Revelation: An Analysis of Revelation 5," *NovT* 50 (2008) 58–77. On the correct reading of the form of βασιλεύω (βασιλεύουσιν or βασιλεύσουσιν) in v. 10 see below.

[24] Giesen, *Offenbarung*, 158; Blount, *Revelation*, 99.

[25] Aune, *Revelation 1–5*, 338. See also Blount, *Revelation*, 99.

[26] Contra Giesen who sees the divisions as vv. 1–5, 6–7, 8–14 (*Offenbarung*, 158).

ticiple κηρύσσοντα (v. 2).[27] The aorist tense form, then, carries along the story line. The basic dilemma of the vision, that no one is found worthy to open the book, is summarized by aorist tense forms (εὑρέθη; cf. ἀνοῖ-ξαι, λῦσαι, vv. 2–4). Against the background aorist forms, the imperfect tense form, though not as frequent in Revelation,[28] depicts the inability (ἐδύνατο) of anyone to open the book (v. 3) and the seer's response to the dilemma in v. 4 (ἔκλαιον).[29] According to Porter, the imperfect tense form, against the background aorist, is the more heavily marked form.[30] Yet as the tense form which grammaticalizes remoteness, they are less marked than the present forms (cf. λέγει, v. 5). Hence, the imperfects provide the staging or setting: they are used for the dilemma and John's weeping, while the more marked present tense is reserved for the solution offered by the angel in v. 5 (λέγει). The present (imperfective) imperative of prohibition (μὴ κλαῖε) aspectually matches the weeping (ἔκλαιον) of the seer.[31]

One non-indicative example deserves brief comment. The present infinitive βλέπειν is paired with the aorist ἀνοῖξαι in vv. 3 and 4. Mussies notices that the usual pattern in Revelation, present-aorist, is not followed here (aorist-present) though he offers no explanation for this.[32] Osborne thinks that the contrast should be understood in terms of a single opening of the book (aorist) followed by a careful perusal (present) of its contents.[33] However, Osborne's conception is too dependent on an

---

[27] According to Beale, the faint outlines of Dan 4.13–14, 23 can be seen here in 5.2. Beale points to the LXX and Theod. However, in contrast to John's κηρύσσοντα, the LXX of Dan 4.14 has ἐφώνησεν and εἶπεν (cf. Theod). MGK has λέγοντα.

[28] According to Bousset, "Der Gebrauch des Imperfektum ist nicht haüfig in der Apk, aber wo dasselbe eingeführt wird, geschieht es mit Bedacht" (*Offenbarung*, 169).

[29] Smalley thinks that the imperfect ἔκλαιον has the effect that "it is almost as if we come across John, to discover that his great grief has long been in progress" (*Revelation*, 130). However, Smalley's conception is too dependent on both a temporal and *Aktionsart* view of the imperfect tense (a continuous activity in the past).

[30] Porter, *Verbal Aspect*, 199. Cf. also Aune, *Revelation 1–5*, 347. As Robertson observes, "The aorist tells the simple story. The imperfect draws the picture" (*Grammar*, 883).

[31] On interpreting imperative constructions in light of verbal aspect, rather than traditional, *Aktionsart*- or time-based taxonomies, see Mathewson, "Aspect in Imperatival Constructions." Cf. K.L. McKay, "Aspect in Imperatival Constructions in NT Greek," *NovT* 34 (1992) 209–228; James L. Boyer, "A Classification of Imperatives: A Statistical Study," *GTJ* 8 (1987), 35–54. This is an example of where the traditional translation "stop ..." is possible ("stop weeping"). Yet this is only true because of contextual justification—John is clearly weeping when this command is uttered by the angel.

[32] Mussies, *Morphology*, 340.

[33] Osborne, *Revelation*, 252 n. 5.

Aktionsart approach to Greek tenses (point vs. durative action). In fact, as the rest of the book makes clear, the opening of the book is anything but a single or punctiliar act, since the seals are removed one at a time in Ch. 6. This would be even more true if, following Richard J. Bauckham, narratively the sealed scroll is not open until Ch. 10 where an angel is depicted as holding a scroll (βιβλαρίδιον, v. 2).[34] Rather, verbal aspect can account for the difference. Aspectually, the switch to the present infinitive suggests that the author chooses to draw more attention to the act of looking into the scroll as the more salient of the pair. By contrast the activity of opening the book serves as the background for the act of looking into it.

5:6–11: The καὶ εἶδον in v. 6 introduces the next novel element in the vision.[35]

Like βιβλίον, the introduction of the Lamb is also achieved with three accompanying perfect participles: ἑστηκός, ἐσφαγμένον (cf. v. 12), ἀπεσταλμένοι, the latter describing the seven spirits which are, however, identified as the Lamb's seven eyes.

> Καὶ εἶδον ἐν μέσῳ τοῦ θρόνου καὶ τῶν τεσσάρων ζῴων καὶ ἐν μέσῳ τῶν πρεσβυτέρων ἀρνίον **ἑστηκὸς** ὡς **ἐσφαγμένον** ἔχων κέρατα ἑπτὰ καὶ ὀφθαλμοὺς ἑπτὰ οἵ εἰσιν τὰ πνεύματα τοῦ θεοῦ **ἀπεσταλμένοι** εἰς πᾶσαν τὴν γῆν.

What is significant is that the author has clustered participles in the more heavily marked perfect tense form around the two new and central features of this vision: the book and the Lamb.[36] Moreover, the fact that the Lamb has already been introduced in v. 5 does not contravene its treatment as a frontground element in v. 6. The Lamb who overcomes is mentioned in the angel's speech (what John *heard*), with aorist verbs summarizing his activity (ἐνίκησεν). Though John is told about the Lamb (what John *heard*), the actual appearance of the Lamb (what John *saw*)

---

[34] For convincing argumentation see Richard J. Bauckham, *The Climax of Prophecy: Studies in the Book of Revelation* (Edinburgh: T. & T. Clark, 1993) 243–266. In contrast to the sealed book here in Ch. 5 (κατεσφραγισμένον), in 10.2 it is now presented to the seer as opened, again using a perfect participle (ἠνεῳγμένον). A further reason for identifying the two books is that the same OT *Vorlage* lies behind both texts (Ezek 2.8–3.3). Cf. also Blount, *Revelation*, 100–104.

[35] Blount, *Revelation*, 107.

[36] "The sealed scroll and the Lamb constitute the narrative focus of Rev 5" (Aune, *Revelation 1–5*, 338). This insight receives linguistic corroboration in light of the clustering of perfect participles around these two features.

is delayed until vv. 6–7;[37] with the appearance of the Lamb the perfect tense forms function to frontground the main character of this vision. Thus the participles themselves do not receive attention, but the main elements that they modify: the scroll and the Lamb.

The narrative aorist, then, summarizes background events and functions to propel the story forward. Thus, the Lamb's initial approach to the throne (ἦλθεν), and his taking the book (ἔλαβεν) are all recorded with the basic narrative aorist aspect. The response of the four living creatures and twenty four elders of falling down (ἔπεσαν), as well as the content of their response (ἐσφάγης, ἠγόρασας, ἐποίησας) are summarized with the background aorist in vv. 8–9.[38] The chapter ends with the elders falling (ἔπεσαν) and worshiping (προσεκύνησαν), both activities summarized with the narrative aorist tense form.

In contrast to the aorist tense form, the present (and imperfect) tenses occur throughout the vision to add descriptive color and/or to highlight or foreground certain events and features in the vision. Following the background aorist (ἔπεσαν) which simply records their act of falling (v. 8), in v. 9 ἄδουσιν introduces the initial song of the four living creatures and twenty-four elders following the Lamb's reception of the scroll, and interpreting its significance.[39] Thus, the present tenses function to draw attention to this important speech. If the correct reading in v. 10 is βασιλεύουσιν, the author uses the present tense to draw attention to this activity, which is the primary reward for the martyrs (cf. 20.4; 22.5). The final responsory word (Ἀμήν) from the four living creatures in v. 14 is introduced by the imperfect ἔλεγον, the remote form being used perhaps in contrast to the hymn sung be all creation in v. 13. The present tense form also occurs in several non-indicative forms, mainly

---

[37] A notorious feature of Revelation is the "what John heard" vs. "what John saw" dialectic. Cf. Boxall, *Revelation*, 97. Usually the juxtaposition of these two perceptual categories (cf. Revelation 7) is understood in terms of the hearing interpreting and giving significance to the seeing. Cf. J.L. Resseguie, *Revelation Unsealed: A Narrative Critical Approach to John's Apocalypse* (Biblical Interpretation Series 32; Leiden: Brill, 1998) 33–37. However, while this is often the case, at least here in Revelation 5 what is *seen* is marked as the more salient element of the see/hear pairing based on verbal aspectual usage. Boxall thinks that the tension between the two is never finally resolved (*Revelation*, 97–98).

[38] The latter depicts the reason (ὅτι) that the Lamb is deemed worthy to open the scroll. Accordingly, it is depicted with the aorist aspect since background material often consists of supporting material for the more thematic or prominent material. Cf. Wallace, "Figure and Ground," 208.

[39] Though it is unnecessary, following Dougherty ("Syntax," 430), to see ἄδουσιν as a description rather than a narration.

participles, to add descriptive color to the vision (ἔχων, v. 6; ἔχοντες, γεμούσας, v. 8) and to introduce the contents of the hymns in vv. 9, 12, 13 (λέγοντες/λέγοντας). Since speech tends to slow down the narrative, the present tense is a suitable aspectual choice to focus on the speech.[40] Further, there is no need to postulate a Semitism for this use of the present participle, since as seen above, it was an acceptable Greek construction.[41]

The perfect tense form occurs only once in the indicative mood in this section. The sole perfect indicative form is found in v. 7: καὶ ἦλθεν καὶ **εἴληφεν** ἐκ τῆς δεξιᾶς τοῦ καθημένου ἐπὶ τοῦ θρόνου. As seen in the previous chapter, the perfect here is most commonly explained as "Aoristic" with little or no "perfective" force.[42] But I suggested above that rather than reducing the perfect to an aorist in meaning εἴληφεν should be given its full semantic force as aspectually stative. The use of the perfect is far from arbitrary, but appears highly motivated at this point and plays an important discourse function. At the place where the crucial transition of the book from the hand of the one seated on the throne to the Lamb takes place, the author marks it with the frontground perfect tense as the most central narrative event.[43] The aorist ἦλθεν functions to provide the necessary background (approaching the throne) to this act. Then once the crucial transition takes place, the author reverts back to the background aorist tense to record what has already taken place (ἔλαβεν, v. 8; λαβεῖν, v. 9; λαβεῖν, v. 12).[44] The aorist ἔλαβεν in v. 8 in the dependent clause probably also functions to background the taking of the scroll now in order to draw attention at this point to the response of the onlookers in the section that follows introduced by the present ᾄδουσιν (v. 9). Thus, the focal activity of the visionary discourse is marked with the frontground perfect tense form in v. 7, an activity

---

[40] This is one of the valid insights of Campbell (*Verbal Aspect*, 54).

[41] *Contra* Thompson, *Semitic Syntax*, 69–70. Cf. Porter, *Verbal Aspect*, 138–141.

[42] Fanning, *Verbal Aspect*, 303; BDF § 343; Charles, *Revelation, I*, 144; Lohmeyer, *Offenbarung*, 55; Beale, *Revelation*, 357.

[43] Aune is the only commentary I have found subsequent to the work of Porter who seems to recognize this based on verbal aspect: "The center of the action is highlighted by using the perfect εἴληφεν, 'took', which contrasts with the aorist, the characteristic background tense used in narrative" (Aune, *Revelation 1–5*, 354). However, Aune does not discuss the function of this highlighting in the context or the shift back to the aorist in the following verses.

[44] As Swete says, "The ordinary aorist of narration is resumed" (*Apocalypse*, 79), though he does not explain the function of this resumption in contrast to the perfect tense form.

that is subsequently celebrated liturgically in vv. 9–14.[45] As commentaries have often noted, usually without linguistic justification, the worthiness of the Lamb to open the scroll is the "centre de la présente vision."[46] This also confirms linguistically Aune's assessment of Ch. 5 as the "investiture of the Lamb."[47]

Verbal aspect, then, functions to structure Revelation 5 in significant ways. The occurrences of the aorist καὶ εἶδον serves to mark off the main sections of the vision, introducing novel elements: the scroll, the angel, and the lamb. It also introduces the final hymns sung by the heavenly hosts. The aorist serves as the primary narrative tense, while the imperfect and present tenses highlight certain activities. The clustering of perfect participles around the scroll and the Lamb suggest that they play the most important roles in the section. The sole use of the perfect indicative tense form functions to frontground the most significant activity in the narrative. In this way the shift in tense forms throughout Revelation 5 does not function to indicate temporal relationships. Rather, it functions to structure the discourse and indicate levels of prominence within John's vision.

Revelation 7.9–17

Following the sealing of 144,000 from the twelve tribes of Israel (7.1–8), John envisions a great multitude standing in heaven (vv. 9–17).[48] The section consists of a visionary narrative which quickly gives way to a dialogue between the seer and one of the elders in the vision (vv. 13–17). Regarding vv. 9–17, Aune laments that "irregularity is evident in 7:9–17, where the overall pattern is a sequence of past-tense verbs, then a sequence of present-tense verbs, followed by a sequence of future-tense

---

[45] As Aune states, "The focus of the action is the taking or reception of the scroll from the right hand of God by the Lamb, for it is this act that is immediately celebrated by the two narrative hymns in 5:9–10; 5:11–12, followed by the doxology sung by all the living beings of the cosmos in 5:13–14" (*Revelation 1–5*, 336).

[46] Prigent, *l'Apocalypse*, 95. Prigent understands the entire section to be an answer to the question: "Qui est digne d'ouvrir …?"

[47] Aune describes *investiture* as "the act of establishing someone in office or the ratification of the office that someone already holds informally" (*Revelation 1–5*, 336).

[48] On the relationship between these two groups see Bauckham, *Climax*, 215–229. Bauckham has settled the issue by demonstrating that the "hear"/"see" dialectic in 7.1–17 points to the two groups being identical. Cf. also Aune, *Revelation 6–16*, 447–448 for discussion. For the structural relationship of Ch. 7 within the seal sequence see Pattemore, *Souls under the Altar*, 128–130.

verbs."[49] Aune's temporal language is regrettable, and the tense sequence can only be described as an "irregularity" if a temporal model is enforced. But if approached from the standpoint of verbal aspect it can be seen that the author shifts tense forms for reasons other than temporal ones.

> [9]Μετὰ ταῦτα εἶδον, καὶ ἰδοὺ ὄχλος πολύς, ὃν ἀριθμῆσαι αὐτὸν οὐδεὶς ἐδύνατο ... ἑστῶτες ἐνώπιον τοῦ θρόνου καὶ ἐνώπιον τοῦ ἀρνίου περι-βεβλημένους στολὰς λευκάς .... [10]καὶ κράζουσιν φωνῇ μεγάλῃ λέγοντες .... [11]καὶ πάντες οἱ ἄγγελοι εἱστήκεισαν κύκλῳ τοῦ θρόνου καὶ τῶν πρε-σβυτέρων καὶ τῶν τεσσάρων ζῴων καὶ ἔπεσαν ἐνώπιον τοῦ θρόνου ἐπὶ τὰ πρόσωπα αὐτῶν καὶ προσεκύνησαν τῷ θεῷ [12]λέγοντες .... [13]καὶ ἀπε-κρίθη εἷς ἐκ τῶν πρεσβυτέρων λέγων μοι, Οὗτοι οἱ περιβεβλημένοι τὰς στολὰς τὰς λευκὰς τίνες εἰσὶν καὶ πόθεν ἦλθον; [14]καὶ εἴρηκα αὐτῷ, Κύ-ριέ μου, σὺ οἶδας. καὶ εἶπέν μοι, Οὗτοί εἰσιν οἱ ἐρχόμενοι ἐκ τῆς θλίψεως τῆς μεγάλης καὶ ἔπλυναν τὰς στολὰς αὐτῶν καὶ ἐλεύκαναν αὐτὰς ἐν τῷ αἵματι τοῦ ἀρνίου.   (vv. 9–14)

As in the other visionary segments of the Apocalypse, aorist tense forms introduce the vision (εἶδον) and summarize main events in the story (ἀριθμῆσαι,[50] ἔπεσαν, προσεκύνησαν) or introduce and summarize dialogue (ἀπεκρίθη, ἦλθον, εἶπεν, ἔπλυναν, ἐλεύκαναν).[51] Other as-pects are used to select various events to dwell on in more detail. The present tense is then used to introduce and draw attention to the key speech of the multitude in v. 10 (κράζουσιν). As in other visionary seg-ments, attention is drawn to the main figure(s), the great multitude, by introducing them with two perfect (stative) participles (ἑστῶτες, περι-βεβλημένους) in v. 9 (cf. v. 13), focusing on their posture and apparel. In the midst of dialogue between John and one of the elders introduced by aorist tense forms (ἀπεκρίθη, εἶπεν), a perfect form εἴρηκα occurs in v. 14 to introduce John's speech. Osborne thinks the perfect is "out of place here."[52] But why must this be the case, apart from a misconception (temporal) of the meaning of the perfect tense? Though this has often been treated as another example of an "aoristic" use of the perfect,[53] the

---

[49] Aune, *Revelation 6–16*, 438.

[50] ἀριθμῆσαι is part of a complementary infinitive construction with ἐδύνατο in v. 9.

[51] Combining an outmoded and inconsistent *Aktionsart* with a temporal view of the aorist, Mounce comments that the aorist tense of the verbs "washed" and "made them white" "indicates once-for-all actions which took place in the past" (*Revelation*, 174).

[52] Osborne, *Revelation*, 323 n. 10.

[53] Fanning, *Verbal Aspect*, 303; Charles, *Revelation, I*, 212; Osborne, *Revelation*, 323 n. 10; Beckwith, *Apocalypse*, 544; Swete, *Apocalypse*, 102; Smalley, *Revelation*, 196; Aune, *Revelation 6–16*, 472. Aune says that "the juxtaposition of the perfect εἴρηκα, 'replied',

occurrence of the suppletive aorist form εἶπεν in the very next clause renders this unlikely and suggests a conscious semantic choice rather than a semantic blurring. As argued in the previous chapter, the perfect εἴρηκα in Revelation maintains its full semantic force. Bousset thinks that εἴρηκα "verlebendigt die Erzählung,"[54] which may be the case as long as such as observation is tied to verbal aspect and not an assumed temporal transfer of the perfect meaning temporally conceived. But perhaps there is some justification for Osborne's surprise at the perfect tense here: it seldom enters into narrative, and when it does, as the more marked form it draws attention unexpectedly to the action. The perfect may be used here to show John's surprise at being asked this question by the elder, since the elder should already possess (οἶδα) this knowledge.[55] The elder then responds with the less heavily marked aorist εἶπεν.

It is in 7.11 that we encounter the sole use of the pluperfect tense form, εἱστήκεισαν, in Revelation. This raises the question of whether it is possible to provide a rationale for the use of the pluperfect at this point. Campbell sees the pluperfect as indicating imperfective aspect and "heightened remoteness."[56] But given the understanding of the perfect articulated above, it is better to see the pluperfect tense form as indicating stative aspect with the additional semantic feature of remoteness.[57] The verb ἵστημι occurs frequently in Revelation in the perfect tense form (especially in participles) to depict the posture of various persons or groups, including angelic beings, especially in relationship to the throne. Yet as seen in the previous chapter it also occurs in the less heavily marked aorist form (cf. 8.3; 12.18; 18.17) and in the future (cf. 18.15). So it would appear that the choice of the pluperfect εἱστήκεισαν here in 7.11 is semantically motivated. Here it introduces the angelic beings who stand, which prepares them for the acts of falling (ἔπεσαν) and worshipping (προσεκύνησαν) summarized with the aorist aspect.[58] Since important

with the aorist εἶπεν, 'said' (v. 14b), suggests that the perfect functions as an aorist" (472). However, Aune's logic does not follow. The juxtaposition just as readily suggests a conscious semantic distinction.

[54] Bousset, *Offenbarung*, 285.

[55] For a similar explanation see Porter, *Verbal Aspect*, 279.

[56] Campbell, *Verbal Aspect*, 231.

[57] For discussion and statistics outside of the Gospels see Porter, *Verbal Aspect*, 289. Cf. Aune, *Revelation 6–16*, 430 for discussion of the pluperfect here, though he gives no clear rationale for its usage rather than the perfect here.

[58] Aune thinks that the pluperfect is used here because "it refers to the position the angels had before they fell down to worship God" (*Revelation 6–16*, 430). But this is too dependent on a temporal view of the pluperfect (a state existing in the past).

figures are often introduced with the stative form of this verb throughout
Revelation it is fitting here. Yet the author has chosen the more remote
pluperfect form so as not to displace the innumerable multitude which is
standing (ἑστῶτες) and is focal at this point.⁵⁹ Furthermore, the more
remote pluperfect form may be used because the angelic beings form
the outer ring around the throne, encircling the elders and the living
creatures. Thus they are "spatially" the furthest removed from the throne.
Though we are to perhaps envision the saints who stand before the throne
as encircling the throne, elders, creatures, and the angels, it is possible that
with the more remote pluperfect form the angles form the outer circle and
encircle the great multitude, though the author is probably unconcerned
with the precise spatial relation of the two groups at this point.⁶⁰

This section then ends in vv. 15–17 with a present tense form (λατρεύουσιν) followed by a cluster of future tense verb forms in vv. 15b–17.

> ¹⁵διὰ τοῦτό εἰσιν ἐνώπιον τοῦ θρόνου τοῦ θεοῦ καὶ *λατρεύουσιν* αὐτῷ
> ἡμέρας καὶ νυκτὸς ἐν τῷ ναῷ αὐτοῦ, καὶ ὁ καθήμενος ἐπὶ τοῦ θρόνου
> **σκηνώσει** ἐπ᾽ αὐτούς. ¹⁶οὐ **πεινάσουσιν** ἔτι οὐδὲ **διψήσουσιν** ἔτι οὐδὲ
> μὴ πέσῃ ἐπ᾽ ὁ ἥλιος οὐδὲ πᾶν καῦμα, ¹⁷ὅτι τὸ ἀρνίον τὸ ἀνὰ μέσον τοῦ
> θρόνου **ποιμανεῖ** οὐτοὺς καὶ **ὁδηγήσει** αὐτοὺς ἐπὶ ζωῆς πηγὰς ὑδάτων,
> καὶ **ἐξαλείψει** ὁ θεὸς πᾶν δάκρυον ἐκ τῶν ὀφθαλμῶν αὐτῶν.

The marked present tense λατρεύουσιν draws attention to the continual
(day and night) service of the great multitude. Regarding the future
tenses which follow, Aune concludes: "the future tenses describe the final
state of the innumerable host, but John does not actually claim to see
them enjoying that state."⁶¹ Aune may be correct, but this cannot be

---

⁵⁹ There are a number of occurrences of the pluperfect of ἵστημι in the LXX of Isaiah,
Ezekiel, and Daniel (the three books which have had a profound influence on Revelation).
Cf. Isa 6.2; Ezek 1.21; 3.23; 10.3, 9; 40.3; Dan 2.31; 12.5. The closest reference conceptually
and lexically is Isa. 6.2.

Isa 6.2 (LXX): καὶ Σεραφιμ εἱστήκεισαν κύκλῳ αὐτοῦ

Rev 7.11: καὶ πάντες οἱ ἄγγελοι εἱστήκεισαν κύκλῳ τοῦ θρόνου

However, the Isa 6.2 reference forms the intertextual backdrop for the author's description of the four living creatures in 4.6–8, which John clearly distinguishes from the angels
here in 7.11, making it unlikely that Isa 6.2 has directly influenced his use of the pluperfect
εἱστήκεισαν at this point.

⁶⁰ Aune, *Revelation 6–16*, 471; Smalley, *Revelation*, 193. Cf. the configuration in Rev
4.4–6; 5.6–14.

⁶¹ Aune, *Revelation 6–16*, 438. Aune goes on to explain that "the presence of this
innumerable host before God in the heavenly temple is *not* a final state of salvation, since
the destruction of the old heaven and earth and the creation of a new heaven and earth
provide the necessary setting for the earthy presence of the New Jerusalem" (438).

tied temporally to the presence of future verb forms. The solution lies in that verses 15–17 are still the speech of the elder. So this is not part of the narrated vision. Rather, they form the anticipation of what can be expected to take place. That is, the elder now articulates the expected reward of those seen in the vision in vv. 9–10. The presence of some of the future tense forms in vv. 15–17 may be due to Old Testament (LXX) influence.

σκηνώσει	Ezek 37.27 (LXX)[62]
πεινάσουσιν, διψήσουσιν	Isa 49.10 (LXX)[63]
ποιμανεῖ	Ezek 34.23 (LXX); Ps. 22.1 (LXX)

Further the future tense of these verbs may also function to anticipate their reappearance in future tense forms in the climactic segments of Revelation's vision.

σκηνώσει	21.3
ποιμανεῖ	19.15
ἐξαλείψει	21.4

Hence, the tense forms function to provide cohesion between earlier and later sections of the book. Altogether, this clustering of future tense forms indicates that the elder's speech presents these processes as things that God will do for his people. Thus the primary function of the present in contrast to the future forms is that the present λατρεύουσιν (v. 15, future referring or timeless-descriptive, see above) should be understood in terms of the present indicating what the people will do in response to God, and the futures used of what God can be expected to do for his people who serve him.[64] It is nevertheless clear that time cannot explain the tense usage in 7.9–17. Once again, verbal aspect and its ability to structure discourse and indicate prominence can explain the various tense forms throughout this visionary segment.

---

[62] Ezek 37.27 LXX does not have σκηνώσει, but does have the future ἔσομαι with κατεσκήνωσις. But John may be providing an independent rendering of the Hebrew text at this point: והיה משכן עליהם

[63] Cf. Charles, *Revelation*, I, 216.

[64] Dougherty, influenced by a temporal approach to the tense shift, concludes that the shift from the present to futures is a shift from time to intention ("Syntax," 431).

Revelation 9

Chapter 9 comprises a section that narrates the content of the fifth and sixth trumpet in the trumpet-plagues hepted. As such, this "doublet of judgments"[65] receives considerable expansion in comparison to the other members of the hepted. This expanded narration of the fifth and sixth trumpets exhibits numerous important tense changes that require explanation.

Verses 1–4 set the stage for this visionary segment with typical narrative aorist tense forms which form the backdrop for the unleashing of the fifth plague (ἐσάλπισεν, εἶδον, ἐδόθη, ἤνοιξεν, ἀνέβη, ἐσκοτώθη, ἐξῆλ-θον, ἐδόθη, ἐρρέθη). Yet in the midst of the aorists a perfect participle πεπτωκότα introduces a star as the object of John's vision. Commentaries typically observe that the significance of the perfect is that John does not actually see the star falling. Representative of a common explanation of the perfect form here, Aune concludes of the author, "he says only that he saw the star *after* it had fallen."[66] Yet this assessment depends on an inconsistently applied temporal scheme for understanding the perfect tense (as past act—which is apparently *not seen* here—with ongoing effects—which *are seen*) and misses the potential discourse significance of the perfect.[67] The use of the perfect at this point is more likely to draw attention to (frontground) the star since it will perform the crucial act of releasing the locusts from the abyss in the narrative which follows.

---

[65] Osborne, *Revelation*, 361.

[66] Aune, *Revelation 6–16*, 525; cf. Swete, *Apocalypse*, 112: "a star lying where it fell"; Beale, *Revelation*, 491; Blount, *Revelation*, 173; Mounce, *Revelation*, 192; Smalley, *Revelation*, 225; Kistemaker, *Revelation*, 285; Boxall, *Revelation*, 142. See Maximilian Zerwick and Mary Grosvenor, *A Grammatical Analysis of the Greek New Testament* (5th edn; Rome: EPIB, 1996) 755 who translate it *"that had fallen."* However, see Osborne (*Revelation*, 362 n. 7) who refers to Porter and recognizes that the notion "had fallen" is too time-based. He is virtually the only commentary I have found that entertains this possibility based on recent work on verbal aspect. Aune's initial discussion of verb tenses in his introduction begins with reference to Porter's work, but his explanation of the perfect here betrays his inability (or unwillingness) to shed traditional conceptions of the perfect tense.

[67] Aune's tacit admission in his introduction that the verb tenses signal aspect and not time should have been sufficient to dispel him of this notion. See also the confusion in Kistemaker, who says that the perfect *"had fallen* indicates that time had elapsed since its occurrence" (*Revelation*, 285). But this does not follow. His conception of the perfect is framed in temporal language.

The locusts' activity is then limited through instruction in the form of ἵνα and a future ἀδικήσουσιν (v. 4), a construction that functions imperatively.[68] Two further constructions with ἵνα follow in v. 5: ἵνα μὴ ἀποκτείνωσιν and ἵνα βασανισθήσονται, alternating aorist subjunctive and future forms. The future, rather than the subjunctive, in ἵνα clauses in Revelation occurs several times (cf. Rev 2.10; 3.8; 6.4, 11; 8.3; 9.4, 5, 20; 13.12; 14.13; 22.14).[69] The similar constructions should not be understood as proof of semantic blurring. Functional similarity does not necessitate lack of semantic differentiation. As Porter notes, "where a choice is offered between the Subjunctive and the Future, the Future is more heavily marked semantically."[70] The future with ἵνα in v. 4, then, is used to emphasize the limitation on the locust plagues—they are not permitted to harm the vegetation. Then the two contrasting forms in v. 5 refer to the limitation of the locusts in relationship to their permission to harm human beings. The aorist subjunctive ἀποκτείνωσιν is used of what they are not permitted to do, but which would be preferable to humanity, while the more marked future form βασανισθήσονται is used of what can certainly be expected, though it is the more terrifying of the two options for people: they will not suffer death, but they will be tormented (see v. 6).[71]

In v. 6, which is probably the author's "partial interpretation" of the vision,[72] the future forms function to indicate what one can expect to take place as a result of the limitations in vv. 4–5: ζητήσουσιν, εὑρήσουσιν, ἐπιθυμήσουσιν. Edmondo F. Lupieri explains the future tenses here as an example of "tense interchange" (ἐναλλαγή).[73] That is, though

---

[68] On the imperatival function of the future here see Porter, *Verbal* Aspect, 420; Smalley, *Revelation*, 206; The future ἀδικήσουσιν in A 025 fam 1611 2351 is to be preferred to the aorist subjunctive ἀδικήσωσιν in ℵ 0207 Andreas Byzantine. See Aune, *Revelation 6–16*, 486; Smalley, *Revelation*, 206.

[69] For this phenomenon in Revelation see Porter, *Verbal Aspect*, 414–416; Robertson, *Grammar*, 960–961; BDF §§ 369, 378; Mussies, *Morphology*, 242; Aune, *Revelation 1–5*, clxxxvi; Dougherty, "Syntax," 416–417.

[70] Porter, *Verbal Aspect*, 414.

[71] Though there is evidence for ἵνα + future tense in the LXX (see Conybeare and Stock, *Grammar*, 93), since this construction was not unknown in Hellenistic Greek, and since confusion of the future and subjunctive was well-known even in Classical Greek (cf. the discussion in Porter, *Verbal Aspect*, 414–416; Aune, *Revelation 1–5*, clxxxvi), it is unnecessary to conclude along with Beale, following Thompson (*Semitic Syntax*, 98–99), that this construction constitutes a "stylistic Semitism" (*Revelation*, 496).

[72] Beale, *Revelation*, 498.

[73] Lupieri, *Apocalypse*, 162: "The visionary sees events that take place that he later refers to as being in his own past because it was in the past when he saw them, although

the events were in the past from the perspective of when the author saw them, they are future with regard to time. Thus the future tense is used deliberately to indicate events which are future, while the aorist reflects the past time of the vision, while still referring to future events. But this temporally confusing explanation assumes that the tenses were selected primarily for their temporal values. This string of futures climaxes with a present tense form φεύγει. Dougherty explains the present tense as rhetorical, more vivid, reflecting a temporal orientation to the present tense form.[74] Rather, the future tense forms indicate what humanity will do due to the pain inflicted by the locusts. The present φεύγει, then, is used to highlight what death will do: the awful reality is that it will flee.[75] The locusts and their activity are then described in vv. 7–11. A perfect participle (stative aspect) is used to highlight their preparedness (ἡτοιμασμένοις) for war. The subsequent verses in this section further describe this state of preparedness with verbs in the imperfective aspect. Here the author utilizes both the imperfect and present tense forms of ἔχω.[76] In vv. 8–9 the imperfect εἶχον is used, whereas the author shifts to present forms, ἔχουσιν, in vv. 10–11. The imperfect forms in vv. 8–9, over against the aorist, foreground the description of the locusts.[77] While it is possible that the switch to the present tense forms in vv. 10–11 elicits a sense of immediacy, this overlooks the aspectual force of the present.[78] Rather, though there is no aspectual contrast in the two forms (both grammaticalize imperfective aspect), there is a semantic opposition at the level of +remoteness/-remoteness. The remote imperfect forms, then, are used to describe important features of the locusts (vv. 8–9) to set the stage for the present forms which follow. The non-remote present forms are reserved for their ability to harm humanity under their nefarious leader (vv. 10–11), recalling their main purpose back in v. 5.

---

the events that he foresaw are themselves in the future with regard to the time, whether real or fictitious, at which the vision occurs."

[74] See similarly Dougherty, "Syntax," 433. Charles incorrectly describes this as a "present of habitual avoidance" (*Revelation*, I, 244).

[75] *Contra* Osborne, whose interpretation of the present is incorrectly determined by both time and *Aktionsart*: "John has deliberately switched from future tenses to a dramatic present here, picturing death as it 'keeps on fleeing' away from them" (*Revelation*, 369).

[76] Cf. Dougherty, "Syntax," 433–434.

[77] Porter, *Verbal Aspect*, 199; cf. Aune, *Revelation 1–5*, clxxxvi. Kistemaker says that the imperfect here "'is sort of a moving panorama'" quoting Robertson (*Revelation*, 293).

[78] Kistemaker, *Revelation*, 293; Smalley, *Revelation*, 233.

Verses 13–19 contain a narrative of the sixth trumpet plague. Aorist tense forms predominate in the narration of this plague. Two perfect participles, δεδεμένους and ἠτοιμασμένοι, function to introduce new and significant actors in the drama. Furthermore, two significant present tense forms function to foreground important activities in the midst of the narrative aorists which focus on the harm they inflict on humanity. In v. 17 the present ἐκπορεύεται climaxes the description of the army with a reference to the three plagues that proceed from their mouths, emphasizing this means by which humanity is killed (ἀπεκτάνθησαν) in v. 18 (cf. ἐκπορευομένου).[79] The shift from present to aorist in vv. 17 and 18 is not to be understood, along with Dougherty, as a shift from description to narration, but as a shift from the more marked term used to describe and highlight the means by which humanity is killed, to the less marked aorist which summarizes their effect.[80] The other present indicative form occurs at the end of v. 19, highlighting their ability to inflict harm (ἀδικοῦσιν). In v. 20 another future form occurs after ἵνα in a clause expressing result.[81] The future προσκυνήσουσιν emphasizes the surprising result of the harm done to humans by the locusts: failure of the rest to turn from worshiping idols. While Ch. 9 consists of a vision within a unified narrative framework (though v. 6 may consist of the author's own commentary), this section exhibits a tense variation that does not lend itself easily to temporally oriented explanations. Rather, the variations are explicable in light of verbal aspect and the author's desire to attach significance to certain processes within the discourse by means of grammaticalizing his perspective on the actions.

Revelation 11.1–13

This section of Revelation, which occurs within an "interlude" within the seals, trumpets, bowls structure, presents an interesting patterning of tense forms. Verses 1–10 are characterized by a combination primarily of present and future tense forms. Verses 11–13, then, conclude with a string of aorist tense forms. Charles concluded that with regard to its use of verb tenses this section "seems to be very confused" and reflects "no unity of time."[82] Dougherty is likewise unsure how to explain the

---

[79] Porter, *Verbal Aspect*, 197: a "climactic reference."
[80] See Dougherty, "Syntax," 434.
[81] Aune, *Revelation 6–16*, 542.
[82] Charles, *Revelation, I*, cxxiii n. 1.

alternation of tense forms, and sees this section as an example of an "Inconsistency" in tense usage.[83] As we will see below, such confusion is unnecessary if the verb tenses are seen as indicating aspect rather than strict temporal reference.

Before we examine the usage of tense forms in this section, two preliminary, somewhat related issues need to be addressed. 1) There appears to be some dispute as to the literary character of this segment: should 11.1–13 be characterized as a narrative account of a vision, or is it of a different literary character, since it lacks the characteristic καὶ εἶδον which customarily introduces John's visionary material?[84] Charles thought that 11.1–13 was a prophecy rather than a vision.[85] Thus the present and aorist tense forms (in vv. 11–13) should be understood as futuristic. Aune likewise argues that the "entire section is presented not as a vision that John saw and is now reporting but as a narrative prophesy focusing on the two witnesses."[86] Bauckham also supposes that 11.1–13 is not a vision but a narrative prophecy, and characterizes 11.3–13 as a sort of parable.[87] This section concludes with what is most likely a series of narrative aorists (vv. 11–13), leading Aune to assert without explanation, "Somewhat surprisingly, this section [vv. 11–13] is dominated by verbs in the past tense, as if it were a narrative of a past sequence of events."[88] McKay thought that v. 1a and vv. 11–13 constitute the narrative section of this vision. In between there is an audition (v. 1b–3) followed by an explanation (v. 4), and possibly a prophecy of John (vv. 5–10). The narration is then resumed in v. 11 not from the standpoint of v. 1a but following the prophetic detail in vv. 5–10.[89] Thus the aspectual usage is what we would expect: aorists in the narration, presents and futures in the audition and prophetic sections from the standpoint of the speaker. Therefore, it appears that 11.1–13 is somewhat unique in the Apocalypse in that it does not constitute a vision per se, but a symbolic, narrative prophesy.[90]

---

[83] Dougherty, "Syntax," 435–436.

[84] "Der Seher sieht zwei Zeugen" (Bousset, *Offenbarung*, 317). Cf. Smalley, *Revelation*, 269. Other commentaries seem to merely assume that 11.1–13 records a vision and describe it as such.

[85] Charles, *Revelation, I*, cxxiii n. 1.

[86] Aune, *Revelation 6–16*, 585.

[87] Bauckham, *Climax*, 267, 274: "The story is more like a parable, which dramatizes the nature and result of the church's prophetic witness to the nations" (274).

[88] Aune, *Revelation 6–16*, 587.

[89] McKay, "Time and Aspect," 224.

[90] Bousset labels it a "Zukunftsweisagung" (*Offenbarung*, 325), though his temporal language is probably too strong.

However, as Aune notes, the prophecy, which commences with future and present tense forms (vv. 3–10), ends with a series of narrative aorists (vv. 11–13).[91] McKay is likely correct that the aorists in vv. 11–13 resume the narrative (v. 1a), but from the perspective of the prophetic section (vv. 4–10), though below I will explore an additional, possible reason for the shift to the aorists. The ensuing discussion will attempt to give an account for the aspectual usage across these segments.

2) A further related issue is the extent of the voice that speaks to the seer beginning in v. 1.[92] It is extremely difficult to determine where this voice ends. 11.1b begins with an unidentified voice which addresses the seer which continues at least through v. 3.[93] Verse 3 addresses the seer in the first person (δώσω, "I will give;" cf. also μου). It is not necessary to settle on the precise identity of the voice, but to note that the extent of the speech is not clear, though most assume that it ends at v. 4, since the rest of the section is cast in the third person. The deictic reference to "their Lord" (ὁ κύριος αὐτῶν) in v. 8 might suggest that the narrative has been resumed at least at this point.[94] However, I will follow those commentaries who see the voice ending with v. 3, and John's own prophecy beginning with v. 4 with John's own description of the two witnesses with the οὗτοί εἰσιν.[95]

In vv. 1–2 the narrative aorist tense form (ἐδόθη) sets the stage for the commands of the voice which are dominated by aorist tense imperative forms (μέτρησον, ἔκβαλε, μετρήσῃς [aorist subjunctive in negation], and the reason for the commands, ἐδόθη). The imperative in the more heavily marked present tense ἔγειρε is perhaps used to highlight the urgency of performing the following commands in the less heavily marked aorist (μέτρησον, ἔκβαλε).[96] The aorists then give way to

---

[91] Aune, *Revelation 6–16*, 586–587. Aune does conclude regarding 11.1–13 that "John has couched this narrative in a style very similar to the visions found in the rest of the book" (585). See also Pattemore, *Souls under the Altar*, 136.

[92] I will not address the issue of the ostensible underlying sources for 11.1–2, 3–13. I will treat them as a literary unity in the form in which they are now found in Revelation. For a source-critical perspective see Aune, *Revelation 6–16*, 588–593; Charles, *Revelation*, I, 269–273.

[93] Cf. Smalley, *Revelation*, 275.

[94] Aune, *Revelation 6–16*, 585.

[95] Aune, *Revelation 6–16*, 586.

[96] *Contra* Dougherty, "Syntax," 488, who sees the present and aorist used in parallel here as an indication of no significant difference between the tense forms. However, Dougherty incorrectly assumes that use in similar contexts implies lack of semantic

futures in vv. 2c–3 which indicate what can be expected to take place, which are suitable for a prophetic speech. The outer court of the temple will be trampled (πατήσουσιν) and there will be two witnesses who will prophesy (δώσω, προφητεύσουσιν), preparing for the ensuing narrative prophesy of the two witnesses. The two witnesses, introduced here for the first time, are referred to with two perfect participles in vv. 3–4 which focus attention on them; like other important figures in Revelation they are identified by their clothing and posture (περιβεβλημένοι, ἑστῶτες), the latter emphasizing their heavenly origin, their priestly role, or the sphere of their testimony, and probably also their resistance.[97] The clothing of the two witnesses (σάκκους) is emphasized because it indicates the nature of their ministry: they are primarily God's agents of judgment as is borne out in the following verses.[98]

Following the introduction of the witnesses, vv. 5–10, then, describe the witnesses, their activity, and their rejection by those who dwell on the earth, with present and future tense forms predominating. Temporally, as a prophecy this section is either timeless or future. The present tense forms function to describe the witnesses and their activities, while the futures emphasize what can be expected to take place. Verse 5 begins with a conditional sentence which stipulates and emphasizes what happens (ἐκπορεύεται, κατεσθίει) to anyone who desires (θέλει) to harm the two witnesses with verbs in the present tense. The second conditional statement repeats the first one, and is formed with an aorist tense form in the protasis (θελήσῃ) and an aorist infinitive in the construction δεῖ ... ἀποκτανθῆναι. The latter conditional structure summarizes the first one, thus the summary aorist forms. Two present tense forms of ἔχουσιν, then, further highlight the authority possessed by the two witnesses (v. 6), and are either timeless-descriptive or future referring.

In a transition to the mistreatment and rejection of the two witnesses, v. 7 begins with a conditional-like construction, similar to that found in 4.9–10, with ὅταν τελέσωσιν. The future tense forms (ποιήσει, νικήσει,

---

distinction. The parallel use of the present and aorist imperatives here are due to verbal aspect, or the author's conception of the process. See Mathewson, "Aspect in Imperatival Constructions."

[97] Cf. Osborne, *Revelation*, 420–422. For the notion of resistance see Blount, *Revelation*, 111. The LXX of Zech 4.14, to which this verse alludes, has παρεστήκασιν.

[98] Cf. C. Brütsch, *Die Offenbarung Jesu Christi* (Zürcher Bibelkommentare: Zürich: Zwingli, 1970) II: 21; A. Satake, *Die Gemeindeordnung in der Johannesapokalypse* (WMANT 21; Neukirchen: Neukirchener, 1966) 119–133; Beale, *Revelation*, 576. *Contra* those who emphasize a message of repentance ("Bußprediger").

ἀποκτενεῖ) which follow indicate what can be expected to take place
when the condition in the ὅταν clause is fulfilled (cf. 4.9–10). In v. 8
the city is identified with the present form καλεῖται, whereas the background aorist is used to summarize what they already know: it is the
place where Christ was crucified (ἐσταυρώθη). Present tense forms once
again proliferate and descriptively highlight the response of the nations
to the death of the two witnesses in vv. 9–10 (βλέπουσιν, ἀφίουσιν, χαίρουσιν, εὐφραίνονται). The perfect infinitive τεθῆναι following ἀφίουσιν is an emphatic construction, drawing attention to the extent of the
mistreatment of the two witnesses: refusal of burial.[99] The present tense
forms are probably future referring temporally, as suggested by the future
tense form that concludes the verb sequence (πέμψουσιν), though the
primary information they convey is aspectual. Aspectually, the present
tense forms function to describe and highlight the response of the people, while the future form indicates what can be expected of those who
see the bodies of the two witnesses and emphasizes the extent of their
rejoicing (πέμψουσιν). An aorist form ἐβασάνισαν in a supporting ὅτι
clause states the reason for the rejoicing, summarizing the activity of the
witnesses from vv. 5–6.[100]

With vv. 11–13 the narrative aorist tense form returns and rounds
off this segment: ... εἰσῆλθεν ... καὶ ἔστησαν ... καὶ ... ἐπέπεσεν
.... καὶ ἤκουσαν .... καὶ ἀνέβησαν ... καὶ ἐθεώρησαν .... καὶ ...
ἐγένετο ... καὶ ... ἔπεσεν καὶ ἀπεκτάνθησαν ... καὶ ... ἐγένοντο
καὶ ἔδωκαν ..... Though above it was suggested that the aorists resume
the narration, it is plausible, following Charles, that the aorists should
all be taken as future referring, since this whole section comprises a
prophecy uttered by John.[101] The concluding aorists, then, summarize
what will take place. However, the clustering of aorists probably implicate
past time narrative. As McKay has suggested, they pick up and resume
the narrative framework begun back in 11.1.[102] At this point the author

---

[99] Porter, *Verbal Aspect*, 280: "The bodies are not the point of interest ... but the people
who do not allow the burial." As Aune comments, "To leave a body unburied in the
ancient world was understood as an outrage; it was done to express great anger against
the deceased" (*Revelation 6–16*, 622). Zerwick and Grosvenor incorrectly parse τεθῆναι
as an aorist form (*Grammatical Analysis*, 759).

[100] Mussies incorrectly classifies this as a future referring aorist (*Morphology*, 339).
However, in the narrative sequence it refers back to and summarizes the activity of the
two witnesses in vv. 5–6.

[101] See Charles, *Revelation*, I, cxxiii.

[102] McKay, "Time and Aspect," 224. Cf. also Mussies, *Morphology*, 339.

reverts to his narrative style reflected in the visions which form the basis for Revelation overall.[103] In addition, the aorist tenses and transition to the narrative framework in this final section may have been influenced by John's allusive appeal to the Old Testament. Verse 11 has the spirit of life entering (εἰσῆλθεν) the two witnesses so that they stand (ἔστησαν) upon their feet. This verse alludes intertextually to Ezek 37.10, as indicated by the close lexical correspondences:[104]

> Rev 11.11: πνεῦμα ζωῆς ... εἰσῆλθεν ἐν αὐτοῖς, καὶ ἔστησαν ἐπι τοὺς πόδας αὐτῶν.
> Ezek 37.10: εἰσῆλθεν εἰς αὐτοὺς τὸ πνεῦμα καὶ ... ἔστησαν ἐπὶ τῶν ποδῶν αὐτῶν.

Following the allusion to Ezek 37.10, the author, perhaps triggered by the narrative in Ezek 37.10, then switches to narrative aorists for the remainder of this segment.

Based on aspect distribution this section (vv. 4–10) stands out in contrast to the final section, vv. 11–13, where the background aorist tense form predominates in the depiction of the vindication of the two witnesses and the response of the people. The aorists occur in rapid succession in vv. 10–13 (εἰσῆλθεν, ἔστησαν, ἐπέπεσεν, ἤκουσαν, ἀνέβησαν, ἐθεώρησαν, ἐγένετο, ἔπεσεν, ἀπεκτάνθησαν, ἐγένοντο, ἔδωκαν). By contrast, the present and future tense forms (as well as non-indicative perfect tense forms in vv. 3–4) predominated in the previous section, vv. 3–10, singling out features that are depicted in more detail, or which can be expected to occur. This suggests that the focus in 11.1–13 linguistically and thematically is on the *description* and ministry of the witnesses, yet their expected rejection and mistreatment by the beast and his followers, as Aune correctly recognizes.[105] Their vindication and the response of the nations to judgment are recorded with the less heavily marked aorists. Though Bauckham places most of the emphasis in this section on the vindication of the witnesses and the conversion of the nations, the function of aspect suggests that the main theme of this section, then, is the

---

[103] Cf. Aune, *Revelation 6–16*, 585: "Despite the nonvisionary character of 11:1–13, John has couched this narrative in a style very similar to the visions found in the rest of the book."
[104] Cf. Aune, *Revelation 6–16*, 623; Beale, *Revelation*, 597; Lupieri, *Apocalypse*. 181.
[105] "The focus ... is ... on the fact that whatever it [the message of the two witnesses] is, it will surely be rejected as they themselves will be" (Aune, *Revelation 6–16*, 612). Cf. Smalley, *Revelation*, 275.

suffering and martyrdom of the two witnesses.[106] As with previous sections of Revelation, the tense forms communicate the author's perspective on the various processes that form this unit.

Revelation 12–13

Though Chs. 12–13 raise a number of questions regarding intertextuality, source-criticism, and their relationship to the structure of the book as a whole, for our purposes it is sufficient to note that in their present form these two chapters present a seamless unity.[107] Though not always supported with clear linguistic evidence, these two chapters are frequently characterized as the literary and thematic centerpiece of the entire book.[108] They explore at a deeper level the nature of the church's conflict as described in Ch. 11. As with the other visionary pieces, the verb tense forms play a significant role in structuring the discourse. I will once again focus primarily on verb forms in the indicative mood.

Chapter 12

Rather than the active form εἶδον 12.1 commences with the aorist passive ὤφθη which summarizes the vision which John saw and introduces the first main character of the vision, the woman clothed with the sun.[109] It recurs in v. 3 (ὤφθη) to introduce the second main character of this visionary piece, the dragon. Further, the aorist ἤκουσα found in v. 10 introduces an audition (vv. 10–12), marking off a further section. Additionally, aorist tense forms characteristically carry the story line throughout Ch. 12, summarizing the main events of the visionary narrative. They are particularly clustered in vv. 7–9, which narrates the battle between

---

[106] *Contra* Bauckham (*Climax*, 273–283).

[107] For a discussion of some of these issues see Aune, *Revelation 6–16*, 660–676. On the coherence of this section cf. Beale, *Revelation*, 621–624; Smalley, *Revelation*, 310–312. Aune sees 11.19–12.17 and 12.18–13.18 as two coherent units which redactionally have been linked by 12.18 (*Revelation 6–16*, 725).

[108] Osborne, *Revelation*, 454.

[109] ὤφθη is used elsewhere in Revelation only in 11.19. Cf. Dan 8.1. For a possible explanation for the usage of the passive form over against the more usual εἶδον, see Blount, *Revelation*, 224–225. Blount suggests that the passive forms here are used because the author wants to draw attention to cosmic woman and dragon, and not to himself. However, one wonders why this would not be the case in John's visions of equally significant objects elsewhere in Revelation.

Satan and Michael and the subsequent casting down of Satan, and in
vv. 13–17, which narrates Satan's attempt to destroy the woman and
her offspring after his expulsion from heaven. The more heavily marked
present and perfect tense forms are used for descriptive color and to
highlight and draw attention to certain processes within the discourse
against the backdrop of the aorist forms.

The first major visionary feature, the woman, is introduced with a perfect participle, περιβεβλημένη, which depicts the woman in the state of
being clothed with the constellations (v. 1). The narrative present κράζει
highlights the agony of the woman, and the present participles ἔχουσα,
ὠδίνουσα, and βασανιζομένη describe her condition of imminent deliv-
ery and her consequent pain for which she cries out (v. 2).[110] The narrative
use of the present tense σύρει is also used to draw attention to one particularly salient action of the dragon in v. 4. Dougherty finds it perplexing
that the present and aorist would both be used in v. 4 in narration, and
concludes that "either a present tense verb is narrative or an aorist verb is
descriptive, or there is an abrupt and brief shift from description to narrative," and Osborne thinks this is a "strange concantenation of tenses."[111]
However, Dougherty's perplexity and Osborne's perceived strangeness
are viable only given a strictly temporal orientation to the tenses. In v. 4
σύρει highlights the incredible power of the dragon (the aorist ἔβαλεν
simply records what he then did with the stars) perhaps to contrast with
the magnificent crown of twelve *stars* on the woman's head.[112] The perfect
tense ἕστηκεν locates the dragon before the woman and frontgrounds his
malicious intention which will be described in more detail in the remainder of the chapter. It may also cohesively serve to highlight the contrast

---

[110] Smalley incorrectly seems to include the participles along with "historical presents"
(*Revelation*, 316). He further invests them with the notions of providing immediacy and
pace to the action. This may be true, but it would be based on the aspect of the present
tense, not a temporal or *Aktionsart* explanation.

[111] Cf. Dougherty, "Syntax," 437; Osborne, *Revelation*, 461 n. 5 respectively. As seen
with other such judgments on the tenses in Revelation, apart from temporal criteria for
evaluating the tense forms these assessments are misguided and unnecessary.

[112] Blount (*Revelation*, 230) suggests that "Part of the celestial woman's magnificence is
the crown of twelve stars that she wears on her head. The dragon is unimpressed. It has
the power to sweep a third of the stars from the sky with a flick of its tail." Cf. LXX Dan
8.10. σύρει and κράζει (Rev. 12. 2) are clear examples of the past referring usage of the
present ("narrative present"). Cf. Smalley, *Revelation*, 318. Relying on the usual temporal
definitions, Beale, drawing on Mussies (*Morphology*, 334–336), thinks that the presents
indicate action "seen again in his mind's eye" (*Revelation*, 639).

with the posture of the Lamb and his followers who "stand" (cf. 5.6; 7.9; 11.4). Furthermore, v. 6 is a prominent section within this stretch of discourse:

καὶ ἡ γυνὴ ἔφυγεν εἰς τὴν ἔρημον, ὅπου **ἔχει** ἐκεῖ τόπον **ἡτοιμασμένον** ἀπὸ τοῦ θεοῦ, ἵνα ἐκεῖ **τρέφωσιν** αὐτὴν ἡμέρας χιλίας διακοσίας ἑξήκοντα.

In the midst of narrative aorists, the combination of the present ἔχει and the perfect participle ἡτοιμασμένον, along with the present subjunctive τρέφωσιν, functions to focus attention on the divine preservation of the woman (v. 6) in the face of the dragon's nefarious activities.

Verses 7–12 constitute a heavenly battle scene followed by its hymnic commentary.[113] The heavenly battle that ensues in heaven (vv. 7–9) is narrated in a succession of aorist tenses. Aorist tense forms also predominate in the audition (vv. 10–12), though one particularly significant present tense form is found in the imperative εὐφραίνεσθε in v. 12. The rejoicing of heaven at the downfall of Satan is prominent, and is contrasted with the woe (οὐαί) directed to the earthly sphere, and perhaps also forges a contrast with the rejoicing of the world at the fate of the two witnesses back in 11.10: the tables are turned.[114] The present tense is also used to foreground the reason for the dragon's fury (ἔχει), though from the standpoint of the speakers of the hymn temporally it may describe what the dragon knows to be presently true. As mentioned above, aorist tense forms also predominate in the closing events of vv. 13–17, which narrates the dragon's attempt to destroy the woman and her offspring. In this final section, however, two present tense forms occur (πέτηται [subjunctive], τρέφεται) in order to once again highlight the preservation of the woman (v. 14). The episode ends with the aorist ἐστάθη, which summarizes the dragon's posture in preparation for the emergence of two additional figures in the ensuing visionary narrative (Ch. 13). Thus in addition to introducing and describing important features of the woman and dragon, the present tense forms (ἔχει, τρέφωσιν, τρέφεται, πέτηται) and a perfect participle (ἡτοιμασμένον) are used primarily to highlight an important feature of this vision, the protection of the woman in the face of the dragon's attempt to exterminate her.

---

[113] Aune, *Revelation 6–16*, 663.
[114] Beale, *Revelation*, 667.

Chapter 13

The visionary drama continues uninterrupted with the introduction of two additional beastly figures who will aid the dragon's malicious plans to destroy the woman and her offspring. The main structure of the vision is indicated by the aorist εἶδον, introducing and summarizing the two beastly figures which John saw (vv. 1, 11). As is expected, the main events and story line are summarized with aorist tense forms throughout. The first beast's activities in vv. 1–8 are narrated with indicative verbs in the aorist tense, the standard narrative tense form. While no present tense forms in the indicative mood are used of his activity, present tense participles are used to describe selected features of the beast: his origin (ἀναβαῖνον), his appearance (ἔχον), and his speaking blasphemies (λαλοῦν). But a perfect participle, ἐσφαγμένην, is used in v. 3 to draw attention to a particularly salient feature of the beast, one of his heads appeared in the state of being slain, which functions to link this feature of the beast to the description of Christ in 5.6 (ἐσφαγμένον; cf. 5.12). Thus the use of the perfect here forms and highlights an important intratextual link and "is an intended parody of the Lamb in 5:6."[115] This link is made clear within Ch. 13 itself, where the Lamb is depicted as ἐσφαγμένου (13.8) which also recalls 5.6 (ἐσφαγμένον). Following a string of aorists, the author climaxes the discussion of the beast's activities with a future tense form, προσκυνήσουσιν (v. 8).[116] The future emphasizes the universal worship of the beast that can be expected to take place. The theme of the universal worship of the first beast is continued by identifying the followers of the beast in opposition to the saints: their names are not recorded (γέγραπται) in the book of life. The book in whose names the worshippers of the beast are not written, belongs to the slain (ἐσφαγμένου) Lamb, a description which, as seen above, contrasts with the beast whose head was described as ἐσφαγμένην (v. 3).

Verses 9–10 are of a different character than vv. 1–8 and consist of a series of conditional statements that are temporally unrestricted. The first is an exhortation to hear (ἀκουσάτω) with the present ἔχει being used to emphasize the insight necessary to heed the warning in the

---

[115] Beale, *Revelation*, 689.

[116] The present participle λαλοῦν in v. 5 may be significant in that it introduces and draws attention to the beasts activity of speaking which is described in the rest of vv. 5–6. On the other hand, it may only be due to a conscious allusion to LXX Dan 7.8, 20 which John seems to have reproduced verbatim: Daniel refers to a στόμα λαλοῦν μεγάλα.

following verse, though it is possible that John is simply reflecting the similar saying of Jesus found in the Synoptics (Matt 13.43; Mark 4.9, 23; Luke 8.8), accounting for the present ἔχει. Mark 4.9, 23 are the closest to Rev 13.9 since they exhibit a conditional structure with the present tense ἔχει in the protasis.[117] The second conditional in v. 10 also contains a temporally unrestricted present form, ὑπάγει, emphasizing the fate of believers, though it is possible that ὑπάγει is future in its temporal sphere of reference.[118] The more marked presents draw attention to the urgency of the exhortation.

The final section of this chapter (vv. 11–18) introduces and describes the second beast and his activities. While indicative aorist tense verbs dominated in vv. 1–8, present and imperfect tense forms are more frequent in this section. As we have already noted, the aorist εἶδον introduces a new scene structurally within the visionary narrative.[119] Aorist tense verb forms then carry the story line throughout.[120] Against this backdrop of the aorists there are several significant occurrences of present and imperfect forms. The beast is introduced in v. 11 with two imperfect tense forms: εἶχεν and ἐλάλει.[121] The imperfect grammaticalizes the semantic features of imperfective viewpoint and remoteness.[122] Here they function to provide the setting for the description of the second beast with present tense forms. Thus the beast's description as "having" two horns and his activity of "speaking" are highlighted over against the aorist forms, yet the present tenses which follow to describe in more detail the beast's activities are the more marked forms.[123]

---

[117] Yet it is possible that John's use of tense forms here is still deliberate. All the Synoptics have a slightly different structure for this saying. Matt 13.43; Luke 8.8 have a present participle ὁ ἔχων. All of them have the imperative in the present (ἀκουέτω), and all include an infinite modifying "ears" (ἀκούειν). This may suggest that while John is dependent on the logion of Jesus, he is providing his own rendering, including his choice of tense forms.

[118] John is drawing on similar statements in LXX Jer 15.2; 50.11. However, neither includes a verb.

[119] Aune, Revelation 1–5, 338.

[120] For John's ἐδόθη (vv. 14, 15) see LXX Dan 7.6b: τῷ θηρίῳ καὶ γλῶσσα ἐδόθη αὐτῷ.

[121] The aorist subjunctive form λαλήσῃ occurs in v. 15. Charles' speculation about a Hebrew original behind ἐλάλει is unnecessary (Revelation, I, 358).

[122] Over against the aorist they are more marked forms, depicting key features of the beast; yet they are "used in contexts where the action is seen as more remote than the action described by the (non-remote) present" (Porter, Verbal Aspect, 207).

[123] Though it is possible that John's imperfect εἶχεν is due to LXX Dan 7.7: εἶχε … κέρατα. For John's dependence on LXX Daniel in Ch. 13 see Beale, Revelation, 683–718.

The key word that appears in the present aspect in vv. 12–18 is ποιεῖ, which occurs in vv. 12 (2×), 13 (also in the subjunctive, ποιῇ), and 16.[124] Two other present tense forms in narration are also found in v. 14: πλανᾷ, ἔχει. Osborne attempts to provide a rationale for the present tense forms by suggesting that they are "undoubtedly for greater vividness in describing the ongoing work of the Antichrist and his false prophet."[125] However, while the present may provide a touch of vividness (or better, prominence), Osborne's conception is based on a dubious view of the present tense motivated by *Aktionsart* (ongoing action). Also reflecting an overreliance on temporality is Dougherty, who finds it strange that present tense forms (ποιεῖ, πλανᾷ) would be found in narrative.[126] Porter suggests that ποιεῖ functions to mark out individual subunits within the larger unit of discourse.[127]

The present aspects in this section are explicable in light of verbal aspect. They appear significant in two respects. First, there is a chain of command evident in this passage, where the dragon gives his authority to the first beast (13.2), who now gives all authority to the second beast (13.11). So it is ultimately through the last member of the trio that the dragon's nefarious activity is carried out.[128] The more heavily marked presents function to foreground the second beast's activity as the working out of the authority of the dragon mediated through the first beast.

Second, it appears that Porter is correct in seeing ποιεῖ as a structuring device which marks out subunits within the broader unit of discourse in 13.11–18. In each subunit the first beast is mentioned as the focus of the second beast's activity. After the second beast's introduction and description in v. 11, the main emphasis of v. 12 is the second beast's relationship with the first. Two occurrences of ποιεῖ in v. 12 draw attention to the worldwide activity of the second beast on behalf of the first one (ἐξουσίαν τοῦ πρώτου θηρίου). The future προσκυνήσουσιν with ἵνα emphasizes

---

[124] ποιέω occurs in the aorist tense as both an infinitive (ποιῆσαι, v. 14 [2×]) and a subjunctive (ποιήσῃ, v. 15) to refer to the same activities as the presents. John's ποιεῖ σημεῖα μέγλα in v. 13 probably reflects LXX Dan 4.37a: ποιῆσαι σημεῖα καὶ θαυμάσια μεγάλα. But John has the present in contrast to Daniel's aorist. Cf. Beale, *Revelation*, 709. Dougherty's perplexity over the apparent use of the "imperfect in description" and the "present in narration" shows the extent to which his theory has too heavily influenced his analysis (see "Syntax," 438–439).

[125] Osborne, *Revelation*, 512.

[126] Dougherty, "Syntax," 439. He also finds it odd that aorists and imperfects would be found in a descriptive section (13.11).

[127] Porter, *Verbal Aspect*, 197.

[128] Cf. esp. Osborne, *Revelation*, 512.

the extent of the first beast's authority: universal worship. The following verses describe specifically the activity of the second beast on behalf of its master. In vv. 13–15, which is introduced by the third occurrence of ποιεῖ, the primary emphasis in both verses is on the signs and wonders performed by the beast. The intention of these sinister deeds is to deceive the whole world, indicated with the marked present tense form πλανᾷ, the present tense tying in his activity with the dragon (cf. 12.9, ὁ πλανῶν). This is further reflected in the setting up of an image of the first beast and demanding worship (v. 15). The present ἔχει also occurs in v. 14, continuing the theme of deception by drawing attention to the first beast's ostensible invincibility: he survives a death blow. The final section marked off by ποιεῖ is vv. 16–17, which narrates the activity of the second beast in causing all to receive a mark of the first beast on their hand or forehead. Thus ποιεῖ does appear to mark off three separate subunits: vv. 12; 13–15; 16–17, all dealing with the activity of the second beast as the authoritative representative of the first beast and the dragon.[129] The present tense functions to foreground this activity.

Perhaps the reason for the predominance of present forms in vv. 11–16, over against the aorists in vv. 1–9, is that this is where the situation is most applicable and relevant to the readers in Asia Minor (cf. Chs. 2–3). In other words, it is the second beast that executes the deceptive activity of the dragon and first beast immediately and locally among the readers located in Asia Minor. As Blount explains, with this second beast

> John probably had in mind the people and the infrastructure that institutionally embodied Asia Minor's commitment to the imperial cult. Rome, as the beast from the sea, is a foreign force. Land based, the false prophet has more of an indigenous feel; he rises up out of the very soil on which John's hearers and readers have built their lives and homes. This beast is local.[130]

---

[129] For the same division see rightly Osborne, *Revelation*, 512–516. *Contra* Aune, *Revelation 6–16*, 794–795, who seems unaware of the importance of ποιεῖ as a structuring device.

[130] Blount, *Revelation*, 257. Cf. also Steven J. Friesen, *Imperial Cults and the Apocalypse of John: Reading Revelation in the Ruins* (New York: Oxford University Press, 2001) 188. "Das erste Tier bleibt nicht allein. Allein könnte es für die Christen in Kleinasien auch kaum eine Gefahr sein. Ein zweites Tier tritt auf, das seine Macht dem ersten verdankt" (H. Giesen, *Studien zur Johannesapokalypse* [Stuttgarter Biblische Aufsatzbände 29; Stuttgart: Verlag Katholisches Bibelwerk, 2000] 32). Cf. Aune, *Revelation 6–16*, 756 ("the imperial priesthood, which was centrally concerned with promoting the imperial cult").

To mark this situation the author utilizes the present tense form. This is not to capitulate to a temporal conception of the present, however. The author's use of the present tense form is not due to temporal reasons (to depict the present time of the readers; cf. Osborne), but is due to his desire to conceive of the action as imperfective in order to foreground the activity of the second beast and highlight this section as of particular significance to the readers. In the chain of authority it is the last beast that directly affects the readers.

Once again, the shifting of tenses within John's visionary construct does not communicate temporal information or shifting temporal perspectives in relationship to the visionary experience. Rather, the tenses function to communicate aspect, that is, the author's perspective on the various processes that make up the visionary narrative, and serve to structure the vision in significant ways.

Revelation 17.1–18

One of the two major visionary pieces that concludes Revelation, Chs. 17–18 is paired structurally with 21.1–22.5 in terms of a contrasting vision; the harlot-Babylon is eclipsed by the bride-New Jerusalem.[131] 17.1–18 consists of an introduction to the vision (vv. 1–6b),[132] followed by the seer's reaction (v. 6c), with the bulk of the chapter devoted to the *angelus interpres'* explanation of the vision (vv. 7–18).[133] The function of the various aspectual forms in this chapter is explicable in light of the literary character of this section. The section consisting of 1–6b is static, that is, "it does not consist of any movement or action but rather has the character of a *tableau*."[134] The remainder of the chapter interprets the various visionary elements of vv. 1–6b.

In the visionary section (vv. 1–6) narrative aorist tenses predominate as expected. Yet they are limited to the introductory speech of the angel and the references to seeing. The vision proper (vv. 3–6a) commences typically with aorists of narration (ἀπήνεγκεν and the ubiquitous εἶδον).

---

[131] See the comparison in Richard J. Bauckham, *The Theology of the Book of Revelation* (Cambridge: University Press, 1993) 130–132.

[132] 17.1–2 forms the introduction not just to Ch. 17 but to 17.3–19.10. Cf. Osborne, *Revelation*, 606 n. 1; Aune, *Revelation 17–22*, 915.

[133] Revelation 17 is unique within the book of Revelation in this regard. See Aune, *Revelation 17–22*, 915.

[134] Aune, *Revelation 17–22*, 919. See also Smalley, *Revelation*, 435. Aune labels 17.1–6 an *Ekphrasis*, (*Revelation 17–22*, 923–928).

Εἶδον also recurs in v. 6a to introduce a new feature within the vision: the woman is drunk with the blood of her victims.[135] Outside of these instances, the rest of the section lacks indicative verb forms. The present tense form only occurs with participles that describe the seven angels (ἐχόντων), the beast (γέμοντα, ἔχων), those who dwell on the earth (κατοικοῦντες), and to introduce a quotation (λέγων). As is typical in Revelation, the main character in this section, the woman which John sees, is introduced in vv. 4–5 with a cluster of perfect participles (cf. also the present ἔχουσα) which draw attention to and introduce new or significant features in John's vision all focusing on her appearance (cf. 18.16).

> ⁴Καὶ ἡ γυνὴ ἦν **περιβεβλεμένη** πορφυροῦν καὶ κόκκινον καὶ **κεχρυ-σωμένη** χρυσίῳ καὶ λίθῳ τιμίῳ καὶ μαργαρίταις, ἔχουσα ποτήριον χρυ-σοῦν ἐν τῇ χειρὶ αὐτῆς γέμον βδελυγμάτων καὶ τὰ ἀκάθαρτα τῆς πορ-νείας αὐτῆς ⁵καὶ ἐπὶ τὸ μέτωπον αὐτῆς ὄνομα **γεγραμμένον** ....

This description also functions to forge an intratextual link with the woman (bride) in 21.2, whose appearance is described in a similar way with perfect participle forms, forming a clear contrast (ἡτοιμασμένην, κεκοσμημένην) to 17.4–5.

The seer's response is summarized in v. 6b with the aorist of narration (ἐθαύμασα), as is the angel's initial response to John in v. 7 (εἶπεν, ἐθαύμασας). The future tense ἐρῶ then conveys what the angel intends to do, introducing and anticipating the rest of the section. This verse, then, functions as an effective summary for the content of the rest of the chapter, since it introduces the four major features that will be developed in the angel's interpretation (ἐρῶ).[136] With the exception of the first mention of the seven horns in v. 9, each of the main features from v. 7 are marked off in the remainder of the angelic interpretation with the aorist εἶδες, itemizing and summarizing the features of John's vision from vv. 1–6 which will now be explicated in more detail.[137] Aune's explanation, followed by Smalley, that εἶδες implies that the author is no longer seeing the vision seems to state the obvious.[138]

---

[135] For this function of εἶδον see Aune, *Revelation 1–5*, 338.

[136] Aune, *Revelation 17–22*, 917.

[137] Cf. Osborne, *Revelation*, 615.

[138] "The aorist tense of εἶδες suggests that he is no longer seeing the vision presented in vv. 3b–6 (in contrast to the present tenses used in describing the New Jerusalem in 21:9–22:5)" (Aune, *Revelation 17–22*, 939). Cf. Smalley, *Revelation*, 434. Moreover, the aorist εἶδον is ubiquitous in Revelation, describing what John saw, so that John never claims to be seeing a vision, but only records what he saw.

v. 8: τὸ θηρίον ὃ εἶδες
(v. 9: αἱ ἑπτὰ κεφαλαὶ εἰσίν)
v. 12, 16: τὰ δέκα κέρατα ἃ εἶδες
v. 15: τὰ ὕδατα ἃ εἶδες[139]
v. 18: ἡ γυνὴ ἣν εἶδες

The primary feature of vv. 8–11 is a repetition of a three-fold formula. Here the tenses are apparently *used* temporally in a threefold repetition of a threefold formula which is meant to mimic the similar formula used of God: "the one who is (ὤν), who was (ἦν), and who is coming (ἐρχόμενος)" (1.4, 8; 4.8). The formula is now applied three times to the beast in Ch. 17.[140]

17.8a: ἦν καὶ οὐκ ἔστιν καὶ μέλλει ἀναβαίνειν ... καὶ εἰς ἀπώλειαν
ὑπάγει
17.8d: ἦν καὶ οὐκ ἔστιν καὶ παρέσται
17.11: ὃ ἦν καὶ οὐκ ἔστιν ... καὶ εἰς ἀπώλειαν ὑπάγει

The middle formula concludes with the aspectually vague πάρειμι, which may parody references to Christ's coming scattered throughout Revelation (1.7; 2.5, 16; 3.11; 16.15; 22.6, 12, 22).[141] The term that concludes the first and last occurrence of this formula is the present tense form ὑπάγει, which temporally is probably future in its sphere of reference (see the μέλλει ἀναβαίνειν in v. 8a), emphasizing the destruction of the beast. In addition to the references to the coming of God in 1.4, 8; 4.8, the present tense forms that end the formulas in Ch. 17 probably function to draw attention to the contrast with the references to Christ's coming in the above mentioned passages which all include the imperfective ἔρχομαι.[142] Further, both ὑπάγω and ἔρχομαι are verbs of motion and fall within Louw and Nida's Semantic Domain number 15 of Linear Move-

---

[139] The waters upon which the woman sits are not mentioned in the vision proper in vv. 3–6, but they are mentioned in the speech of the angel to John in v. 1. Aune regards this as a clear gloss (*Revelation 17–22*, 917).

[140] Bauckham may be correct that the threefold use of the formula in Ch. 17 intentionally mirrors the threefold use in reference to God in 1.4, 8; 4.8 (*Climax*, 435). Cf. Lupieri, *Apocalypse*, 275.

[141] Bauckham, *Climax*, 435. It is also possible that it is meant to parody Christ's παρουσία (from πάρειμι), though this term is not used of Christ's coming in Revelation. Cf. Smalley, *Revelation*, 343.

[142] Beale also suggests that the ὑπάγει contrasts with the third element in the altered form of the threefold formula in 11.17 ("you have taken your great power and did reign") and 16.5 ("you did judge these things"), contrasting God's victory and judgment with the defeat of the beast (*Revelation*, 864).

ment.[143] As such they form a fitting contrast to Christ's coming aspectually and semantically. The effect of this parody with the coming of God and Christ is to contrast the eschatological roles of God and Christ with the beast. Thus "The eschatological coming of God in Christ results in victory, and judgment on the unfaithful; but the attempt by the beast to assume authority, which rests on a false claim to sovereignty, ends in defeat and its own judgment."[144] Moreover, ὑπάγει frames this entire section (vv. 8–11) emphasizing the destruction of the (apparently invincible) beast. By contrast, aorists (ἔπεσαν, ἦλθεν) summarize the course of the seven kings (v. 9), while the focus remains on the beast. In the midst of these formulas two other indicative forms are important. The future θαυμασθήσονται (v. 8) depicts what can be expected to occur because of the beast's display of authority (the earth dwellers will marvel), while the perfect γέγραπται (v. 8) draws attention to the identifying feature of those who marvel at the beast (their names are not written in the book of life), also anticipating 20.15 (γεγραμμένος).

With v. 12–13 the ten horns of the beast are interpreted. The less heavily marked aorist (ἔλαβον) summarizes what the kings have not yet received, while the more heavily marked presents (λαμβάνουσιν, ἔχουσιν, διδόασιν) describe the authority they will receive in collusion with the beast and are either temporally future in their sphere of reference or timeless-descriptive.[145] The author then shifts to the future tense to emphasize the expected outcome of these events: they will make war (πολεμήσουσιν) with the Lamb but the Lamb will conquer (νικήσει) them (v. 14).

The final two features of John's vision which receive interpretation (vv. 15–18) are introduced by the present tense form λέγει.[146] The more heavily marked present tense (in contrast to the εἶπεν in v. 7) introduces the final two elements and perhaps is used to draw attention to the unexpected turn of events, where the kings turn on the woman, leading to her destruction and anticipating the fuller explication in Ch. 18. In v. 16 the future tense forms portray what can be expected to take place in this

---

[143] Louw and Nida, *Greek-English Lexicon, vol. 1*, 183, 187. According to Campbell, verbs of motion or propulsion frequently occur in the present tense in narrative (*Verbal Aspect*, 52–53).

[144] Smalley, *Revelation*, 434. Cf. Beale, *Revelation*, 864.

[145] See Smalley, *Revelation*, 437–438.

[146] Aune says that v. 17 "provides a commentary on some, but not all, of the events predicted in vv. 12–16" (*Revelation 17–22*, 957). The commentary is structured according to three summary aorist infinitives: ποιῆσαι, ποιῆσαι, δοῦναι.

unexpected turn of events. The beast and the kings turn on the woman and destroy her (μισήσουσιν, ποιήσουσιν, κατακαύσουσιν), and these events reflect the certainty of fulfillment of God's word (τελεσθήσονται). The perfect participle ἠρημωμένην emphasizes the expected desolate state of the woman in which her new enemies will leave her. The switch from the future to the present tense φάγονται may be to highlight a particularly gruesome detail in the description of the woman's downfall. As mentioned earlier, the literary character of Ch. 17 helps to explain the aspectual usage. In vv. 1–6 the only indicative forms are aorists which, however, do not describe activities of the woman or beast, though the woman is introduced with stative (perfect) participles and her features are described with imperfective (present) participles. This is because the vision is static.[147] In vv. 7–18, which interpret the vision, present and future tenses dominate, which is what we would expect.[148] The static nature of the vision allows the angel to interpret its main features by describing in more detail what the woman and beast do or what happens to them and what they can be expected to do or what can be expected to happen to them.

Revelation 18.4–20

As part of the ideological and economic critique of the Roman Empire, this section comprises a lengthy speech of one of Revelation's enigmatic voices in v. 4 (ἤκουσα ἄλλην φωνὴν), though Osborne incorrectly identifies this chapter as a vision.[149] The voice from heaven encompasses this entire section, though there are other voices embedded within this voice. As Kraft says of this section, "Hier beginnt ein geschlossener Abschnitt, der bis V. 20 reicht."[150] This segment is prefaced by two narrative sections, v. 4 which introduces the speech with a narrative aorist (ἤκουσα), and v. 21 which introduces a symbolic action by another angel, again with

---

[147] Aune, *Revelation 17–22*, 919.

[148] See Smalley, *Revelation*, 435.

[149] Osborne, *Revelation*, 631, though obviously it occurs within the framework of John's entire visionary narrative. For the overall structure of this section see Bauckham, *Climax*, 341.

[150] Kraft, *Offenbarung*, 231. Cf. also Dougherty, "Syntax," 441–442; Beale, *Revelation*, 905; Aune, *Revelation 17–22*, 976, though Aune inconsistently includes two examples of present tense forms from this chapter in the category of historical present in narration (18.11, cf. *Revelation 1–5*, clxxxiv). The punctuation of the UBSGNT 4th edn is unclear. Cf. the punctuation of the NIV.

an aorist tense in narration (ἦρεν).[151] Dougherty was perplexed at the apparent inconsistency of shifting between future (v. 9), present (v. 11), and aorists (vv. 17–19) within the same temporal context.[152] Moreover, Prigent recognized "l'emploi des temps passes et futures" (note his temporal language to describe the tenses).[153] Based on this alternation of tenses Prigent wonders: "Maladresse de l'auteur?"[154] He finds the solution in the Christ-event which subverts (douleverse) our temporal categories, which our human language is inadequate to capture. However, all of these assessments falter on an overreliance on a temporal conception of the Greek tense system. And Prigent's observation, though perhaps correct, is a theological construct and does not offer a grammatical explanation for the author's choice of tense forms. Furthermore, as Aune and Beale have recognized, Ch. 18 is not arranged chronologically.[155] Rather, the progression in this section appears to be a logical one.[156]

Roughly, the events in vv. 4–8 appear to have taken place before the fall of Babylon (the command to "come out" in v. 4), while the events in vv. 9–20 record events following her fall. Despite the fact that it is not explicitly narrated, the fall of Babylon may be assumed to have taken place with ἔπεσεν, ἔπεσεν. Thus at least in this case, the aorists ἔπεσεν, ἔπεσεν seem to have past time implicature in v. 2.[157] The solution is to

---

[151] Resseguie thinks that Chs. 17 and 18 relate to each other in terms of the "hear"/"see" dialectic in Revelation. In Ch. 17 Johns *sees* the harlot, Babylon, while in Ch. 18 he *hears* of her destruction (*Revelation*, 227). While there is some truth to this, in that John does not actually see her downfall, there is auditory material in Ch. 17 by way of the interpretation of the *angelus interpres*.

[152] Dougherty, "Syntax," 440–443.

[153] Prigent, *l'Apocalypse*, 265.

[154] Prigent, *l'Apocalypse*, 265.

[155] Aune, *Revelation 17-22*, 975 ("In this chapter the author presents surrounding the fall of Babylon, not in chronological order or in logical sequence but rather in such a way as to create an emotional effect on the hearers."); Beale, *Revelation*, 891; Mussies, *Morphology*, 338–339. Resseguie advocates the following divisions temporally: vv. 1–3: takes place immediately after the fall of Babylon; vv. 4–8: takes place before the fall of Babylon; vv. 9–20: takes place after the fall of Babylon (*Revelation*, 227). Charles, *Revelation, II*, 87–95 postulated that Revelation 18 was a Greek translation of an underlying original Hebrew source which has suffered some dislocation in its present form.

[156] Bauckham, *Climax*, 342.

[157] The actual fall is not narrated in Ch. 18, though it is anticipated and expected from 17.1–3. "Der Seher beschreibt den Vorgang der Nernichtung nicht, sondern schildert die Reaktionen derer, die vom Reichtum und Prunk der Stadt profitiert haben …" (Giesen, *Offenbarung*, 389–390). Given the fact that this section is not arranged chronologically, as Beale (*Revelation*, 891) and Aune (*Revelation 17-22*, 975) have recognized, it is possible that the aorists ἔπεσεν ἔπεσεν in 18.2 are past referring, so that it is assumed that the

see the tenses in vv. 4–20 in terms of verbal aspect: the aorist summarizes
and backgrounds certain processes, the present dwells on and describes
certain processes, and the future indicates what can be expected to take
place.

Aorist tense forms are predominant in vv. 4–8 as the reasons for the
call to come out (ἐξέλθατε) and the reason for Babylon's judgment are
summarized. Verse 8 concludes with two future forms (ἕξουσιν, κατα-
καυθήσεται) which express what can expected to take place as a result
of Babylon's crimes (διὰ τοῦτο). The remaining segment (vv. 9–20) contains the lament of three groups who benefited from Babylon's wealth.
The three threnodies belong to vv. 9–10: the kings; vv. 11–16: the merchants; vv. 17–19: the shipowners.[158] The aspects play a crucial function
in the depiction of the activities of these three groups. In vv. 9–10, with
the future tense the kings will mourn and weep (κλαύσουσιν καὶ κόψονται) because of the destruction of Babylon. A perfect participle, ἑστηκότες, highlights their distance from the city on which they depended for
their well-being, and perhaps is to be seen in contrast to other instances
of "standing" throughout the book. In the next section, vv. 11–16, the
indicative verbs which depict the response of the merchants (ἔμποροι)
are found in the present and future tense forms. In v. 11 the present tense
is used to describe and highlight their weeping and mourning (κλαίουσιν
καὶ πενθοῦσιν). Smalley's view, that the shift to the present tense has
the effect of "switch[ing] the audience into the action of the drama, and
mak[ing] the visionary material vivid and immediate,"[159] is acceptable
as long as it is not determined by a rhetorical, temporal shift. Osborne
thinks that the switch from the futures in 18.9 to the presents in 18.11 is
a stylistic variation, with the futuristic presents emphasizing the certainty

---

city has fallen at this point. Cf. Mussies, *Morphology*, 338–339. In other words, they may
not be future referring as their counterpart in 14.8, which 18.2 is clearly meant to echo.
Most commentaries assume that the fall referred to in 18.2 is future and that the aorists
reflect the "prophetic perfect." Smalley labels the aorists in 18.2 as prophetic perfects,
since "the final judgment of Babylon ... has yet to be brought about" (*Revelation*, 444).
But Smalley does think the judgment in 18.2 is more imminent. Cf. Aune, *Revelation*
17–22, 985; Blount, *Revelation*, 326. However, it is possible that the judgment has already
taken place between Ch. 17 and Ch. 18, so that the aorists may be past referring. The
angel now announces the fall of Babylon which has already taken place by 18.2. Though
v. 4 is a call for God's people to come out of her, suggesting that Babylon has not fallen.
Yet, as already suggested this section is not necessarily arranged chronologically.

[158] Cf. Charles, *Revelation*, II, 87; Aune, *Revelation 17–22*, 978–979; Prigent, *l'Apocalypse*, 265. For further details on this section see Bauckham, *Climax*, 371–378.

[159] Smalley, *Revelation*, 453. Cf. also Beale, *Revelation*, 909, following Mussies, *Morphology*, 335–336.

of the events.[160] Yet, not only does Osborne follow a typical temporal orientation, it is not clear how they are any more certain than the verbs in the future in v. 9 or the verbs that follow in the aorist (vv. 17–19). While temporally these presents are future-referring, their primary function is an aspectual one, to highlight and describe the mourning of the merchants.[161] The other indicative verb is a future, στήσονται, expressing that they can be expected to stand far off due to fear of Rome's torment. Hence, the combination of future and present forms with these two groups draws attention to the response of these two groups to the fall of Babylon, the future tense grammaticalizing what can be expected to occur because of Babylon's fall, and the present describing their responses.

The response of the final group, the shipowners (vv. 17–19), differs from the other two groups in that the indicative verbs that describe their response are in the aorist (ἔστησαν, ἔβαλον), the former verb occurring as a perfect participle and future tense form to describe the other two groups. Even the verbs that introduce their crying and weeping, though standing out against the aorists, are in the more remote imperfect form (ἔκραζον). Therefore:

Kings (vv. 9–10): κλαύσουσιν, κόψονται (ἑστηκότες)
Merchants (vv. 11–16): κλαίουσιν, πενθοῦσιν, στήσονται
Shipowners (vv. 17–19): ἔστησαν, ἔλαβον, ἔκραζον (2×)

There may be a motivation for this tense shift. The final response in the triology of responses is recorded in the aorist (and more remote imperfect) due to the fact that it functions to background the response of the onlookers in order to transition to the response of God's people to Babylon's fall in v. 20. Hence, v. 20 is the climax of the responses to Babylon's fall, indicated by the more heavily marked present imperative form (εὐφραίνου)[162] along with the vocative and nominative forms (οὐρανὲ καὶ οἱ ἅγιοι καὶ οἱ ἀπόστολοι καὶ οἱ προφῆται) over against the aorists (and imperfects) which characterize the activity of the final group of onlookers in vv. 17–19. Thus the mourning of the earthly groups in vv. 9–19 contrasts with the rejoicing of heaven and the saints in v. 20, marked by the

---

[160] Osborne, *Revelation*, 646 n. 14.

[161] For the importance of this section among the three responses to Babylon's fall recorded in 18.9–19, see Bauckham, *Climax*, 342; Osborne, *Revelation*, 647: "The list of cargoes in 18:12–13 is intended to demonstrate the kind of wealth involved in the lucrative trade." Textually the variants κλαύσουσιν and πενθήσουσιν are found in fam 1611 2030 Byzantine it^a vg. cop. See Aune, *Revelation 17–22*, 968.

[162] This form in itself also contrasts aspectually with the aorist imperative in v. 4: Ἐξέλθατε.

shift in tenses (and mood).[163] The call to rejoice in v. 20 anticipates and is apparently fulfilled in the hymnic episode in 19.1–4.[164] While not a narrative of a vision per se, this section nevertheless exemplifies important shifts in tenses which function not to communicate temporal information but to indicate the author's conception of the processes and their pragmatic function of indicating levels of prominence.

Revelation 19.11–21

The second half of Revelation 19 narrates one of the final battle scenes (cf. 16.12–16; 20.7–10). In these final chapters of Revelation the Parousia of the Lamb is depicted metaphorically from various standpoints.[165] Following the downfall of Babylon, the Lamb is depicted as a warrior who comes from heaven in order to avenge his people (19.11–21). This segment (19.11–21) structurally can be divided into two sections which incidentally correspond generally with a difference in usage of aspect: vv. 11–16, 17–21 (see below). The first section (vv. 11–16) comprises a description of the rider on the white horse, while the second section (vv. 17–21), marked off by καὶ εἶδον, consists of a record of the battle itself containing an invitation by an angel which sets the scene for the battle, followed by the narration of the battle.[166]

The opening section (vv. 11–16), where the Warrior-Messiah is introduced, is a highly prominent section within the discourse, with a significant clustering of perfect participles and a perfect indicative verb form, as well as a number of indicative verbs and participles in the present tense (**Perfect**, *Present*).

> [11]Καὶ εἶδον τὸν οὐρανὸν **ἠνεῳγμένον**, καὶ ἰδοὺ ἵππος λευκὸς καὶ ὁ καθήμενος ἐπ᾽ αὐτὸν πιστὸς καὶ ἀληθινός, καὶ ἐν δικαιοσύνῃ *κρίνει* καὶ *πολεμεῖ.* [12]οἱ δὲ ὀφθαλμοὶ αὐτοῦ φλὸξ πυρός, καὶ ἐπὶ τὴν κεφαλὴν αὐτοῦ διαδήματα πολλά, ἔχων ὄνομα **γεγραμμένον** ὃ οὐδεὶς **οἶδεν** εἰ μὴ αὐτός, [13]καὶ **περιβεβλημένος** ἱμάτιον **βεβαμμένον** αἵματι, καὶ **κέκληται** τὸ ὄνομα αὐτοῦ ὁ λόγος τοῦ θεοῦ. [14] καὶ τὸ στρατεύματα ἐν τῷ οὐρανῷ ἠκολούθει αὐτῷ ἐφ᾽ ἵπποις λευκοῖς, **ἐνδεδυμένοι** βύσσινον λευκὸν

---

[163] "Contrastant avec les lamentations des diverses catégories des habitants de la terre, le ciel et les chrétiens sont invites à la jubilation" (Prigent, *l'Apocalypse*, 273). Cf. also Resseguie, *Revelation*, 231; Smalley, *Revelation*, 460 ("Verse 20 represents a sudden change of mood and thought as, instead of the lamentation over the destruction of Babylon, the people of God are called upon to rejoice in his justice").

[164] Cf. Aune, *Revelation 17–22*, 1007; Giesen, *Offenbarung*, 397.

[165] Cf. R.W. Wall, *Revelation* (NIBC; Peabody, MA: Hendrickson, 1991) 227.

[166] Aune, *Revelation 17–22*, 1046.

καθαρόν. ¹⁵καὶ ἐκ τοῦ στόματος αὐτοῦ *ἐκπορεύεται* ῥομφαία ὀξεῖα, ἵνα ἐν αὐτῇ πατάξῃ τὰ ἔθνη, καὶ αὐτὸς ποιμανεῖ αὐτοὺς ἐν ῥάβδῳ σιδηρᾷ, καὶ αὐτὸς *πατεῖ* τὴν ληνὸν τοῦ οἴνου τοῦ θυμοῦ τῆς ὀργῆς τοῦ θεοῦ τοῦ παντοκράτορος, ¹⁶καὶ *ἔχει* ἐπὶ τὸ ἱμάτιον καὶ ἐπὶ τὸν μηρὸν αὐτοῦ ὄνομα **γεγραμμένον**· Βασιλεὺς βασιλέων καὶ κύριος κυρίων.

As Aune says, this unit is a *"symbolic description,* which focuses on the *description, identity,* and *tasks* of the rider on the white horse."¹⁶⁷ This accounts for the distribution of verbal aspect in this section. The section begins (v. 11) with a prominent statement where the object of the seer's vision (οὐρανόν) is modified by a perfect participle (ἠνεῳγμένον). The author sees heaven in the state of standing open, which functions to introduce and frontground another significant scene in the Apocalypse: the disclosure and consummation of God's activity of judgment through Christ (cf. Chs. 4–5). This is a prominent section in the discourse—a judgment scene which will now set off a series of images of judgment and salvation that extend to the end of the vision (22.5). In 4.1 John sees a vision of the heavenly throne room. Now in 19.11 he envisages "the consummation of God's acts in human history."¹⁶⁸

The introduction of the warrior (and his army) is then marked by a significant cluster of perfect participles (γεγραμμένον, περιβεβλημένος, βεβαμμένον, ἐνδεδυμένοι, γεγραμμένον), all depicting significant characteristic features focusing on the appearance of the rider and his army.¹⁶⁹ Two indicative verbs also occur in the perfect tense: the name that is written on him no one knows (οἶδεν). The title "word of God" is also the name which he will be called (κέκληται). Nowhere else in the Apocalypse is such a concentrated usage of perfect tense forms found.

In addition, there are a number of present tense forms which also describe important features of the warrior, filling out the details and adding further descriptive color by drawing attention to these features. Present tense indicative verb forms are used to describe important characteristic activities of the Warrior-Messiah. With two 'timeless' presents in v. 11 the author introduces the two main characteristic activities of

---

¹⁶⁷ Aune, *Revelation 17–22,* 1047. Italics his.

¹⁶⁸ Cf. Osborne, *Revelation,* 679; Prigent, *l'Apocalypse,* 288. For the prominence of this section, though not for reasons of verbal aspect, see also Lupieri, *Apocalypse,* 302.

¹⁶⁹ Overly relying on a temporal conception of tenses, Giesen incorrectly concludes that the perfect tense form ἐνδεδυμένοι suggests that "haben die Christen dieses Gewand für immer erhalten" (*Offenbarung,* 423). This is a theological construct which does not necessarily reflect the grammatical state of affairs.

the warrior in this scene as judging and making war (κρίνει, πολεμεῖ).[170] These two verb forms do not refer to any specific war, but highlight characteristic features of the warrior more generally, hence I classify them as timeless-descriptive. His portrait as a warrior is further enhanced in v. 15 by the sword issuing from his mouth (ἐκπορεύεται) and the fact that he treads the winepress of the wrath of God (πατεῖ). He also possesses (ἔχει) the name "king of kings and Lord of Lords" (v. 16; cf. also ἔχων in v. 12). The sole imperfect tense form is found in v. 14: ἠκολούθει to describe the accompanying army. Dougherty thinks that the imperfect here is an intrusion in a descriptive section, and hence a narrative of what is happening rather than a description.[171] But this can be true if the imperfect is restricted to past time narration, and since the next verbs return to future and present forms, it is unlikely that the readers were meant to shift between description and narrative, then back to description, so abruptly. Perhaps the more remote imperfect form (ἠκολούθει) is used since the focus is on the Warrior rather than the accompanying army, which actually plays a minor role (if any at all) in the conquest (cf. vv. 19–21): the focus is on the activity of the Warrior-Messiah. The presence of one future form in v. 15, ποιμανεῖ, may serve to emphasize what can be expected to take place given the description of the warrior. However, the future may also only be due to an Old Testament allusion to LXX Ps. 2.9 (ποιμανεῖς αὐτοὺς ἐν ῥάβδῳ σιδηρᾷ).[172]

This analysis of verbal aspect suggests that the primary focus of this section is on the description and identity of the warrior,[173] and verbal aspect marks this section out as highly prominent. This is the climax to

---

[170] Cf. Smalley, *Revelation*, 488, who classifies them as gnomic. Cf. Swete, *Apocalypse*, 251 ("A principle feature in the Messianic character"); Aune, *Revelation 17–22*, 1053. But even this is not quite correct, in that this is not a reference to a habitual action on the part of the rider but a characteristic feature. Swete also thinks that "it [the present tense form] may possibly imply that Christ's work as Judge and Warrior is already proceeding in the world …." (*Apocalypse*, 247). This is unnecessarily temporal and does not fit contextually with the vision of the consummation of history. Note the confusion in Kistemaker, *Revelation*, 519. Isa 11.3–4, upon which John draws intertextually, has the future κρινεῖ. For other possible OT background cf. Charles, *Revelation, II*, 131–132.

[171] Dougherty, "Syntax," 444: "the verb ἠκολούθει, an imperfect, is narrative of what is happening in the vision, not descriptive of the horse or rider."

[172] Cf. 12.5. The verbal correspondence here in 19.15 to LXX Ps. 2.9 is even closer. The change from the second person (Ps. 2.9) to the third person is contextually appropriate. For further discussion see Beale, *Revelation*, 962–963.

[173] This confirms Aune's conclusion, who notes that 19.11–16 is a *symbolic description*, focusing on the description and identify of the rider on the horse (*Revelation 17–22*, 1047).

the question of the saints who have longed for vindication, a question that has received partial answer, but not received its climactic visionary response: ἕως πότε, ὁ δεσπότης ὁ ἅγιος καὶ ἀληθίνος, οὐ κρίνεις καὶ ἐκδικεῖς τὸ αἷμα ἡμῶν ἐκ τῶν κατοικούντων ἐπὶ τῆς γῆς; (6.10). The answer comes in the climactic return to earth of the Warrior-Messiah in 19.11–21, a section made focally prominent by the proliferation of heavily marked verb tense forms. Furthermore, in this section all the references to Christ as the conquering Lamb who will come now culminate in this passage. "[T]he consummation of God's acts in human history has arrived. The eschaton is here."[174] This act now sets off the remaining scenes of judgment and salvation (20.1–22.5). Thus the distribution of highly marked tenses is appropriate here at this crucial juncture.

Now that the warrior has been introduced and described, the battle itself is narrated (vv. 17–21). In this section aorist tense forms clearly dominate. Two characteristic aorist forms, εἶδον, introduce and delimit the two main sections of this segment: the invitation of the angel (vv. 17–18), and the battle itself (vv. 19–21). In the first segment the angel who plays a significant role here is introduced with the perfect participle ἑστῶτα. The exhortation of the commanding angel to the birds to gather, along with the purpose of their gathering, is issued in the summary aorist tense (συνάχθητε, φάγητε). The next section (vv. 19–21) begins with an important perfect participle (συνηγμένα), which highlights the intention of the kings of the earth and their armies and the magnitude of what they will attempt to do.[175] Yet as has often been observed, there is no actual fighting narrated: the Warrior-Messiah destroys all his foes apparently without any fighting actually taking place.[176] The battle (if it can be called that) itself, then, is narrated with a quick succession of aorist indicative tense forms (ἐπιάσθη, ἐπλάνησεν, ἐβλήθησαν, ἀπεκτάνθησαν, ἐχορτάσθησαν), though a handful of present participles add descriptive detail (προσκυνοῦντας, ζῶντες, καιομένης).

Thus 19.11–16 constitutes a highly prominent section, marked with a significant concentration of perfect tense forms (both participles and indicatives) and several important present tense forms. 19.17–21 is less marked, where the aorist tense in narration clearly dominates the

---

[174] Osborne, *Revelation*, 679.

[175] The implied agent of the passive form here is most likely the beast, who gathers them for warfare. See Osborne, *Revelation*, 688.

[176] Aune, *Revelation 17–22*, 1065, who notes that this seems to be true of all the narratives of battles in Revelation. Cf. Osborne, *Revelation*, 684.

description. Consequently, more attention is focused on the warrior and his characteristic features, appearance, and activities (vv. 11–16) than on the actual battle itself in vv. 17–21.

Summary

In the preceding section I have examined the tense forms in eight major sections in the Apocalypse. The sections were chosen because they exemplify significant shifting of tense forms, and because most of them have been the cause of confusion among commentaries and grammarians and have elicited a variety of explanations. The following is a tabulation of the distribution of the *indicative* tense forms (excluding aspectually vague verbs such as εἰμί) from the selected texts discussed in the preceding section. As can be observed the full range of tense forms in the Greek verbal system is well-represented throughout the Apocalypse.

Chap. 5

Aorist – 16
Present – 3[177]
Imperfect – 3
Perfect – 1

7.9–17

Aorist – 8
Present – 2
Imperfect – 1
Perfect – 1
Pluperfect – 1
Future – 6

Chap. 9

Aorist – 20
Present – 7
Imperfect – 2
Future – 4 (1 in ἵνα clause)

11.1–13

Aorist – 15
Present – 10
Future – 6

Chap. 12

Aorist – 32
Present – 7
Perfect – 1

Chap. 13

Aorist – 18
Present – 8
Imperfect – 2
Perfect – 1
Future – 2

---

[177] As noted above, this count is based on the argument that the textual variant in the present tense form (βασιλεύουσιν) is the correct reading over against the future form (βασιλεύσουσιν) in 5.10. Otherwise the count would reflect two presents and one future.

Chap. 17   *18.4–20*

Aorist – 19   Aorist – 16
Present – 8   Present – 5
Perfect – 1   Imperfect – 2
Future – 10   Future – 6

19.11–21

Aorist – 8
Present – 5
Imperfect – 1
Perfect – 2 (8 perfect participles)

The following summary remarks can be made concerning the tense distribution across these various literary segments of the Apocalypse compared above. 1) Consistent with an aspectual scheme and its function in narrative, the aorist is the unmarked form, the basic narrative tense which is utilized to summarize the actions that carry along the story line or even dialogues. Quantitatively it functions as the predominant aspectual form in all of the major sections surveyed above, in both visionary and auditory sections.

2) The present and imperfect forms provide the fundamental opposition with the aorist and are more marked, and are used to describe and highlight certain processes in the narrative of what John saw/heard. Though both function to foreground action over against the aorist, we have suggested above that the imperfect grammaticalizes the additional feature of remoteness, with the present being slightly more focal.

3) The perfect tense is far less common in occurrence through Revelation's visions. This is consistent with the fact that it is the most heavily marked form and functions to frontground actions that stand out somewhat unexpectedly. However, the above tabulation does not reveal the number of perfect participles that tend to cluster around new or main characters/features in the vision.

4) The future tense form is particularly visible in 7.9–17; 11.1–13; 17; 18.4–20. Probably the literary character of these segments has to do with the high number of future tense forms. These segments appear to have a slightly higher number of present tense forms as well. What these sections all have in common is the fact that they are dominated by speech or prophetic speech rather than narratives of visions per se. Hence, 7.9–17 ends with a lengthy discourse of one of the elders; 11.1–13 is probably prophetic rather than a narration of a vision; Ch. 17 contains a lengthy interpretation by an *angelus interpres* (vv. 7–18) following

a static vision (vv. 1–6); 18.4–20 is a lengthy speech from a voice from heaven.

5) Dougherty is generally correct in the pattern he has observed.[178] The combination of the aorist and imperfect tend to implicate past time narration while the present and future tend to be used in descriptive and predictive material in the Apocalypse.

> Aorist, imperfect—past time narration
> Present, Future—descriptive, predictive, speech

However, this is not the whole story, as aorists function within speeches and prophecies to provide supporting and background information, and presents, futures, and perfects "intrude" into narrative section as more heavily marked forms.

6) One of the shortcomings of a mere tabulation of the number of tense forms that occur in each segment is that it masks the distribution of tense forms within the sections of discourse. So in 7.9–17 the future form is confined to vv. 15–17; in Ch. 13, which contains eight present tense forms, while there is only one present tense form in vv. 1–10, there are five in vv. 11–18. This latter section (vv. 11–18) also contains both imperfect forms found in this segment. "The use of tense to create paragraph patterns together with semantic organizing features such as episode or topic is very common."[179] Thus each section must be studied on its own to examine how the tense forms are distributed and function across the discourse.

7) 19.11–21 is a highly marked section, which contains a high number of presents and perfects, along with a significant clustering of perfect participles (8) within a rather condensed textual space. This suggests that 19.11–21 functions as a "peak" in the discourse, or creates significant "turbulence" in the flow of information (see above for possible reasons).[180]

Other New Testament Texts

To buttress his case for the Semitic flavor of Revelation's tense usage, Thompson concludes that the phenomenon of shifting tenses is some-

---

[178] Dougherty, "Syntax," 426–427.
[179] Westfall, *Hebrews*, 40.
[180] See Longacre, "Discourse Peak."

what unique to the Apocalypse, and so he attributes it to Semitic influence, though he does admit that alternation of tenses occurs elsewhere in the New Testament, but to a more limited degree.[181] Thus in completing our examination of verbal aspect in the Apocalypse it would be helpful to note briefly examples elsewhere in the New Testament and also in the Greek outside of the New Testament which demonstrate a marked distribution of tense forms over extended sections of texts similar to that found in the Apocalypse.

Though no other canonical Apocalypses (as a literary genre in the New Testament) offer themselves for comparison, the closest analogy to how tense forms function would be narrative literature since Revelation purports to be a first person narrative of a visionary experience of the seer.[182] The purpose of this brief section is not to provide a detailed exegesis of additional texts, nor to offer a detailed analysis of how verbal aspect functions as such, but only to highlight the distribution of tense forms over extended sections within a selection of two New Testament narrative texts. One could possibly further analyze these texts in light of the function of the various aspects to structure the discourse and indicate prominence. In these representative texts the authors employ a range of tense forms to depict the processes that comprise the narrative accounts, all while largely maintaining the same temporal sphere of reference (past time narration). I will only include indicative tense forms, since most of the question regarding tense forms in Revelation lies with the use of indicative mood forms. I have also limited my list to narrative material within each text (excluding speeches since the tense forms could be from the perspective of the speaker). Not counting the speeches themselves, the following table tabulates the tenses used in *narration* within two New Testament texts: Mark 5.21–43; John 20.1–10.[183]

Mark 5.21–43[184]
    Aorists – 14
    Presents – 11
    Imperfects – 7
    Perfects – 1

---

[181] Thompson, *Semitic Syntax*, 47.

[182] See Resseguie, *Revelation Unsealed*; David L. Barr, *Tales of the End: A Narrative Commentary on the Book of Revelation* (Santa Rosa, CA: Polebridge, 1998).

[183] As indicated earlier, I will not include the forms of εἰμί, in this tabulation since it offers no aspectual choice beyond imperfective forms; i.e. it is aspectually vague.

[184] For a thorough treatment of verbal aspect in Mark see Decker, *Temporal Deixis*.

John 20.1–10[185]
  Aorists – 9
  Presents – 9
  Imperfects – 2
  Pluperfect – 1

Extra-Biblical Texts

The phenomenon of shifting tenses can also be found in Greek outside of New Testament literature. The proceeding is just a sampling of texts which reveal a tendency to alternate tense forms. The following text by Polybius, treated by Porter,[186] describes the constitution of the Roman military. Present tense forms are inserted in the description of the selection of various groups which is otherwise dominated by aorists. The aorist is used to summarize the selection of the first group of centurions (ἐξέλεξαν), while the present draws attention to the selection of another group of ten centurions (ποιοῦνται) and highlights the fact that the first appointed serves on the council (κοινωνεῖ). The centurions themselves select (προσεκλέγονται) rearguard officers. The remaining selection and naming of various groups are then recorded in a string of the least heavily marked aorist forms.

Key: **Aorist**
      Present

Plb 6.24.1–6

ἐξ ἑκάστου δὲ τῶν προειρημένων γενῶν πλὴν τῶν νεωτάτων **ἐξέλεξαν** ταξιάρχους ἀριστίνδην δέκα. μετὰ δὲ τούτους ἑτέραν ἐκλογὴν ἄλλων δέκα *ποιοῦνται.* καὶ τούτους μὲν ἅπαντας **προσηγόρευσαν** ταξιάρχους, ὧν ὁ πρῶτος αἱρθεὶς καὶ συνεδρίου *κοινωνεῖ· προσεκλέγονται* δ᾽ οὗτοι πάλιν αὐτοὶ τοὺς ἴσους οὐραγούς. ἑξῆς δὲ τούτοις μετὰ τῶν ταξιάρχων **διεῖλον** τὰς ἡλικίας, ἑκάστην εἰς δέκα μέρη, πλὴν τῶν γροσφομάχων· καὶ

---

[185] W.D. Chamberlain noted that John 20.1–10 provides "an excellent example of weaving together historical presents, imperfects, aorists, perfects and pluperfects with great dramatic effect" (*An Exegetical Grammar of the Greek New Testament* [New York: Macmillan, 1941] 71). Cf. also the significant tense shifts in John 1.1–18. In the first five verses there is a shift from aorist tense forms (ἐγένετο, 2×) to a perfect (γέγονεν) to a present (φαίνει) and back to an aorist (κατέλαβεν), all while apparently maintaining the same temporal sphere of reference. Cf. vv. 14–18: ἐγένετο (aorist), ἐθεασάμεθα (aorist), μαρτυρεῖ (present), κέκραγεν (perfect), γέγονεν (perfect in speech), ἐλάβομεν (aorist), ἐδόθη (aorist), ἐγένετο (aorist), ἑώρακεν (perfect), ἐξηγήσατο (aorist).

[186] See Porter, *Verbal Aspect*, 243–244. For his treatment of a lengthier text, Plato, *Phaedr* 244–256 see 240–243. For other brief examples see 213–216.

προσένειμαν ἑκάστῳ μέρει τῶν ἐκλεχθέντων ἀνδρῶν δύ' ἡγεμόνας καὶ δύ' οὐραγούς, τῶν δὲ γροσφομάχων τοὺς ἐπιβάλλοντας κατὰ τὸ πλῆθος ἴσους ἐπὶ πάντα τὰ μέρη **διένειμαν**, καὶ τὸ μὲν νέρος ἕκαστον **ἐκάλεσαν** καὶ τάγμα καὶ σπεῖραν καὶ σημαίαν, τοὺς δ' ἡγεμόνας κεντυρίωνας καὶ ταξιάρχους. οὗτοι δὲ καθ' ἑκάστην σπεῖραν ἐκ τῶν καταλειπομένων **ἐξελεξαν** αὐτοὶ δύο τοὺς ἀκμαιοτάτους καὶ γενναιοτάτους ἄνδρας σημαιαφόρους.[187]

Two present tenses follow in 6.25.1 (προκρίνουσιν) and 6.26.9 (καλοῦσι).

An instructive example is a Christian Apocalypse which is closest generically and temporally to Revelation: The *Shepherd of Hermas*. Like Revelation, *Hermas* is a first person narrative account of a visionary experience. I have selected just one section from Vision 4 (1.1–10) in which the author narrates one of his visions, and in which he shifts back and forth between various tense forms in order to do so. Interestingly, though the author commences his vision with the aorist εἶδον (cf. Revelation), in two cases in the cited text the author switches to the present tense βλέπω (vv. 5, 6) with past time implicature to refer to what the author saw. Like Revelation, Herm. *Vis* 4.1.1–10 reveals an intriguing alternation of tense forms that cannot be explained on temporal grounds.

Key: **Aorist**
Present
<u>Imperfect</u>
<u>Pluperfect</u>

Hermas *Vis* 4.1.1–10

[1]*Ὅρασις δ ἣν* **εἶδον** ἀδελφοί μετὰ ἡμέρας εἴκοσι *τῆς προτέρας ὁράσεως τῆς γενομένης* εἰς τύπον τῆς θλίψεως τῆς ἐπερχομένης [2] <u>ὑπῆγον</u> εἰς ἀγρὸν τῇ ὁδῷ τῇ Καμπανῇ *ἀπὸ τῆς ὁδοῦ τῆς δημοσίας ἐστὶν* ὡσεὶ στάδια δέκα *ῥαδίως δὲ ὁδεύεται ὁ τόπος* [3] μόνος οὖν *περιπατῶν ἀξιῶ* τὸν κύριον ἵνα τὰς ἀποκαλύψεις καὶ τὰ ὁράματα *ἅ μοι* **ἔδειξεν** διὰ τῆς ἁγίας

---

[187] "And from each of the appointed groups except for the youngest they select ten taxiarchs according to merit. With these they make another selection of ten others. And all of these they name taxiarchs, of whom the first who is selected participates in the council; and these themselves again select equal members of the rearguard officers. Then with the taxiarchs they divide up the group, each into ten parts, apart from the javelin throwers; and they place with each part from the selected men two leaders and two rearguard officers. And from the javelin throwers they assign according to the number equal portions over all parts. And each part they call tagam and speiran and semaian, and the leaders centurions and taxiarchs. And these themselves appoint, from those remaining according to each speiran the two strongest and noblest men as standard bearers."

Ἐκκλησίας αὐτοῦ τελειώσῃ ἵνα με ἰσχυροποιήσῃ καὶ δῷ τὴν μετάνοιαν τοῖς δούλοις αὐτοῦ τοῖς ἐσκανδαλισμένοις ἵνα δοξασθῇ τὸ ὄνομα αὐτοῦ τὸ μέγα καὶ ἔνδοξον ὅτι με ἄξιον **ἡγήσατο** τοῦ δεῖξαί μοι τὰ θαυμάσια αὐτοῦ [4] καὶ δοξάζοντός μου καὶ εὐχαριστοῦντος αὐτῷ ὡς ἦχος φωνῆς μοι **ἀπεκρίθη** Μὴ διψυχήσεις Ἑρμᾶ ἐν ἐμαυτῷ **ἠρξάμην** διαλογίζεσθαι καὶ λέγειν Ἐγὼ τί ἔχω διψυχῆσαι οὕτω τεθεμελιωμένος ὑπὸ τοῦ κυρίου καὶ ἰδὼν ἔνδοξα πράγματα [5] καὶ **προσέβην** μικρόν ἀδελφοί καὶ ἰδοὺ βλέπω κονιορτὸν ὡς εἰς τὸν οὐρανόν καὶ **ἠρξάμην** λέγειν ἐν ἐμαυτῷ Μήποτε κτήνη ἔρχονται καὶ κονιορτὸν ἐγείρουσιν οὕτω δὲ ἦν ἀπ᾽ ἐμοῦ ὡς ἀπὸ σταδίου [6] γινομένου μείζονος καὶ μείζονος κονιορτοῦ ὑπενόησα εἶναί τι θεῖον μικρὸν **ἐξέλαμψεν** ὁ ἥλιος καὶ ἰδοὺ *βλέπω* θηρίον μέγιστον ὡσεὶ κῆτός τι καὶ ἐκ τοῦ στόματος αὐτοῦ ἀκρίδες πύριναι ἐξεπορεύοντο ἦν δὲ τὸ θηρίον τῷ μήκει ὡσεὶ ποδῶν ρ τὴν δὲ κεφαλὴν *εἶχεν* ὡσεὶ κεράμου

[7] καὶ **ἠρξάμην** κλαίειν καὶ ἐρωτᾶν τὸν κύριον ἵνα με λυτρώσηται ἐξ αὐτοῦ καὶ **ἐπανεμνήσθην** τοῦ ῥήματος οὗ *ἀκηκόειν* Μὴ διψυχήσεις Ἑρμᾶ [8] ἐνδυσάμενος οὖν ἀδελφοί τὴν πίστιν τοῦ κυρίου καὶ μνησθεὶς ὧν **ἐδίδαξέν** με μεγαλείων θαρσήσας εἰς τὸ θηρίον ἐμαυτὸν **ἔδωκα** οὕτω δὲ ἤρχετο τὸ θηρίον ῥοίζῳ ὥστε δύνασθαι αὐτὸ πόλιν λυμᾶναι [9] *ἔρχομαι* ἐγγὺς αὐτοῦ καὶ τὸ τηλικοῦτο κῆτος *ἐκτείνει* ἑαυτὸ χαμαὶ καὶ οὐδὲν εἰ μὴ τὴν γλῶσσαν προέβαλλεν καὶ ὅλως οὐκ **ἐκινήθη** μέχρις ὅτε **παρῆλθον** αὐτό [10] *εἶχεν* δὲ τὸ θηρίον ἐπὶ τῆς κεφαλῆς χρώματα τέσσερα μέλαν εἶτα πυροειδὲς καὶ αἱματῶδες εἶτα χρυσοῦν εἶτα λευκόν[188]

---

[188] "Twenty days after the former vision I saw another vision, brethren—a representation of the tribulation that is to come. [2] I was going to a country house along the Campanian road. Now the house lay about ten furlongs from the public road. The district is one rarely traversed. [3] And as I walked alone, I prayed the Lord to complete the revelations which He had made to me through His holy Church, that He might strengthen me, and give repentance to all His servants who were going astray, that His great and glorious name might be glorified because He vouchsafed to show me His marvels. [4] And while I was glorifying Him and giving Him thanks, a voice, as it were, answered me, "Doubt not, Hermas;" and I began to think with myself, and to say, "What reason have I to doubt—I who have been established by the Lord, and who have seen such glorious sights?" [5] I advanced a little, brothers, and, lo! I saw dust rising even to the heavens. I began to say to myself, "Are cattle approaching and raising the dust?" It was about a furlong's distance from me. [6] And, lo! I saw the dust rising more and more, so that I imagined that it was something sent from God. But the sun now shone out a little, and, lo! I saw a mighty beast like a whale, and out of its mouth fiery locusts proceeded. But the size of that beast was about a hundred feet, and it had a head like an urn. [7] I began to weep, and to call on the Lord to rescue me from it. Then I remembered the word which I had heard, "Doubt not, O Hermas." [8] Clothed, therefore, my brethren, with faith in the Lord and remembering the great things which He had taught me, I boldly faced the beast. Now that beast came on with such noise and force, that it could itself have destroyed a city. [9] I came near it, and the monstrous beast stretched itself out on the ground, and showed nothing but its tongue, and did not stir at all until I had passed by it. [10] Now the beast had four colors on its head—.black, then fiery and bloody, then golden, and lastly white." The vision continues in section two with a vision of a woman and reveals similar shifts in tenses: v. 1—

The point of this brief discussion and limited sampling of texts has been to demonstrate that the phenomenon of shifting tenses is not unique to Revelation, but can be found elsewhere in the New Testament and extra-biblical Greek, especially in narration, rendering the proposal that Revelation's shifting tenses is inconsistent or unnatural or due to Semitic influence even more difficult to sustain. As Porter observes, "the most common pattern in narration throughout the NT, and within Greek literature as a whole, is to find an alteration of tenses."[189] This suggests that in all of these examples something other than time is the motivating factor for tense choice. In all these places verbal aspect can account for the shifting tenses, rather than temporal concerns or Semitic interference. The aorist is the normal tense of narration, functioning to summarize main processes and move the story along, as well as to provide background material. The present and imperfect tenses, then, select specific items to vividly describe in more detail and draw attention to. The perfect (stative) tense form, which enters into narrative less frequently, is used to focus attention of processes that stand out unexpectedly. Thus the shifting of tense forms that one encounters in the Apocalypse is different only in degree, not in kind, from what is found elsewhere in the New Testament and other extra-biblical Greek texts.

Conclusion

The focus of this chapter has been on the phenomenon of shifting tenses in the visions of the Apocalypse. I have considered only a handful of examples of sustained visionary accounts in order to examine the function of the various aspects that depict the processes which make up these visionary segments (Revelation 5; 7.9–17; 9; 11.1–13; 12–13; 17; 18.4–20; 19.11–21). These texts were chosen due to the notable shifts in tense forms and due to the varied responses (often confused) from commentators and grammarians that they have engendered. Obviously, further analysis could be and needs to be carried out on other visionary segments of the Apocalypse. In examining just a sample of Revelation's visionary (and auditory) material I have focused primarily on indicative forms, but

---

ὑταντᾷ (present), εἶχεν (imperfect); v. 2—ἔγνων (aorist), ἐγενόμην (aorist), ἀσπάζεται (present), ἀντησπασάμην (aorist); v. 3—λέγει (present). Note also the perfect participles used to describe the woman in v. 1 (κεκοσμημένη, κατακεκαλυμμένη). Cf. Rev 21.2.

[189] Porter, *Verbal Aspect*, 207.

have also included analysis of some non-indicative forms at times. As the author narrates his vision for his audience he employs a full range of tense forms to depict the processes that make up his vision, while often retaining the same temporal frame of reference.

It cannot be expected that readers will agree with all the conclusions reached here, and several sections may be patient of different analyses. However, the above analysis should be sufficient to show that the author of Revelation has chosen tense forms to narrate his vision for reasons other than temporal concerns. Rather than indicating temporal information or constraint from an underlying Semitic tense system, the author selected the various tense forms to communicate his conception on the various processes that make up his visionary narrative. The shifts that take place between the various tense forms, then, are explicable in light of verbal aspect, or "the author's reasoned subjective choice of conception of a process."[190] Furthermore, the author employs the various aspects to structure the discourse in significant ways, often indicating levels of prominence (background, foreground, frontground) within the discourse. The aorist and imperfect forms together tend to implicate past time narration, while the present and future indicate speeches and prophetic sections. But the aorist also functions in discourse as a background tense, while the present and future enter into narrative as the more heavily marked forms. The perfect is utilized in both types of discourse as the most heavily marked form and to frontground certain processes.

Perhaps a visual illustration will prove suggestive of the functions of the various aspects within Revelation's visionary narrative. A suggestive illustration is a 3-dimensional picture, or watching a movie with 3-D spectacles.[191] The various verbal aspects, as communicating the author's perspective on the processes, function to allow the reader to see John's vision in 3-D. One of the functions of apocalyptic discourse is a reactualization of the visionary experience of the author. Rather than offering a flat mosaic or photograph, the aspects provide for and effect different perspectives within the visional field. Thus, the aorist is used for the backdrop of the vision, those events, characters, and things that are the furthest away in the field of vision. Yet other characters and events stand out against this backdrop and are more lifelike and are presented with

---

[190] Porter, *Verbal Aspect*, 88.
[191] I owe the observation that the aspects in Revelation could be compared to 3-dimensional vision to my friend, Mike Boyle.

more descriptive color in the more immediate field of 3-D vision. For these the author uses the present tense (and imperfect) forms. But certain elements seem to "jump" off the screen to grab the reader and stand out more starkly in full color and bold relief in the immediate field of our 3-dimensional vision. For these elements the author utilizes the most heavily marked perfect tense form (These three perspectives would correspond to background, foreground, and frontground). So seeing John's visions through verbal aspectual 'glasses' allows us to see the visions in 3-D, to see them in all their spectacular contours and graphic details.[192] This is at least consistent with one of the functions of Revelation, to mediate "a new actualization of the original revelatory experience through literary devices, structures and imagery."[193] Perhaps one of the devices utilized by the author to aid the reader/hearer in reactualizing the visionary experience was his usage of aspect which provided a perspective on the various processes that made up the vision. In this way the author allows his readers to (re)experience his visionary experience in 3-D. It is clear that the shifting verbal aspects in Revelation semantically have a perspectival purpose rather than a temporal one.

---

[192] For a different dimensional illustration see Porter's illustration of a book case to describe planes of discourse (*Idioms*, 23). The entire case of books can be compared to the backdrop or background of discourse (aorist). A featured shelf from the bookcase would form the foreground (present, imperfect). A single volume selected from the shelf, then, would form the frontground (perfect).

[193] Aune, "Problem of Genre," 87. In other words, "the skillful apocalyptic writer may portray the revelatory experience which he purportedly had with such literary skill (particularly enhanced through public performance) that the intended audience may indeed participate in the original experience to such an extent that the experience is 're-presented' or reactualized for them" (89).

CHAPTER FIVE

CONCLUSION:
VERBAL ASPECT AND THE NATURE
OF REVELATION'S GREEK

In the preceding pages I have attempted to apply insights from the semantic category of verbal aspect to Greek verb tenses in the Apocalypse of
John. While the issue of tenses in Revelation has attracted some attention in the past, recent research into verbal aspect theory makes a rein-
vestigation of the tenses in Revelation worthwhile. There has been to my
knowledge no book-length treatment devoted to the issue of verb tenses
in Revelation that takes into account the most recent research into the
semantics of Greek verb tenses. In fact, all of the major treatments of this
issue were produced prior to the most significant work done on aspect
theory. And all of them operated with similar, outmoded time-based or
Aktionsart-based theories of the verb tenses in Revelation, leading to several questionable and unsupported assumptions and explanations. Such
studies, however, have had to overcome the obstacle of how to account
for the numerous instances of tense forms in Revelation that are not utilized according to their assumed temporal values (e.g. present for past
time; aorist for future time).

This difficulty is particularly prevalent in the phenomenon of shifting tenses in Revelation's visionary segments, where the author shifts
between all the major tense forms, often without a corresponding temporal shift. However, in light of recent research into verbal aspect, I have
suggested that the verb tenses in Revelation should be seen as grammaticalizing the semantic category of verbal aspect, rather than time
or *Aktionsart*. When examined from the standpoint of verbal aspect it
becomes clear that the author chose verb tense forms for reasons other
than temporal ones. According to this study, Revelation's use of aspect
falls well within the range of the functions one encounters elsewhere
in the New Testament, rendering judgments regarding its aberrant or
inconsistent nature in Revelation misguided and unnecessary.

The difficulty of accounting for the phenomenon of tense usage in the
Apocalypse from a governing temporal standpoint has led to a variety
of judgments regarding the author's handling of verb tenses. Mussies

argued that the use of tense forms in Revelation, while reflecting Semitic influence (Mishnaic Hebrew and Aramaic), was not at odds with their normal Greek (temporal) functions. According to Mussies, the Greek tense forms in Revelation retain their full temporal value and should be understood from the temporal standpoint of the visionary experience of the seer (past vision, present vividness, future prediction). The other, much more common, approach is to see the apparent violation of the temporal values of the Greek tense forms as the result of appreciable Semitic influence. Following Charles, Lancellotti and others, Thompson in particular has argued that the seemingly inexplicable tense usage in Revelation can be accounted for by recognizing the underlying Semitic influence. Thus Greek verb tenses are not to be understood as having their normal Greek (temporal) meanings, but underlying Hebrew meanings. Dougherty acutely recognized that the various tenses were used in a variety of temporal contexts throughout Revelation. But ultimately he was unable (or unwilling) to part with a temporal model when he found the tense forms often used "inconsistently" in Revelation's visionary material.

What all of these approaches share in common is a conception of Greek tense forms that is heavily temporal in orientation. From a strictly temporal standpoint Revelation's use of the different tense forms appears irregular and inexplicable indeed. And in one sense these conclusions are to be expected, since the grammars upon which these works relied advocated such an approach to the Greek verbal system. However, taking the important work on verbal aspect by Porter in particular and others (McKay, Fanning, Campbell) as a starting point, I have argued that rather than communicating (or mis-communicating) temporal information, the verb tense forms in Revelation are to be seen as grammaticalizing the semantic feature of verbal aspect, "a synthetic semantic category (realized in the forms of verbs) used of meaningful oppositions in a network of tense systems to grammaticalize the author's reasoned subjective choice of conception of a process."[1] That is, rather than indicating time or kind of action (*Aktionsart*) the verb tense forms in Revelation indicate how the author wished to portray the action (aspect).

When seen from this perspective, there is no need to conclude that the author's use of tenses was irregular, confusing, temporally motivated, nor semitically governed. Rather, when we divest ourselves of several past

---

[1] Porter, *Verbal Aspect*, 88.

conceptions of Greek verb tenses and analyze them from the standpoint of verbal aspect, John's use of verb tense forms is not quite so inexplicable. I am not suggesting that there is no Semitic influence on Revelation's Greek at any level, nor that other grammatical categories might not require a separate or different analysis.[2] But the preceding study has demonstrated that at least for verb tenses, direct Semitic influence plays little, if any, role in the author's selection of tense forms. The various tense forms can be construed as the author's desire to portray the processes in his visionary construct from differing perspectives. At the same time there are instances where John's use of a given aspect may be the result of translation by means of citation of or allusion to the Old Testament. Even then, John may have chosen a tense form because it communicated his view of the process aspectually. At other times John's choice of tense form may reflect his dependence on the LXX. Or in other instances an acceptable use of a tense form in Koine Greek may be semitically *enhanced*.

Moreover, in addition to grammaticalizing the author's "conception of a process" the different aspects may function to structure the discourse in significant ways. Often the different tense forms could be used to establish discourse prominence, backgrounding some information (aorist) while foregrounding (present, imperfect, future) or frontgrounding (perfect) other information within Revelation's discourse. This study has attempted to make a contribution to the debate by integrating recent linguistic insights from the recent work done on verbal aspect. In fact, as seen in the introduction, all of the major work done on the issue of verb tenses in the Apocalypses is "pre verbal aspect," making the time ripe to revisit the issue of verb tense usage in the Apocalypse. This study is a sustained effort to fill that void.

The bulk of this work has examined the tense forms individually as they are distributed throughout Revelation, in order to demonstrate that verbal aspect can account for the variety of ways that the various tense forms function throughout the Apocalypse. There it was demonstrated that the various tense forms occur in a variety of temporal contexts and with a variety of pragmatic functions. Furthermore, I also examined the question of the shifting tenses in Revelation's visions, once again suggesting that verbal aspect can account for the manner in which the

---

[2] For some suggestions with regard to other grammatical constructions in Revelation cf. Porter, "Language of the Apocalypse."

author alternates between all the major tense forms in communicating
the processes that make up his visionary narrative, while often maintaining the same temporal sphere of reference. That is, the tense shifts indicate
the author's various conceptions of the different processes. While it cannot be expected that all the conclusions argued for here will elicit complete agreement, the results should be sufficient to demonstrate that the
author used the verb tenses for reasons other than time. I have suggested
that verbal aspect provides the most compelling explanation.

One of the upshots of the conclusions from this study, then, is that
Revelation's use of tense forms appears to correspond with their usage in
the rest of the New Testament literature, and even in some extra-biblical
Greek. Porter has argued that the primary feature grammaticalized in the
verb tense forms in the New Testament consistently is verbal aspect.[3] The
results of this study suggest that this should be extended to include the
book of Revelation. That is, the author of Revelation is doing nothing
fundamentally different from the rest of the New Testament in his use of
verb tenses, when seen as communicating verbal aspect. This latter point
requires brief unpacking.

Part of the issue surrounding verb tenses in Revelation is the issue of
the nature of John's Greek. In this conclusion I will not attempt to com-
prehensively address the question of the nature of Revelation's Greek, but
wish only to make some very brief comments on the issue as it relates to
the author's use of verb tenses and verbal aspect in Revelation. As seen
above, it has frequently been concluded that John's use of verb tenses
reflects significant Semitic influence and is not representative of Koine
Greek in general, a judgment that usually extends to John's use of grammar more generally. Charles' well-known dictum that "while he writes in
Greek, he thinks in Hebrew" can be applied to the use of verb tenses in the
Apocalypse.[4] Similarly, based on his study of tense forms and other grammatical constructions in the Apocalypse Thompson concluded that "the
Greek language was little more than a membrane, stretched tightly over a
Semitic framework."[5] This is not just a matter of a handful of Greek constructions being affected by the Hebrew tense system, but a widespread
and thoroughgoing semantic innovation. The Greek verb tenses reveal a
more significant underlying semantic contour provided by the Hebrew

---

[3] Porter, *Verbal Aspect*. Cf. Fanning, *Verbal Aspect*.
[4] Charles, *Revelation, I*, cxliii. On the nature of New Testament Greek more generally
along these lines cf. Turner, *Syntax*, 2–9.
[5] Thompson, *Semitic Syntax*, 108.

tense system. Another way of putting it is that, for the reader, John's use of verb tenses can be seen as a kind of parody of his "hear"/"see" dialectic: *"see" Greek, but "hear" Hebrew.* When the reader "sees" a Greek verb tense, (s)he should "hear" a Hebrew meaning.[6]

One suspects that much of the discussion related to Semitic influence of the verbal system in Revelation would not have progressed as it has if the aspectual nature of the Greek verb system had been recognized. It is, of course, possible that John's use of tenses could have been influenced by his Hebrew background. But the more verbal aspect is seen to lie behind Revelation's verb tense usage the less necessary it is to resort to Semitic influence to explain them. Yet other methodological questions are raised by assessing Revelation's use of tenses in light of widespread Semitic influence. As we have noticed earlier, much of Thompson's argument is cumulative in nature, so that even when he admits that a given usage of a tense form is acceptable Greek, he is compelled to diminish this evidence in favor of finding Semitic influence. However, judgments on the nature of Revelation's use of tenses such as one finds in Charles, Lancellotti, Thompson, and others raises other important questions that have exegetical implications. According to Thompson, the Greek verb tenses apparently cannot be understood according to the standards of first century Greek, but only according to the standards of biblical Hebrew. Regarding the New Testament in general Turner reflected a similar sentiment when he concluded that grammatically "it is not that Biblical Greek has no standards at all, but pains must be taken to discover them outside the sphere of classical Greek, even outside secular Greek altogether."[7] And such judgments are not without their exegetical implications.

For example, in his treatment of the perfect tense form in the Apocalypse Thompson concluded:

> It hardly requires saying that if the proposal maintained here is accepted—i.e. that a Greek perfect is used in the NT in a manner not acceptable to Greek syntax where translation from a Semitic source has occurred—the *tense can be ignored*, since it merely indicates a derived conjugation Semitic

---

[6] Though this could be turned the other way around to "hear" a Greek tense/"see" a Hebrew meaning, since the earliest recipients "heard" the Apocalypse in oral enactment. Cf. Rev 1.3 (οἱ ἀκούοντες); 22.18 (τῷ ἀκούοντι). My use of this dialectic with the 'reading' element first simply reflects that fact that most modern-day interpreters encounter the Apocalypse through reading/readings of the text.

[7] Turner, *Syntax*, 3. Notice his standard of comparison with Classical Greek. Turner further suggested that "Bibl. Greek is a unique language with a unity and character of its own" (4).

verb. The temporal sense of the verb would thus be determined by the
context. This would *remove the need for exegetes to account for the 'perfect'
or 'completed' nature of the action of verbs where this was not evident.*[8]

In other words, besides Thompson's inadequate understanding of the
perfect tense form (a past action with present results), the tense endings
are simply a thin veneer which covers over the true, underlying Semitic
meanings of those forms. Therefore, the exegete must apparently ignore
their Greek meanings in exchange for the underlying Hebrew meanings.
Yet I have tried to argue that if seen as representative of the Greek
aspectual system the tenses do have important exegetical implications.
And the perfect (stative) aspect in particular has significant implications
for interpretation.

Though they do not explicitly explore the question, presumably
Thompson and others would conclude that the readers of Revelation were
privy to this special kind of semitized Greek. But this creates a fundamental difficulty with the fact that *John still wrote in Greek.* Thus our starting
point must be the fact that John chose to write in the Greek vernacular
of the day, and this meant for verbs choosing a specific tense form which
semantically communicated an aspectual viewpoint. Besides the prob-
lematics of postulating a hybrid language (a Jewish Greek), it is difficult
to conceive of why John chose this vehicle of expression if he did not
intend to communicate Greek meanings with his choice of tenses, not
to mention what the (Greek-speaking) readers/hearers residing in Hellenistic cities thought they were reading/hearing.[9] Again, if Greek does
not provide the standard for John's Greek, if it is merely a thin veneer
that the exegete must strip away to uncover the true Hebrew meanings,
or a Hellenistic cover soil that must be quickly cleared away in order to
unearth the true Semitic bedrock beneath, one must explain why John
wrote in Greek at all and how his readers could have grasped the underlying Hebrew meanings.

Indeed, if this is the case, it is difficult not to conclude that John's
employment of tenses would have been confusing to and seriously mis-
understood by his readership, if not outright misleading. As the messages
to the seven churches clearly indicate (Revelation 2–3), however, John

---

[8] Thompson, *Semitic Syntax*, 45. Italics mine.
[9] For a discussion of bilingualism or multilingualism as it relates to New Testament
Greek see Porter, *Verbal Aspect*, 112–113; and esp. Moises Silva, "Bilingualism and the
Character of Palestinian Greek," *Bib* 61 (1980) 198–219. Cf. also Joseph Fitzmyer, "The
Language of Palestine in the First Century," *CBQ* 32 (1970) 501–531.

was writing to churches in Asia Minor, thoroughly ensconced in Greek culture and at the center of Imperial Roman rule.[10] That is, John's "text came to life in a Greco-Roman context. John chose to write in Greek, idiosyncratic as his may be, because it was the language of the eastern Empire and of the early Christian communities."[11] In such a context it is difficult to conceive of the author (and the readers) treating the tense system of the Apocalypse as anything other than standard Koine Greek. Methodologically, in order for Thompson's (and others) theory to work, one would need to argue that the communities which John addressed, living in Greco-Roman Asia Minor, and who used Greek every day as the common language of commerce, were familiar with this heavily semitized use of Greek verb tenses and that they would have possessed the Semitic grammatical sophistication necessary to find the correspondences that Thompson and others hypothesize. Porter aptly concludes that though the view that the speakers of Greek themselves took is difficult to determine, "there is little chance anyone thought he [John] was using anything other than the Hellenistic Greek of the day."[12] And given the widespread and influential affect of Koine Greek as the imperial language in the Greco-Roman world, it is just as possible that any Semitic language spoken by the author would have been influenced by Greek, rather than the other way around.[13]

As Porter has further argued, this all raises the methodological issue of where the burden of proof lies. Thompson and others place the burden of proof squarely on those who would argue for the normal Hellenistic meaning of the Greek tense forms (albeit a temporal meaning). Thus even when a given construction is deemed acceptable (however uncommon) Greek, Semitic influence is still preferred and posited. However, given the fact that John wrote in Greek, that his text emerged in a Greco-Roman context, and given that as seen above the Greek verb tense forms, when analyzed from the standpoint of verbal aspect, reflect acceptable Greek standards, the burden of proof must necessarily shift to those who would argue for any appreciable Semitic influence in the Greek

---

[10] For the importance of the Greco-Roman environment for interpreting Revelation 2–3 see Colin J. Hemer, *The Letters to the Seven Churches of Asia in their Local Setting* (JSNTSS 11; Sheffield: JSOT Press, 1986).

[11] Robert W. Royalty Jr., *The Streets of Heaven: The Ideology of Wealth in the Apocalypse of John* (Macon, GA: Mercer, 1998) 81.

[12] Porter, "Language of the Apocalypse," 603.

[13] See Silva, "Bilingualism," 208; Porter, "Language of the Apocalypse," 603.

tense system in Revelation.[14] Furthermore, as Porter has demonstrated, Semitic influence should be understood to affect the language of the Apocalypse (if at all) at the level of text rather than code.[15] More generally, Silva evokes the Saussurian terminology of "langue" and "parole."[16] While the former may be affected, the latter is not, at least in any lasting way. That is, any Semitic influence should not be "seen as affecting the essential grammatical structure or code of the language."[17]

Moreover, some semantic distinctions or choices in a language are nearly impossible to avoid in certain languages; in Greek this applies to synthetic verbal aspect which is a morphologically-based semantic property that exists in a network system of obligatory semantic choices on the part of the author. Thus for "Greek, ... there is no way to abandon verbal aspect, since every verbal form (with the exception of the future and a handful of aspectually vague verbs) has a morphologically-bound aspectual designation."[18] Such a consideration makes explanations of Revelation's use of verb tenses based on widespread Semitic interference into the Greek tense system and Revelation's use of tense forms difficult to sustain. As the chart at the beginning of Ch. 3 of this work indicates, the Greek verbal system finds full expression across all its tenses and moods throughout Revelation (aorist, present, imperfect, perfect, future, pluperfect; subjunctive, participle, infinitive, imperative; also active, passive, middle voices).[19] This fact in itself suggests that it is the Greek verbal system, not a supposed underlying Semitic verbal system, that is affecting John's use of tenses.[20] Neither is it methodologically legitimate, as

---

[14] "The burden of proof must rest upon those arguing for a Semitic source to prove that a particular construction is impossible in the NT or at least highly unlikely to occur as often as it does. Since the NT documents are extant Greek documents in a Greek linguistic milieu ..., the burden of proof must lie with those who argue for Semitic influence" (Porter, "Language of the Apocalypse," 587).

[15] Cf. Porter, "Language of the Apocalypse," 597.

[16] Silva, "Bilingualism," 216–218.

[17] Porter, "Language of the Apocalypse," 597. Porter also demonstrates that the discussion more broadly is fundamentally related to understanding of the distinction between "language" and "dialect." See pp. 595–596.

[18] Porter, "Language of the Apocalypse," 602.

[19] For a similar conclusion regarding the verbal system in the Pentateuch, clearly a translation document, see Evans, *Verbal Syntax*.

[20] For example, the Hebrew infinitive does not grammaticalize tense or aspect. Yet within the Greek verbal system the selection of verbal aspect encoded in the morphological ending (aorist, present, perfect) is obligatory when choosing an infinitive form. Thus even in instances where a Greek infinitive might translate or represent a Hebrew infinitive, the aspectual choice is in the Greek construction is obligatory and is unaffected semantically by its Hebrew counterpart.

Thompson consistently does, to draw on the evidence of the LXX for his theory, since the latter is clearly a translation document, whereas Revelation is not, except for the instances where John may be quoting from/explicitly alluding to the Old Testament.[21] But aside from those instances, if the Greek verb tenses indicate verbal aspect, as I have tried to argue, rather than time or *Aktionsart*, then it is simply unnecessary to look outside of Koine Greek itself for the semantics of the Greek tense forms in Revelation. As seen above, much of the motivation for postulating Semitic influence/interference came from the assumption that the Greek tenses were essentially temporal in meaning.

Taking these observations into consideration, Revelation's use of verb tenses can be seen as acceptable first century Greek rather than as a thin "membrane" of Greek tense forms "stretched tightly over a Semitic framework."[22] Again, it is not my purpose to argue that no grammatical structure in Revelation has been semitically influenced. This study is far more restricted, and has demonstrated that at least the verb tense system has not been so influenced. Porter's conclusion regarding the language of the Apocalypse in general is certainly true for the verb tense system in particular, when the verb tense forms are seen as communicating verbal aspect as this study has argued: "the language of the Apocalypse can be understood as falling within the range of possible registers of Greek usage of the 1st century."[23] Therefore, starting from the perspective of verbal aspect, the interpreter should analyze Greek verb usage in Revelation from the perspective of its normal, Koine semantics. The verb tenses in the Apocalypse, as a network system of specific semantic choices, as with the New Testament in particular and Koine Greek more generally, communicate verbal aspect or the "author's reasoned subjective choice of conception of a process."[24]

---

[21] Even if Thompson were correct that Revelation has undergone Semitic influence, his conclusion does not necessarily follow. As mentioned earlier, Evans has done initial work on the translation techniques of the LXX in the Pentateuch as it relates to its verbal structure. His findings suggest that the verb tense usage in the LXX is nothing less than idiomatic Greek. Evans summarizes his own work: "The central argument is that verbal syntax in the translation documents [of the Pentateuch] represents essentially idiomatic Greek, which needs to be viewed in the light of contemporary Koine vernacular usage" (*Verbal Syntax*, 2).

[22] Thompson, *Semitic Syntax*, 108.

[23] Porter, "Language of the Apocalypse," 603.

[24] Porter, *Verbal Aspect*, 88.

BIBLIOGRAPHY

Aune, David E. *Prophecy in Early Christianity and the Ancient Mediterranean World*. Grand Rapids: Eerdmans, 1983.

———. "The Apocalypse of John and the Problem of Genre." *Sem* 36 (1986): 65–96.

———. *Revelation 1–5*. WBC 52a. Dallas: Word Books, 1997.

———. *Revelation 6–16*. WBC 52b. Nashville: Thomas Nelson, 1998.

———. *Revelation 17–22*. WBC 52c. Nashville: Thomas Nelson, 1998.

———. *Apocalypticism, Prophecy, and Magic in Early Christianity: Collected Essays*. Grand Rapids: Baker Academic, 2006.

Bache, C. "Aspect and Aktionsart: Towards a Semantic Distinction." *Journal of Linguistics* 18 (1982): 57–72.

Barnard, Jody A. "Is Verbal Aspect a Prominence Indicator? An Evaluation of Stanley Porter's Proposal with Special Reference to the Gospel of Luke." *FN* 19 (2006): 3–29.

Barr, David L. *Tales of the End: A Narrative Commentary on the Book of Revelation*. Santa Rosa: Poleridge Press, 1998.

———. (ed.). *Reading the Book of Revelation*. Atlanta: Society of Biblical Literature, 2003.

———. (ed.). *The Reality of Apocalypse: Rhetoric and Politics in the Book of Revelation*. Atlanta: Society of Biblical Literature, 2006.

Barr, James. *The Semantics of Biblical Language*. Oxford: University Press, 1961.

Battle, J. "The Present Indicative in New Testament Exegesis." Th.D. Dissertation. Grace Theological Seminary, 1975.

Bauckham, Richard J. *The Climax of Prophecy: Studies on the Book of Revelation*. Edinburgh: T & T Clark, 1993.

———. *The Theology of the Book of Revelation*. Cambridge: Cambridge University Press, 1993.

Bauer, W., Danker, F.W., Arndt, W.F., and Gingrich, F.W. *A Greek-English Lexicon of the New Testament and Other Early Christian Literature*. 3rd edn. Chicago: University Press, 2000. (BDAG).

Baugh, Steven M. "Twelve Theses on Greek Verbal Aspect." Unpublished Paper, Westminster Theological Seminary, California, 1997.

Beale, Gregory K. *John's Use of the Old Testament in Revelation*. JSNTSS 166. Sheffield: Sheffield Academic Press, 1998.

———. *The Book of Revelation*. NIGTC. Grand Rapids: Eerdmans/Carlisle: Paternoster, 1999.

Beasley-Murray, G.R. *Revelation*. The New Century Bible Commentary. Grand Rapids: Eerdmans, 1974.

Beckwith, I.T. *The Apocalypse of John*. New York: Macmillan, 1919.

Black, David A. "Greek Verbs: Tense and Aspect." *BibRev* 8/6 (1992): 17.

Black, David A., Barnwell, Katharine, and Levinsohn, Stephen (eds.). *Linguistics and New Testament Interpretation: Essays on Discourse Analysis*. Nashville: Broadman, 1992.

Black, David A. *Linguistics for Students of New Testament Greek: A Survey of Basic Concepts and Application.* 2nd edn. Grand Rapids: Baker, 2000.

Black, Matthew. *An Aramaic Approach to the Gospels and Acts.* 3rd edn. Oxford: Oxford University Press, 1967.

Black, Stephanie L. "The Historic Present in Matthew: Beyond Speech Margins." In *Discourse Analysis and the New Testament: Results and Applications.* Edited by Stanley E. Porter and Jeffrey T. Reed. JSNTSS 170. Sheffield: Sheffield Academic Press, 1999: 120–139.

Blass, F. *Grammatik der Neutestametlichen Griechisch.* Göttingen: Vandenhoeck und Ruprecht, 1902.

Blass, F., A. Debrunner, and Robert A. Funk. *A Greek Grammar of the New Testament and Other Early Christian Literature.* Chicago: University of Chicago Press, 1961. (*BDF*)

Blount, Brian K. *Revelation.* NTL. Louisville: JohnKnox Press, 2009.

Bousset, W. *Die Offenbarung Johannis.* Göttingen: Vandenhoeck and Ruprecht, 1906.

Boyer, James L. "The Classification of Participles: A Statistical Study." *GTJ* 5 (1984): 163–179.

———. "The Classification of Infinitives: A Statistical Study." *GTJ* 6 (1985): 3–27.

———. "The Classification of Subjunctives: A Statistical Study." *GTJ* 7 (1986): 3–19.

———. "The Classification of Imperatives: A Statistical Study." *GTJ* 8 (1987): 35–54.

Boxall, Ian *The Revelation of Saint John.* Black's New Testament Commentary. Peabody: Hendrickson/London: Continuum, 2006.

Brook, Matthew D. "Authorial Choice and Verbal Aspect in the NT: An Investigation Using Corpus Linguistics to Identify Patterns of Aspectual Usage Linked with Lexis, Syntax and Context." M.Div. thesis, Gordon-Conwell Theological Seminary, 1997.

Brook O'Donnell, Matthew. *Corpus Linguistics & the Greek of the New Testament.* New Testament Monographs 6. Sheffield: Sheffield Phoenix Press, 2005.

Brütsch, C. *Die Offenbarung Jesu Christi I–II.* ZBK. Zürich: Zwingli, 1970.

Brooks, James A. and Winbery, Carlton L. *Syntax of New Testament Greek.* Lanham, MD: University of America Press, 1979.

Burton, E.D.W. *Syntax of the Moods and Tenses in New Testament Greek.* 3rd edn. Edinburgh: T & T Clark, 1898.

Buth, Randall. "Mark's Use of the Historical Present." *Notes on Translation* 65 (1977): 7–13.

———. "Verbs Perception and Aspect: Greek Lexicography and Grammar." In *Biblical Greek Language and Lexicography: Essays in Honor of Fredrick W. Danker.* Edited by B.A. Taylor *et al.* Grand Rapids: Eerdmans, 2004: 177–198.

Caird, G.B. *A Commentary on the Revelation of St. John the Divine.* New York: Harper & Row, 1966.

Callahan, A.D. "The Language of the Apocalypse." *HTR* 88 (1995): 453–457.

Callow, Kathleen. *Discourse Considerations in Translating the Word of God.* Grand Rapids: Zondervan, 1974.

Campbell, Constantine R. *Verbal Aspect, the Indicative Mood, and Narrative: Soundings in the Greek of the New Testament.* SBG 13. New York: Peter Lang, 2007.

———. *Verbal Aspect and Non-Indicative Verbs: Further Soundings in the Greek of the New Testament.* SBG 15. New York: Peter Lang, 2008.

———. *Basics of Verbal Aspect in Biblical Greek.* Grand Rapids: Zondervan, 2008.

Caragounis, Chrys C. *The Development of Greek in the New Testament.* Grand Rapids: Baker, 2006.

———. "The Development of Greek and the New Testament: A Response to Dr. M. Silva." *WTJ* 67 (2005): 405–415.

Carson, D.A. "An Introduction to the Porter/Fanning Debate." In *Biblical Greek Language and Linguistics: Open Questions in Current Research.* Edited by Stanley E. Porter and D.A. Carson. JSNTSS 80. Sheffield: Sheffield Academic Press, 1993: 18–25.

———. *Exegetical Fallacies.* 2nd edition. Grand Rapids: Baker, 1996.

Chamberlain, W.D. *An Exegetical Grammar of the Greek New Testament.* New York: Macmillan, 1941.

Charles, R.H. *Studies in the Apocalypse.* Edinburgh: T & T Clark, 1912.

———. *The Revelation of St. John.* 2 Vols. ICC. New York: Scribner's, 1920.

Collins, J.J. "Introduction: Towards the Morphology of a Genre." *Semeia* 14 (1979): 1–20.

———. *The Apocalyptic Imagination: An Introduction to the Jewish Matrix of Christianity.* 2nd edn. Grand Rapids: 1998.

Comrie, B. *Aspect: An Introduction to the Study of Verbal Aspect and Related Problems.* Cambridge Textbooks in Linguistics. Cambridge: Cambridge University Press, 1976.

———. *Tense.* Cambridge Textbooks in Linguistics. Cambridge: Cambridge University Press, 1985.

Conybeare, F.C. and Stock, St. George. *Grammar of Septuagint Greek.* Peabody: Hendrickson, 1995. Reprint from the original edn published by Gin and Company, Boston, 1905.

Cotterell, Peter & Turner, Max. *Linguistics & Biblical Interpretation.* Downers Grove: IVP, 1989.

Dana, H.E. and Mantey, J.R. *A Manual Grammar of the Greek New Testament.* New York: Macmillan, 1955.

Decker, Rodney J. *Temporal Deixis of the Greek Verb in the Gospel of Mark with Reference to Verbal Aspect.* SBG 10. New York: Peter Lang, 2001.

Dougherty, E.C.A. "The Syntax of the Apocalypse." Ph.D. Dissertation. Catholic University of America, 1990.

Dry, H.A. "Foregrounding: An Assessment." In *Language in Context: Essays for Robert E. Longacre.* Edited by S.J.J. Hwang and W.R. Merrifield. Dallas: Summer Institute of Linguistics, 1992: 435–450.

Du Plooy, G.P.V. "Aspect and Biblical Exegesis." *Neot* 25 (1991): 19–53.

Edwards, Ruth B. "Review of Stanley E. Porter, *Verbal Aspect in the Greek of the New Testament, with Reference to Tense and Mood.*" *The Bible Translator* 42 (1991): 345–348.

Evans, T.V. *Verbal Syntax in the Greek Pentateuch: Natural Greek Usage and Hebrew Interference*. Oxford: Oxford University Press, 2001.

———. "Future Directions for Aspect Studies in Ancient Greek." In *Biblical Greek Language and Lexicography: Essays in Honor of Frederick W. Danker*. Edited by B.A. Taylor et al. Grand Rapids: Eerdmans, 2004: 199–206.

Fanning, Buist M. *Verbal Aspect in New Testament Greek*. Oxford: Clarendon Press, 1990.

———. "Approaches to Verbal Aspect in New Testament Greek: Issues in Definition and Method." In *Biblical Greek Language and Linguistics: Open Questions in Current Research*. Edited by Stanley E. Porter and D.A. Carson. JSNTSS 80. Sheffield: JSOT Press, 1993: 46–62.

———. "Review of *Verbal Aspect, the Indicative Mood, and Narrative: Soundings in the Greek of the NT* by C. Campbell," *JETS* 51 / 2 (2008): 394–397.

Fekkes, Jan. *Isaiah and Prophetic Traditions in the Book of Revelation: Visionary Antecedents and Their Development*. JSNTSS 93. Sheffield: JSOT Press, 1994.

Fitzmyer, Joseph. "The Language of Palestine in the First Century." *CBQ* 32 (1970): 501 31.

Ford, J. Massygnberde. *Revelation*. Anchor Bible 38. Garden City: Doubleday, 1975.

France, R.T. "The Exegesis of Greek Tenses in the NT." *Notes on Translation* 46 (1972): 3–12.

Friesen, Steven J. *Imperial Cults and the Apocalypse of John: Reading Revelation in the Ruins*. New York: Oxford University Press, 2001.

Giesen, Heinz. *Die Offenbarung des Johannes*. Regensburger Neues Testament. Regensbug: Pustet, 1997.

———. *Studien zur Johannesapokalypse*. Stuttgartes Biblische Aufsatzbände 29. Stuttgart: Verlag Katholisches Bibelwerk, 2000.

Goodwin, William W. *Syntax of the Moods and Tenses of the Greek Verb*. Boston: Ginn and Co., 1890.

Guite, Harold F. "A Review of *Verbal Aspect in New Testament Greek*, by B. Fanning." *ExpT* 103 (1991): 54.

Halliday, M.A.K. *An Introduction to Functional Grammar*. 3rd edn. Revised by Christian M.I.M. Matthiessen. London. Arnold, 2004.

Hatina, Thomas R. "The Perfect Tense-Form in Colossians: Verbal Aspect, Temporality and the Challenge of Translation." In *Translating the Bible: Problems and Prospects*. Edited by Stanley E. Porter and Richard S. Hess. JSNTSS 173. Sheffield: Sheffield Academic Press, 1999: 224–252.

———. "The Perfect Tense-Form in Recent Debate: Galatians as a Case Study." *FN* 15.8 (1995): 3–22.

Hellholm, David. "The Problem of Apocalyptic Genre and the Apocalypse of John." *Semeia* 36 (1985): 13–64.

Hemer, Colin J. *The Letters to the Seven Churches of Asia in their Local Setting*. JSNTSS 11. Sheffield: JSOT Press, 1986.

Hill, David. *New Testament Prophecy*. Atlanta: John Knox Press, 1979.

Hopper, P.J. "Aspect and Foregrounding in Discourse." In *Discourse and Syntax*. Edited by T. Givón. New York: Academic Press, 1979: 213–241.

———. "Aspect Between Discourse and Grammar: An Introductory Essay for this Volume." In *Tense-Aspect: Between Semantics and Pragmatics*. Edited by P.J. Hopper. Amsterdam: Benjamins, 1982: 1–18.

Hoskier, H.C. *Concerning the Text of the Apocalypse*. Vol. II. London: Quartich, 1929.

Jobes, Karen H. "The Syntax of 1 Peter: Just how Good Is the Greek?" *BBR* 13.2 (2003): 159–173.

Kistemaker, Simon J. *Revelation*. NTC. Grand Rapids: Baker, 2001.

Kraft, H. *Die Offenbarung des Johannes*. HNT 16a. Tübingen: Mohr, 1974.

Kuehne, C. "Translating the Aorist Indicative." *Journal of Theology* 18 (1978): 19–26.

Lancellotti, A. *Sintassi ebraica nel Greco dell'Apocalisse. Vol. 1. Uso delle forme verbali*. Collectio Assisiensis I. Assisi: Studio Teologico, 1964.

Lee, G.M. "Tense, Voice, and Case." *Bib* 51 (1970): 238–239.

Levinsohn, Stephen H. "Preliminary Observations on the Use of the Historical Present in Mark." *Notes on Translation* 65 (1977): 13–28.

———. *Discourse Features of New Testament Greek: A Coursebook*. 2nd edn. Dallas: Summer Institute of Linguistics, 2000.

———. "The Relevance of Greek Discourse Studies to Exegesis." *Journal of Translation* 2/2 (2006): 11–21.

Levinson, Stephen C. *Pragmatics*. Cambridge Textbooks in Linguistics. Cambridge: University Press, 1983.

Liddell, H.G. and Scott, R. *A Greek-English Lexicon*. Ed. by H.S. Jones and R. McKenzie. 9th edn. Oxford: Clarendon, 1996. (*LJS*)

Lindars, Barnabas. "Review of S. Thompson, *The Apocalypse and Semitic Syntax*." *JSS* 30 (1985): 289–291.

Lohmeyer, E. *Die Offenbarung des Johannes*. Handbuch zum Neuen Testament 16. Tübingen: Mohr, 1970.

Loney, Alexander. "Narrative Structure and Verbal Aspect Choice in Luke." *FN* 18 (2005): 3–31.

Long, Gary A. *Grammatical Concepts 101 for Biblical Hebrew*. Peabody: Hendrickson, 2005.

———. *Grammatical Concepts 101 for Biblical Greek*. Peabody: Hendrickson, 2006.

Longacre, R.E. "Discourse Peak as a Zone of Turbulance." In *Beyond the Sentence: Discourse and Sentential Form*. Edited by J.R. Worth. Ann Arbor: Karoma, 1985: 81–98.

Louw, J.P. "On Greek Prohibitions." *Acta Classica* 2 (1959): 43–57.

———. "Discourse Analysis and the Greek New Testament." *The Bible Translator* 24/1 (1973): 101–118.

———. "Verbal Aspect in the First Letter of John." *Neot* 9 (1975): 98–104.

———. *Semantics of New Testament Greek*. SBL Semeia Studies. Philadelphia: Fortress Press, 1982.

Louw, J.P. and Nida, E.A. *Greek-English Lexicon of the New Testament Based on Semantic Domains*. 2 vols. New York: United Bible Societies, 1988.

Lupieri, Edmondo F. *A Commentary on the Apocalypse of John*. Grand Rapids: Eerdmans, 2006.

Lyons, J. *Language and Linguistics: An Introduction*. Cambridge: University Press, 1981.

Martín-Asensio, Gustavo. *Transitivity-Based Foregrounding in the Acts of the Apostles: A Functional-Grammatical Approach to the Lukan Perspective*. JSNTSS 202; Sheffield: Academic Press, 2000.

Mathewson, David. "Verbal Aspect in Imperatival Constructions in Pauline Ethical Injunctions." *FN* 17 (Mayo 1996): 21–35.

———. "Verbal Aspect in the Book of Revelation: An Analysis of Revelation 5." *NovT* 50 (2008): 58–77.

McKay, K.L. "The Use of the Ancient Greek Perfect Down to the End of the Second Century." *Bulletin of the Institute of Classical Studies* 12 (1965): 1–21.

———. "Syntax in Exegesis." *TynB* 23 (1972): 39–57.

———. "On the Perfect and Other Aspects in New Testament Greek." *NovT* 23 (1981): 289–329.

———. "Aspect in Imperatival Constructions in NT Greek." *NovT* 27 (1985): 201–226.

———. "Time and Aspect in New Testament Greek." *NovT* 34 (1992): 209–228.

———. *A New Syntax of the Verb in New Testament Greek: An Aspectual Approach*. SBG 5. New York: Peter Lang, 1994.

Metzger, Bruce M. *A Textual Commentary on the Greek New Testament*. 2nd edn. Stuttgart: United Bible Society, 1994.

Millhouse, Roy R. "The Use of the Imperfect Verb Form in the New Testament: An Investigation into Aspectual and Tense Relationships in Hellenistic Greek." M.A. Thesis, Trinity Evangelical Divinity School, 1999.

Morris, Leon. *Revelation*. Rev. edn. Tyndale New Testament Commentaries. Grand Rapids: Eerdmans, 1987.

Moule, C.F.D. *An Idiom Book of New Testament Greek*. 2nd edn. Cambridge: Cambridge University Press, 1959.

Moulton, James H. *A Grammar of New Testament Greek. Prolegomena*. Vol. 1. 3rd edn. Edinburgh: T & T Clark, 1908.

Mounce, Robert H. *The Book of Revelation*. NICNT. Rev. edn. Grand Rapids: Eerdmans, 1998.

Mounce, William D. *The Morphology of Biblical Greek*. Grand Rapids: Zondervan, 1994.

———. *The Basics of Biblical Greek Grammar* (2nd edn; Grand Rapids: Zondervan, 2003).

Moyise, Steve. *The Old Testament in the Book of Revelation*. JSNTSS 115; Sheffield: Academic Press, 1995.

———. "The Language of the Old Testament in Revelation." *JSNT* 76 (2000): 97–113.

Mussies, G. *The Morphology of Koine Greek as Used in the Apocalypse of John: A Study in Bilingualism*. NovTSup 27. Leiden: Brill, 1971.

———. "The Greek of the Book of Revelation." In *L'Apocalypse johannique et l'Apocalyptique dans le Nouveau Testament*. Edited by J. Lambrecht. Leuven: Leuven University Press, 1980: 167–177.

Newport, Kenneth G.C. "Semitic Influence in Revelation: Some Further Evidence." *AUSS* 25 (1987): 249–256.

Nida, E. and Louw, J.P. *Lexical Semantics of the Greek New Testament*. Atlanta: Scholars Press, 1992.

Olsen, Mari B. *A Semantic and Pragmatic Model of Lexical and Grammatical Aspect*. Outstanding Dissertations in Linguistics. New York: Garland Publishing, 1997.

O'Rourke, J.J. "The Historical Present in the Gospel of John." *JBL* 93 (1974): 585–590.

Osborne, Grant R. *Revelation*. BECNT. Grand Rapids: Baker, 2002.

Ozanne, C.G. "The Language of the Apocalypse." *TynB* 16 (1965): 3–9.

Pattemore, Stephen. *Souls under the Altar: Relevance Theory and the Discourse Structure of Revelation*. UBS Monograph Series 9. New York: UBS, 2003.

Pearson, Brook R.W. and Porter, Stanley E. "The Genres of the New Testament." In *A Handbook to the Exegesis of the New Testament*. Edited by Stanley E. Porter. Leiden: Brill, 1997: 131–163.

Picirilli, Robert E. "The Meaning of the Tenses in New Testament Greek: Where Are We?" *JETS* 48 (2005): 533–555.

Porter, Stanley E. "Tense Terminology and Greek Language Discussion: A Linguistic Re-evaluation." *Sheffield Working Papers in Language and Linguistics* 3 (1986): 77–86.

———. "Review of S. Thompson, *The Apocalypse and Semitic Syntax*." *JSNT* 29 (1987): 122–124.

———. *Verbal Aspect in the Greek of the New Testament, with Reference to Tense and Mood*. SBG 1. New York: Peter Lang, 1989.

———. "The Language of the Apocalypse in Recent Discussion." *NTS* 35 (1989): 582–603.

———. "Studying Ancient Languages from a Modern Linguistic Perspective: Essential Terms and Terminology." *FN* 2 (1989): 147–172.

———. *Idioms of the Greek New Testament*. Sheffield: JSOT Press, 1992.

———. "In Defense of Verbal Aspect." In *Biblical Greek Language and Linguistics: Open Questions in Current Research*. Edited by Stanley E. Porter and D.A. Carson. JSNTSS 80. Sheffield: Sheffield Academic Press, 1993: 26–45.

———. "How Can Biblical Discourse Be Analyzed: A Response to Several Attempts." In *Discourse Analysis and Other Topics in Biblical Greek*. Edited by Stanley E. Porter and D.A. Carson. JSNTSS 113. Sheffield: Academic Press, 1995: 107–116.

———. *Studies in the Greek of the New Testament: Theories and Practice*. SBG 6. New York: Peter Lang, 1996.

———. "The Greek Language of the New Testament." In *Handbook to the Exegesis of the New Testament*. Ed. by Stanley E. Porter. Leiden: Brill, 1997: 99–130.

———. "Greek Grammar and Syntax." In *The Face of New Testament Study: A Survey of Recent Research*. Edited by Scot McKnight and Grant R. Osborne. Grand Rapids: Baker Academic, 2004: 76–103.

———. "Aspect Theory and Lexicography." In *Biblical Greek Language and Lexicography: Essays in Honor of Frederick W. Danker*. Edited by Bernard A. Taylor et al. Grand Rapids: Eerdmans, 2004: 307–322.

Porter, Stanley E. and Matthew B. O'Donnell. "The Greek Verbal Network from a Probabilistic Standpoint: An Exercise in Hallidayan Linguistics." *FN* 14 (2001): 3–41.

Porter, Stanley E. and Matthew B. O'Donnell (eds.). *The Linguist as Pedagogue: Trends in the Teaching and Linguistic Analysis of the Greek New Testament.* NTM 11; Sheffield: Sheffield Phoenix Press, 2009.

Prigent, Pierre. *L'Apocalypse de saint Jean.* CNT XIV. Lausanne: Delachaux & Niestlé, 1981.

Reddish, Mitchell G. *Revelation.* Smyth & Helwys Bible Commentary. Macon: Smyth & Helwys, 2001.

Reed, Jeffrey T. "Identifying Theme in the New Testament: Insights from Discourse Analysis." In *Discourse Analysis and Other Topics in Biblical Greek.* Edited by Stanley E. Porter and D.A. Carson. JSNTSS 113. Sheffield: Sheffield Academic Press, 1995: 75–101.

———. *Discourse Analysis of Philippians: Method and Rhetoric in the Debate over Literary Integrity.* JSNTSS 136. Sheffield: Sheffield Academic Press, 1997.

Reed, Jeffrey T. and Ruth A. Reese. "Verbal Aspect, Discourse Prominence, and the Letter of Jude." *FN* 18 (1996): 181–199.

Resseguie, J.L. *Revelation Unsealed: A Narrative Critical Approach to John's Apocalypse.* Biblical Interpretation Series 32. Leiden: Brill, 1998.

———. *The Revelation of John: A Narrative Commentary.* Grand Rapids: Baker, 2009.

Rijksbaron, Albert. *The Syntax and Semantics of the Verb in Classical Greek: An Introduciton.* 3rd edn. Chicago and London: University of Chicago Press, 2002.

Robertson, A.T. *A Grammar of the Greek New Testament in the Light of Historical Research.* Nashville: Broadman, 1934.

Roloff, Jürgen. *The Revelation of John: A Continental Commentary.* Translated by John E. Alsop. Minneapolis: Fortress Press, 1993.

Royalty, Robert W. Jr. *The Streets of Heaven: The Ideology of Wealth in the Apocalypse of John.* Macon: Mercer, 1998.

Satake, A. *Die Gemeindordnung in der Johannesapokalypse.* WMANT 21. Neukirchen: Neukirkener, 1966.

Schmidt, Daryl D. "Semitisms and Septuagintalisms in the Book of Revelation." *NTS* 37 (1991): 592–603.

———. "Review of Buist M. Fanning, *Verbal Aspect in New Testament Greek*, and Stanley E. Porter, *Verbal Aspect in the Greek of the New Testament, with Reference to Tense and Mood.*" *JBL* 111 (1992): 714–718.

———. "Verbal Aspect in Greek: Two Approaches." In *Biblical Greek Language and Linguistics: Open Questions in Current Research.* Edited by Stanley E. Porter and D.A. Carson. JSNTSS 80. Sheffield Academic Press, 1993: 63–73.

Schüssler Fiorenza, Elisabeth. *The Book of Revelation: Justice and Judgment.* 2nd edn. Minneapolis: Fortress, 1998.

Scott, R.B.Y. *The Original Language of the Apocalypse.* Toronto: University of Toronto, 1928.

Selwyn, E.C. *The Christian Prophets and the Prophetic Apocalypse.* London: Macmillan, 1900.

Seow, C.L. *A Grammar for Biblical Hebrew.* Nashville: Abingdon Press, 1987.

Shive, Ronald. "The Use of the Historical Present and its Theological Significance." Th.M. Thesis. Dallas Theological Seminary, 1982.

Silva, Moises. "Bilingualism and the Character of Palestinian Greek." *Bib* 61 (1980):

———. *Biblical Words and their Meaning: An Introduction to Lexical Semantics.* 2nd end. Grand Rapids: Zondervan, 1994.

———. *God, Language and Scripture: Reading the Bible in Light of General Linguistics.* Foundations of Contemporary Interpretation. Vol. 4. Grand Rapids: Zondervan, 1990.

———. "A Response to Fanning and Porter on Verbal Aspect." In *Biblical Greek Language and Linguistics: Open Questions in Current Research.* Edited by Stanley E. Porter and D.A. Carson. JSNTSS 80. Sheffield: Sheffield Academic Press, 1993: 74–82.

———. "Biblical Greek and Modern Greek: A Review Article." *WTJ* 67 (2005): 391–404.

———. "Some Comments on Professor Caragounis's Response." *WTJ* 67 (2005): 417–418.

Silzer, Peter James & Finley, Thomas John. *How Biblical Languages Work.* Grand Rapids: Kregal, 2004.

Smalley, Stephen S. *The Revelation to John: A Commentary on the Greek Text of the Apocalypse.* Downers Grove: InterVarsity Press, 2005.

Smith, Charles R. "Errant Aorist Interpreters." *GTJ* 2 (1981): 205–226.

Smith, C.S. "A Theory of Aspectual Choice." *Language* 59 (1983): 480–501.

Smyth, Herbert W. *Greek Grammar.* Harvard: Harvard University Press, 1920.

Stagg, Frank. "The Abused Aorist." *JBL* 91 (1972): 222–231.

Sweet, J.P.M. *Revelation.* Westminster Pelican Commentaries. Philadelphia: Westminster Press, 1979.

Swete, H.B. *The Apocalypse of St. John.* 3rd edn. London: Macmillan, 1911.

Talbert, C.H. *The Apocalypse: A Reading of the Revelation of John.* Louisville: Westminster John Knox, 1994.

Thompson, Leonard L. *The Book of Revelation: Apocalypse and Empire.* New York: Oxford, 1990.

Thompson, Steven. *The Apocalypse and Semitic Syntax.* SNTSMS 52. Cambridge: Cambridge University Press, 1985.

Torrey, C.C. *The Apocalypse of John.* New Haven: Yale University Press, 1958.

Turner, Nigel. *A Grammar of New Testament Greek. Syntax. Vol. III.* Edited by J.H. Moulton. Edinburgh: T & T Clark, 1963.

———. *A Grammar of New Testament Greek. Style. Vol. IV.* Edited by J.H. Moulton. Edinburgh: T. & T. Clark, 1976.

Voelz, James W. *Fundamental Greek Grammar.* St. Louis: Concordia, 1986.

———. "Present and Aorist Verbal Aspect: A New Proposal." *Neot* 27 (1993): 153–164.

Vorster, W.S. "'Genre' and the Revelation of John: A Study in Text, Context, and Intertext." *Neot* 22 (1988): 103–123.

Wall, R.W. *Revelation.* New International Biblical Commentary. Peabody: Hendrickson, 1991.

Wallace, Daniel B. *Greek Grammar Beyond the Basics: An Exegetical Syntax of the New Testament*. Grand Rapids: Zondervan, 1996.

——. *The Basics of New Testament Syntax*. Grand Rapids: Zondervan, 2000.

Wallace, S. "Figure and Ground: The Interrelationship of Linguistic Categories." In *Tense-Aspect: Between Semantics and Pragmatics*. Edited by P.J. Hopper. Amsterdam: Benjamins, 1982: 201–223.

Waltke, Bruce K. and O'Conner, M. *An Introduction to Biblical Hebrew Syntax*. Winona Lake: Eisenbrauns, 1990.

Westfall, Cynthia Long. *A Discourse Analysis of the Letter to the Hebrews: The Relationship Between Form and Meaning*. Library of New Testament Studies 297. London: T & T Clark, 2005.

Whiteley, Iwan M. "An Explanation for the Anacolutha in the Book of Revelation." *FN* 20 (2007): 33–50.

Witherington, Ben III. *Revelation*. NCBC. Cambridge: University Press, 2003.

Young, Richard A. *Intermediate New Testament Greek*. Nashville: Broadman & Holman, 1994.

——. "A Review of *Verbal Aspect in the Greek of the New Testament, with Reference to Tense and Mood*, by S.E. Porter." *JETS* 37 (1994): 145–147.

Zerwick, Maximilian. *Biblical Greek: Illustrated by Examples*. Rome: Pontificio Instituto Biblico, 1963.

Zerwick, Maximilian and Grosvenor, Mary. *A Grammatical Analysis of the Greek New Testament*. 5th edn. Rome: EPIB, 1996.

AUTHOR INDEX

REFERENCE INDEX

Linguistic Biblical Studies

Series Editor
Stanley E. Porter

Professor of New Testament at McMaster Divinity College
Hamilton, Ontario

1. Foley, T. *Biblical Translation in Chinese and Greek*. Verbal Aspect in Theory and Practice. 2009. ISBN 978 90 04 17865 6
2. Park, Y.-M. *Mark's Memory Resources and the Controversy Stories (Mark 2:1-3:6)*. An Application of the Frame Theory of Cognitive Science to the Markan Oral-Aural Narrative. 2010. ISBN 978 90 04 17962 2
3. Lee, J.H. *Paul's Gospel in Romans*. A Discourse Analysis of Rom 1:16-8:39. 2010. ISBN 978 90 04 17963 9
4. Mathewson, D.L. *Verbal Aspect in the Book of Revelation*. The Function of Greek Verb Tenses in John's Apocalypse. 2010. ISBN 978 90 04 18668 2